QUICK
Sum & Substance
REVIEW

CRIMINAL LAW
3RD EDITION

Steven Friedland

WEST GROUP

ISBN 0-314-24320-8

ISBN 0-314-24320-8

Sum & Substance Quick Review of Criminal Law
is a publication of The West Group.

This product was printed and published in the United States.

TABLE OF CONTENTS

Sum & Substance Criminal Law	Criminal Law - Cases & Materials (4th Ed.) George E. Dix, M. Michael Sharbot	Criminal Law Cases, Materials and Text (5th Ed.) Phillip E. Johnson	Modern Criminal Law - Cases, Comments and Questions (2nd Ed.) Wayne R. LaFave	Criminal Law Cases and Comments (5th Ed.) Andre Moenssens, Fred Inbau, Ronald Bacigal	Criminal Law and Approaches to the Study of Law; Cases and Materials (2nd Ed.) John M. Brumbaugh
IV. Purposes and General Requirements of the Criminal Law	39-108		23-95		
A. Purposes	59-76		23-42		12-39, 50-60
B. Forms of Criminal Law			42-71	156-276	
C. Principle of Legality					
D. Constitutional Limitations		83-104	71-95	268-437	62-106
1. No Ex Post Facto Laws			52, 60		88, 92-93
2. No Bills of Attainder					
3. Due Process	39-58		52, 57, 60, 92-93, 366	274-304	62, 75-79, 84-92, 153-164, 303-320, 422-429, 518-519, 557-561, 653
4. Void for Vagueness	108-122 (precision)	83-104	44,74-75, 80-81, 584, 636	274-304	96-106
5. Narrowing Construction					
6. Cruel and Unusual Punishment	78-108 (proportionality)		94, 335, 422, 429, 513	366-437	678-714
V. Crime Components Basic Principles & Overview		9-34, 49-63, 96-105		17-101	
C. Actus Reus Requirement	129-265	49-63	187-237	17	121-135
1. Voluntary Act Requirement	151-159	49-63	187-203	17-22	129-135
2. Omissions	169-180	49-63	217-225	23-32	122-129
D. Mens Rea - General Principles	267-331	9-14, 18-34, 96-105	96-186	33-101	121-122, 135-147
E. Concurrence Requirement					147-151
F. Causation	514-544		315-334	102-119	121-122, 631-643, 667-678

Sum & Substance Criminal Law	Criminal Law - Cases & Materials (4th Ed.) George E. Dix, M. Michael Sharbot	Criminal Law Cases, Materials and Text (5th Ed.) Phillip E. Johnson	Modern Criminal Law - Cases, Comments and Questions (2nd Ed.) Wayne R. LaFave	Criminal Law Cases and Comments (5th Ed.) Andre Moenssens, Fred Inbau, Ronald Bacigal	Criminal Law and Approaches to the Study of Law; Cases and Materials (2nd Ed.) John M. Brumbaugh
1. Embezzlement	187-196, 309-312	679-718		716-718	248-258
2. False Pretenses	196-201	738-757	875	719-731	273-298
3. Forgery			875		323-326
4. Receiving Stolen Property		707-710		732-744	320-323
5. Theft	201-205	679-757	60, 164, 871	722-731, 776-793	229-232
6. Statutory Rape	587-590		174	626-637	209-213
7. Incest					
VII. Vicarious Liability	673-733	622-656	762-807	832-633	717-770, 805-875
A. Vicarious Liability	723-733		762-807	925-933	752-770
B. Conspiracy Liability	703-722		596-696	832-893	805-875
C. Accomplice Liability	673-703	622-656	704-762	898-925	717-752
VIII. Defenses					
A. Defenses to Inchoate Crimes	614-623, 646-660	581-597	563-581, 640-645, 668-670, 700-701	810-826, 894-898	789-809
1. Defenses to Solicitation			700-701		
2. Defenses to Attempt	614-623	581-597	563-581	810-826	794-804, 789-792
3. Defenses to Conspiracy	646-660		640-645, 668-670	894-898	805-807, 809
4. Abandonment of Accomplice Status			575-581	916	789-792, 805-809
B. Defenses Negating an Element of the Crime	331-386	14-30, 77-81, 348-353	165-186, 439-454	53-102	
1. Mistakes	332-369	14-30, 77-81	165-186	53-102	217-228
2. Intoxication	369-386	348-353	439-454	1027-1031	576-610
C. Affirmative Defenses	734-884	283-459	354-418, 460-539	934	
1. Justification and Excuse Compared	736-737		460-462		

Sum & Substance Criminal Law	Criminal Law - Cases & Materials (4th Ed.) George E. Dix, M. Michael Sharbot	Criminal Law Cases, Materials and Text (5th Ed.) Phillip E. Johnson	Modern Criminal Law - Cases, Comments and Questions (2nd Ed.) Wayne R. LaFave	Criminal Law Cases and Comments (5th Ed.) Andre Moenssens, Fred Inbau, Ronald Bacigal	Criminal Law and Approaches to the Study of Law; Cases and Materials (2nd Ed.) John M. Brumbaugh
2. Justification	739-800	353-440	460-514	934-1110	432-495
3. Excuse	801-884	283-352, 440-459	514-539, 455-459, 354-418	988-1027	495-517, 611
a. Entrapment	801-821	440-459	831	934-987	
b. Mental Illness/Insanity	822-884	283-352	354-418	1058-1110	517-576

CAPSULE OUTLINE

I.   INTRODUCTION

II.   10-5-2 HOUR STUDY GUIDE FOR CRIMINAL LAW

III.   ANALYTICAL AND EXAM APPROACH

IV.   THE PURPOSES AND GENERAL REQUIREMENTS OF THE CRIMINAL LAW.

A. PURPOSES [§10]

1. PUNISHMENT (RETRIBUTION) [§11]

2. DETERRENCE [§12]

3. REHABILITATION [§13]

4. SAFETY [§14]

5. COMPARISON WITH CIVIL LAW [§16]

Criminal law, unlike civil law areas such as torts and contracts, is designed to **morally condemn** and **punish** violators through incarceration or death. **Civil law** is primarily intended to **compensate** an injured party through damages or other remedies.

Civil cases permit a finding of liability based on a preponderance of the evidence; **criminal cases** require **proof beyond a reasonable doubt**.

B. FORMS OF CRIMINAL LAW [§17]

Common law and **statutory law**.

C. "THE PRINCIPLE OF LEGALITY" [§18]

Sets forth **limitations** on the formation, creation, and interpretation of the criminal law.

Requires **advance notice** and **fair warning** of what is criminal; **retroactive crime creation** is **unacceptable**.

D. CONSTITUTIONAL LIMITATIONS [§20]

1. NO EX POST FACTO LAWS. [§21]

The United States Constitution, Art. 1, §9, §10, prohibits the federal and state legislatures from enacting **ex post facto** laws (laws which look backward or are retroactive). Laws must be **prospective** in application only.

2. NO BILLS OF ATTAINDER. [§23]

The United States Constitution, Article 1, §9 and §10, prohibit bills of attainder, which are essentially laws that **punish** specific individuals or members of a group without the benefit of a judicial trial.

3. DUE PROCESS. [§26]

The due process clauses of the **Fifth** and **Fourteenth Amendments** to the United States Constitution restrict the states and the federal government, respectively, in the way in which criminal laws are created and applied.

a. The Incorporation Doctrine. [§27]

Due process clause of the Fourteenth Amendment **selectively "incorporates"** most of the Bill of Rights as limitations on the states.

b. Fundamental Fairness. [§29]

Criminal laws, at a minimum, must be "fundamentally fair" under due process.

c. Burden of Proof. [§31]

Because of the high stakes, due process requires that all elements of a crime be proven by the government "**beyond a reasonable doubt**."

d. What the Prosecutor Must Prove. [§33]

The State must prove all of the elements listed in the crime beyond a reasonable doubt.

4. VOID FOR VAGUENESS. [§35]

Prohibits criminal laws from being **so vague** that **reasonable people must necessarily guess** as to the **meaning** of the law and its **application**.

5. NARROWING CONSTRUCTION. [§38]

A law that is excessively vague on its face can be interpreted narrowly by courts, legislatures, or appropriate administrative bodies to create "**tolerable vagueness**."

6. CRUEL AND UNUSUAL PUNISHMENT. [§40]

The **Eighth Amendment** prohibits punishment grossly **disproportionate** to the crime charged.

V. CRIME COMPONENTS

A. BASIC PRINCIPLES. [§42]

Act + Result + Mental State = Crime - Defense

All crimes require an act (**actus reus**) and most require a concurrent mental state (**mens rea**). Many crimes also require a **result**; whether the defendant **proximately** and **in fact caused** the result to occur is a relevant issue.

B. BRIEF OVERVIEW.

Each of the basic elements of a crime — the act and mental state, in particular, give rise to various sub-issues. These sub-issues often pose obstacles to the existance of a crime.

C. THE ACTUS REUS REQUIREMENT. [§51]

All crimes must have an "actus reus," or act. The act must be "voluntary," a fuzzy word meaning there must be a mind-body connection (e.g., a reflexive movement or epilepsy is not enough).

Includes all types of **conduct**, from physical movements, to words inciting other people to act, to the use of mechanical objects, and to the manipulation of other people to do one's bidding.

1. VOLUNTARY ACTS REQUIREMENT. [§52]

The act must be voluntary. A reflexive or unconscious movement does not qualify.

a. "Voluntariness" Does Not Mean "Blameworthiness". [§53]

Blameworthiness or culpability depends on the person's **mental state** at the time of the act; it is not related to voluntariness.

b. Exception: A Voluntary Act in the Course of Involuntary Conduct. [§59]

Some courts still will hold a defendant responsible **if the involuntary conduct occurs during the course of voluntary, culpable conduct**.

c. The Model Penal Code. [§60]

MPC § 2.01, states that "a person is not guilty unless his liability is based on conduct which includes a voluntary act ...".

d. Constitutional Limitations. [§62]

The United States Constitution requires that crimes be based on a **voluntary act**, and not on the status of a person or a sickness over which a person has no control. (e.g., Alcoholism is a sickness, but drunkeness is a voluntary act.)

2. OMISSIONS. [§65]

Unless there is a **legal duty to act**, an individual will not be subject to criminal penalties for omitting or failing to act.

a. A Legal Duty to Act. [§67]

There are **five** general situations in which a legal duty to act exists: "**SCRAP.**"

S = **S**tatutory creation of the duty.

C = **C**ontractual creation of the duty.

R = **R**elationship of a special nature that creates the duty.

A = Assumption of voluntary care and seclusion of an injured person creates the duty.

P = Peril to another, wrongfully caused by the actor, creating a duty.

(1) Statute. [§68]

Legislature may require people to act on certain occasions. Failure to act in these situations may result in a crime, provided that the requisite mental state also exists.

(2) Contract. [§71]

An individual may create a legal duty to act by entering into a contract. Results from a voluntary agreement by the person to be bound.

(3) Relationship. [§75]

A special non-contractual relationship creates a legal duty to act. The relationship depends on the **status** of the individuals involved, such as husband-wife, parent-child, employer-employee, and land owner-invitee.

(4) Assumption of Voluntary Care and Seclusion. [§79]

An individual who voluntarily assumes the care of another, and then secludes that person from assistance by others, has a duty to continue assisting the person in need, provided that abandonment of care would leave the person worse off.

(5) Peril. [§81]

If an individual **wrongfully creates another's peril**, an obligation may arise to assist the person in danger and to minimize further harm. (Note: Duty to mitigate harm can be viewed as falling within the doctrine of proximate causation, where a person who wrongfully harms another can be held liable for all reasonably foreseeable harm resulting from the wrongful conduct.)

(a) Prerequisites to Liability for Failure to Comply with a Legal Duty to Act. [§83]

Even if one of the five legal duty categories in "SCRAP" exists, liability may occur only if two prerequisites also are met: (1) there must be **capacity to assist**; and (2) there must be **no substantial danger to the person assisting.**

(i) Capacity to Assist. [§84]

A person who, through no fault of his or her own, lacks the capacity to render assistance, will not be held responsible despite a legal duty to act.

(ii) No Substantial Danger to the Person Assisting. [§86]

A person will not be held responsible for failing to assist another if compliance with a legal duty to act places the person in substantial danger.

(6) The Model Penal Code. [§88]

The MPC is substantially similar to the common law. It provides for liability for sufficient omissions made "by the law defining the offense." The actor also must be physically capable of performing the act in question.

C. MENS REA — GENERAL PRINCIPLES. [§89]

To paraphrase Oliver Wendall Holmes, "even a dog can tell the difference between being stumbled over and being kicked."

The determination of what constitutes a crime, and how severe that crime is, generally depends on the mental state of the actor at the time the act was committed. Some actors are more morally **blameworthy** or **culpable** than others because of their mental state — or lack thereof. The degree of culpability often determines not only whether punishment is appropriate, but the severity of that punishment as well.

There are **two** major **types** of criminal mental state: **subjective** (what is **in the actor's mind**) and **objective** (what should have been in the actor's mind had she been a **reasonable person**). **Motive** is different. It explains why the actor has a particular mental state.

1. TYPES OF MENS REA. [§90]

There are four different criminal mental states: "**purpose**," "**knowledge**," "**recklessness**," and "**negligence**" ("**P-K-R-N**"). Mental states may be subjective or objective. A subjective mental state embraces the thoughts or beliefs of the person in question. An objective mental state ignores the thoughts and beliefs of the person in question and looks solely to the reasonably prudent person as a reference. The more heinous the mental state, the more subjective it is.

a. Purpose. [§91]

Purposeful behavior occurs when it is the actor's **intent** that certain consequences occur.

b. Knowledge. [§93]

Knowledge exists when the actor is **consciously aware** that the **results** will be **practically certain to occur**. The results that actually occur, however, need not be desired.

c. Recklessness. [§95]

Recklessness exists when a person **consciously disregards** a **substantial and unjustifiable risk** of harm. The requirement that the individual "consciously disregard a risk" is **subjective** and depends solely on whether the individual is in fact aware of the risk. Whether the risk of harm is substantial and unjustifiable is measured **objectively** and based on a reasonable person standard.

d. Negligence. [§97]

Negligence is a mental state imputed to a person who **acts reasonably**, in disregard of a **substantial** and **unjustifiable** risk of harm to others. It is based solely on **objective** criteria — specifically, a "reasonable person" standard. People are deemed negligent if they **should have known** that the risk created was unjustifiable and substantial — what they were thinking is irrelevant.

e. Criminal Versus Civil Negligence. [§100]

Criminal negligence generally requires a **higher level** of "unreasonableness" than **civil** negligence in tort.

f. More Serious Crimes do not Necessarily Require the Most Heinous Mental States. [§101]

g. Specific and General Intent. [§102]

Specific intent comprises conduct performed either purposefully or knowingly. **General intent,** on the other hand, denotes any of the four mental states — negligence, recklessness, knowledge, or purposefulness. Thus, a person acting negligently or recklessly has general, but not specific, intent.

(1) Comparing the Mens Rea of Completed Crimes and Attempt Crimes. [§105]

Attempt crimes require specific intent (either purposeful or knowing conduct). In contrast, the completed crimes might require either general or specific intent.

h. Malice. [§106]

It serves as the mens rea requirement for the common law crimes of **murder** and **arson**. Malice is a **mental state requiring either purpose, knowledge, or recklessness**. In other words, malice can be satisfied if a person acted intentionally (meaning either purposefully or knowingly), or recklessly.

i. "Transferred Intent." [§108]

This fiction generally is not required in the criminal law. In tort law, the **intent** to harm may be "transferred" from the intended victim to the actual one to hold the defendant liable. Some courts have used it in criminal law as well. The **preferable approach** involves determining whether an intent to kill a human being existed, and to hold the defendant liable even though the person killed was not the human being the defendant wanted to kill.

j. Strict Liability. [§110]

"**Public welfare**" **offenses** are strict liability crimes. No mens rea whatsoever is required to commit these offenses. These offenses are generally considered "**malum prohibitum**," which means they are wrong because they are prohibited. Most other crimes, including all crimes requiring mens rea, are "**malum in se**," meaning they are bad in and of themselves.

(1) Crimes with No Stated Mens Rea. [§111]

When no mens rea is expressly stated in the statutory definition of a crime, mens rea will be **implied** in the law because of the integral part played by mens rea in determining criminal culpability.

k. The Model Penal Code. [§113]

Divides mental states into categories of purpose, knowledge, recklessness, and negligence. Recognizes that some crimes require specific circumstances that are accorded their own mental states. Also generally implies a mental state requirement for crimes without a stated mental state. Unlike the common law, which implies negligence, the MPC **implies**, at a minimum, a **recklessness** mens rea.

l. Crimes with More Than One Mens Rea. [§114]

When this occurs, each mental state applies only to a component part of the actus reus.

E. CONCURRENCE REQUIREMENT. [§116]

The requisite **mens rea** and **actus reus** of a crime must occur **simultaneously**, not at different times.

F. CAUSATION. [§118]

Some crimes, such as criminal homicide, require causation, meaning that the actor's conduct must cause a particular **result**. There are two different types of causation: **causation in fact**, (also called "but for" causation, as in, "but for the causal event, the result would not have occurred."), and **proximate causation** (also called "legal" causation).

1. CAUSATION IN FACT. [§119]

A single event may have **numerous causes** in fact (e.g., many of the circumstances surrounding an event may be causes in fact). To satisfy this requirement, the perpetrator must only be **one** of the causes — not **the sole cause** — of the harmful result. An action is a cause in fact of a result if, "but for" that initial action, the result would not have occurred at the time it did.

a. Simultaneous Causes (the "Substantial Factor" Test). [§120]

When there are **two simultaneous causes**, the courts ask whether each cause was a **substantial factor** in the outcome.

b. Hastening an Inevitable Result. [§122]

When the conduct by one actor hastens an inevitable result, such as death, the important question to ask is whether, but for the act, the bad result would have occurred **at the precise time it did**. Remember that the existence of cause in fact does not necessarily mean that either proximate cause or criminal liability also exists. The other elements of the crime must still be proven.

2. PROXIMATE CAUSATION. [§126]

Decides which of the actors who are a cause in fact of harm should be held criminally responsible for that harm. For determining if proximate causation (a.k.a. "Legal Causation") exists, ask whether the bad results were **"reasonably foreseeable"** from the defendant's conduct. Whether consequences are "reasonably foreseeable" depends on different factors and diverse terminology, including: (1) the **remoteness** of the actor's conduct to the harm caused; (2) the **independence** of the **intervening, causes** that occurred after the defendant's act; and (3) whether the actor **intended** the consequences.

a. Subsequent Negligent Medical Care and Independent Intervening Factors. [§127]

If medical care is negligent, whether it breaks the "chain" of proximate causation depends on whether the negligence is deemed gross or simple. **Gross negligence breaks the proximate cause chain; simple negligence does not**.

b. Intended Consequences. [§129]

A finding of proximate causation is more likely to occur with an actor who **intends** harmful consequences, such as the death of another.

3. THE YEAR AND A DAY RULE. [§131]

At common law, a person could not be held responsible for causing a criminal homicide if the **death occurred more than one year and a day after the injury** was inflicted. Since the harm was **too remote**, it would be unfair to hold the defendant responsible.

Under many **modern statutes**, however, the year and a day rule has been **abrogated** and a person could be charged with criminal homicide. The existence of proximate causation, however, is still required.

4. THE MODEL PENAL CODE. [§133]

For crimes requiring mens rea, the MPC asks whether the harmful result was "too remote or accidental in its occurrence to have a bearing on the actor's liability or on the gravity of the offense." [MPC § 2.03(2)(b).] Also provides that with respect to strict liability offenses, no causation exists "unless the actual result is a probable consequence of the actor's conduct." [MPC § 2.03(4).] This is a more restrictive standard than the common law, and focuses on the probability of the result, not simply whether the result is too remote or accidental.

VI. CRIMES.

A. BACKGROUNDS. [§134]

Much of a criminal law course involves defining and interpreting the elements of crimes and their defenses.

B. INCHOATE CRIMES. [§135]

Incomplete and failed crimes.

1. SOLICITATION. [§136]

Occurs when a person (1) **knowingly** (2) **invites, entices, advises, orders, or encourages another person to** (3) **commit either** (a) **a felony or** (b) **a misdemeanor which involves a breach of the peace or the obstruction of justice**.

a. The Problem of a Failure to Communicate. [§138]

Person solicited must have heard or received communication for solicitation to occur at common law.

b. The "Primary Actor" Requirement. [§139]

A solicitation occurs at common law only when the person solicited is asked to be the **primary actor** in committing the crime. If the person solicited is asked merely to assist the solicitor, a common-law solicitation has not occurred.

c. The "Innocent Instrumentality" Rule. [§141]

Individuals who are solicited to commit a crime must be told or made aware of the fact that they are being asked to engage in criminal conduct, and not merely to perform an act that appears to be lawful. If the solicited person is **duped** or **tricked** into committing a crime, that person becomes an "innocent instrumentality," and no solicitation has occurred. The "solicitor" may be held liable for either an attempt or a completed crime, depending on whether the intended harm occurs.

d. Solicitation and Accomplice Liability. [§143]

If a crime is solicited and the solicitee successfully completes the object offense, the solicitor may be held liable for the completed crime. If the object crime does not occur, then the solicitor still can be held liable for solicitation.

e. The Mens Rea. [§144]

Solicitation, like the other inchoate offenses, is a **specific intent offense** requiring either purposeful or knowing conduct by the perpetrator.

f. The Model Penal Code. [§146]

Under the MPC, a person is guilty of solicitation if that person (1) **intentionally** (2) **encourages another to commit a crime**, even if the encouragement is not communicated to the solicitee.

2. ATTEMPT. [§148]

An attempt crime is defined as (1) an **incomplete** or **unsuccessful effort** to commit an **offense** (2) with the **intent** to commit that offense.

a. How Minimal an Act? [§149]

An overt act towards the crime's completion is necessary. The threshold issue is whether the act went far enough towards the completion of the object crime to cross over the line from "mere preparation" to a legally overt act.

b. The Overt Act. [§150]

There must be an **overt act**, one that **goes beyond mere preparation**.

The act must be "close enough" to completion to provide an **unequivocal**, **symbolic**, or **manifest** indication that the individual was intending to commit a crime, and was sufficiently close to the goal to make such conduct dangerous to society. Acts that are "**ambiguous**" or "**equivocal**," on the other hand, are considered mere preparation and insufficient to form the basis of an attempt charge.

c. Attempt Crimes and the Innocent Instrumentality. [§151]

Attempts may be perpetrated by a solitary individual, and may result from group activity. An attempt which involves more than one person usually involves the use of an "**innocent instrumentality**". This occurs when the defendant dupes or tricks another person to assist him in the commission of a crime, without revealing the criminal nature of the endeavor. A defendant who uses an "innocent instrumentality" to do the "dirty work" can still be charged with an attempt crime without having lifted a finger in the commission of the overt act.

d. Mens Rea. [§153]

Attempt requires that the defendant intend to commit the object offense.

e. The Model Penal Code. [§156]

Defines an **attempt** crime as (1) conduct constituting a "**substantial step**" towards the commission of an offense, with (2) the **purpose** of committing that offense. [MPC § 5.01.] An attempt under the MPC also includes an effort to enlist another person's assistance as an accomplice in committing a crime, abrogating the common law requirement that the person be solicited as the primary actor. Recognizes the defense of abandonment, provided that there is a complete and voluntary renunciation of the criminal purpose and a thwarting of the crime.

3. CONSPIRACY. [§157]

A conspiracy is: (1) **an agreement between two or more people to commit a crime** with (2) the **intent** to (a) **agree to commit the offense** and (b) **to commit the offense.**

a. The Actus Reus. [§159]

At **common law**, an express or implied **agreement** satisfies the **actus reus requirement. Modern jurisdictions** have expanded the actus reus by requiring the commission of **an act in furtherance of the conspiracy,** sometimes referred to as an "**overt act**," in addition to the agreement.

b. The Number of Conspiracies. [§161]

The number of conspiracies depends on the number of agreements made, not on the number of crimes the parties agree to commit.

c. The Problem of the Lawful Supplier. [§162]

Unless the supplier knows the sale of goods or services is furthering an egregious felony, **mere knowledge** of the unlawful use of lawfully provided goods or services **will not satisfy the mens rea** requirement for conspiracy.

The situations in which **conspiratorial intent will be inferred** include:

(1) When a merchant charges an **excessive price** because of the unlawful use to which the goods or services are put;

(2) When **no legitimate use** exists for the goods or services provided (even though the goods or services themselves are lawful); or

(3) When the merchant does an **excessively large volume** of business with the unlawful user.

d. Bilateral Versus Unilateral Conspiracies. [§165]

If the jurisdiction adopts a **bilateral approach**, this means that **two or more individuals** must not only **agree** to commit a crime, **but** also **actually intend** at the time of the agreement to carry that agreement out.

In a unilateral jurisdiction, if **one conspirator** with the requisite two intents (the intent to agree and the intent to carry out the object crime), agrees with another person to commit the crime, the sole conspirator **can be held liable** even if the other person did not intend to agree or to carry out the agreement.

e. The Multiple Conviction Requirement. [§167]

In a **bilateral** jurisdiction at common law, if all conspirators but one are acquitted, a conviction of the remaining co-conspirator cannot stand.

f. The Unknown Conspirator. [§168]

Those who are involved in a conspiracy need not know each other personally, but can simply know **of** each other.

g. Types of Conspiracies. [§170]

(1) The "Wheel" Conspiracy. [§171]

The **wheel conspiracy** has a **controlling** person, or persons, located at the figurative **center** of the wheel, and other less central members of the conspiracy connected to the center figuratively by "**spokes**." The controlling center deals with each of the "spokes," who need not deal with each other at all.

(2) The Chain Conspiracy. [§172]

The **chain conspiracy**, on the other hand, looks like a **straight line**, and involves conspirators connected to each other in a linear fashion. There is no controlling center, and participants might only have contact with members of the chain who precede and follow them.

h. Liability for the Acts of Others — The "Pinkerton" Rule. [§175]

The common law rule states that a conspirator is responsible for all acts (and criminal offenses) by co-conspirators committed **during and in furtherance of the conspiracy**. An offense "in furtherance of" a conspiracy has been defined as any offense that is a **natural and probable consequence** of the conspiracy. A natural and probable consequence of the conspiracy is one that is "**reasonably foreseeable**."

i. Wharton's Rule (The "Plus One" Requirement). [§177]

Adultery, **dueling**, **bigamy** and **incest** require at least two persons for the commission of the offense. Under Wharton's Rule, a conspiracy to commit these offenses will be recognized only if: (1) at least **one person more than the minimum number** of individuals required to commit the offense participates in the conspiracy; or (2) **two persons** who are **not required to participate** in the crime enter into a conspiracy to commit the crime.

j. The Model Penal Code. [§179]

Adopts:

(1) a **unilateral approach** to conspiracy;

(2) the "**no identity**" rule similar to the common law, in which a co-conspirator need not know the identities of all of the individuals who participate in the conspiracy;

(3) the "**multiple objectives of one conspiracy**" approach, consistent with the common law, in which a single conspiracy can have multiple criminal objectives;

(4) the **common law approach to impossibility** (i.e., it is **no defense** to conspiracy);

(5) an **affirmative defense of abandonment**, unlike the common law, but only so long as the conspirator **completely** and **voluntarily** renounces his criminal purpose and **thwarts** the commission of the object offense or offenses;

(6) a scheme permitting a conspiracy offense to be tried in any jurisdiction in which the conspiracy was created, or where an overt act in furtherance of the conspiracy was committed;

(7) a position **contrary to Wharton's Rule**, such that there need not be one more person in the conspiracy than the number of persons required to commit the underlying crime;

(8) an actus reus which requires (1) an **agreement** between the parties, **plus**, when the charge is either a **felony in the third degree or a misdemeanor**, (2) an **overt act** by at least one of the conspirators in **furtherance** of the conspiracy; and

(9) conspirators are not held liable for the reasonably foreseeable acts of other co-conspirators.

l. Merger. [§180]

A criminal defendant cannot be convicted of **both a crime and any of its lesser included offenses**.

(1) Exception to the Merger Doctrine. [§183]

Under the **later common law**, **conspiracy convictions did not merge** with the completed offense. Convictions for conspiracy and the object offense of the conspiracy can both occur.

m. Merger Under the Model Penal Code. [§185]

Conspiracy generally merges with the completed object offense. An **exception** to this rule exists if the conspirators intend to commit **other offenses** in addition to the object offense.

4. POSSESSION. [§187]

Requires (1) **the act of exercising dominion and control over the thing possessed,** having had the **opportunity to dispossess** it, along with (2) **the mental state of knowingly doing the act**. A "knowing" mental state means knowingly exercising dominion and control over a thing.

a. Actual and Constructive Possession. [§188]

Possession is considered **actual** if the thing possessed is on the person of the possessor or within arm's reach. Possession is considered **constructive** if it is outside of the individual's actual possession but still within her dominion and control.

b. Joint versus Exclusive Possession. [§189]

Possession of a thing may be joint, **between two or more people**, or **exclusive, by one person only**.

C. CRIMES AGAINST THE PERSON

1. HOMICIDE. [§192]

Occurs when a **person causes the death of another** person or persons. "**Non-criminal homicide**" includes accidents in which the actors were not culpable. **Criminal homicide**, on the other hand, involves a **culpable** perpetrator who engages in morally blameworthy conduct.

a. Elements of Murder. [§193]

Murder is defined as the (1) **unlawful (unexcused or unjustified)** (2) **killing of** (3) **another human being** (4) **with malice aforethought**.

(1) "With Malice Aforethought." [§202]

For most crimes, **malice** is defined as the **intentional** (purposeful or knowing) **or reckless commission** of an act. For the purposes of common law murder, malice equals either **intentional or grossly reckless conduct**.

b. The Four Types of Common Law Murder. [§203]

Includes: (a) **intent to kill**; (b) **intent to commit serious bodily harm** against another; (c) "**depraved heart**" (i.e., gross recklessness) murder; and (d) **felony murder**.

c. Culpability and Common Law Murder. [§207.5]

The most **heinous** type of murder is the intent to kill murder, followed by the intent to commit serious bodily harm murder and certain types of felony murder. The more serious the felony, the more culpable the perpetrator.

d. Statutory Degrees of Murder. [§208]

Many jurisdictions, by statute, **divide** up the crime of murder not just by mental states, but by special categories labeled "**degrees**."

Many jurisdictions have at least **three degrees** of murder. **First degree** murder is punished the most severely, sometimes even by death. Second and third degree murder include crimes with lower levels of culpability, such as depraved heart murder. Murder in the first degree is often defined as a killing that is "**willful, premeditated**, and **deliberate**."

e. Felony Murder at Common Law. [§209]

Originally, defined as a **murder committed during the course of a felony or an attempted felony**. **Over time**, the definition of felony murder changed dramatically. Felony murder today simply requires a killing during the commission of a felony or attempted felony. Malice was presumed from the commission or attempted commission of the felony. In the **later common law**, a **felony murder** was defined as: (1) a **killing** (2) **during the commission of a felony or attempted felony**. The killing, can be accidental, negligent, reckless, knowing, or purposeful. **Attempted felony is sufficient** to serve as the basis for felony murder.

(1) The "D.I.D.I." Limitations of Felony Murder. [§211]

(a) Direct. [§212]

("**D.**"I.D.I.) The death must be directly caused by the felony or attempted felony. The death must be a **natural and probable consequence**; both **actual** and **proximate causation** must exist for the death to be attributable to the felon or felons.

(b) Inherently Dangerous Felonies. [§214]

(D."**I.D.**"I.) Only those felonies or attempted felonies that are considered "inherently dangerous" qualify. Inherent dangerousness depends on how **dangerous** the felony is to **human life**.

(c) Independent Felony. [§219]

(D.I.D."**I.**") The inherently dangerous felony must also be **independent** of murder. This means that the **felony cannot be a lesser included offense** of murder.

> **NOTE:** The independent felony rule only prevents a felony murder charge based on certain non-dangerous felonies; the rule does not preclude a direct charge of intent-to-kill, intent-to-commit-serious-bodily harm or depraved heart murder for any killing.

(2) Felony Murder Liability When a Non-Felon Kills. [§225]

A non-felon is a person who **is not an accomplice** participating in the crime. Non-felons include **bystanders** or **police officers**. If a felon kills, conspirator or accomplice liability will be used to hold the co-felons liable for the death.

(a) The Agency Theory (Majority Rule). [§226]

Co-felons will be held responsible under a felony murder theory **only if one of the felons does the killing**.

(b) The Proximate Cause Theory. [§228]

Defendant felons are **liable for any deaths proximately caused** by the felons' conduct.

(c) The Limited Proximate Cause Theory. [§230]

Co-felons (the perpetrators of the crime) are liable for **all reasonably foreseeable deaths** of **non-felons only**.

f. Manslaughter. [§232]

Manslaughter is the **unlawful (unjustified and unexcused) killing of another human being without malice aforethought**. There are **four types** of manslaughter: (1) **heat of passion** (or **provocation**) **manslaughter**; (2) **imperfect justification manslaughter**; (3) **negligence/recklessness manslaughter**; and (4) **misdemeanor (sometimes called "Bad Act") manslaughter**.

(1) Heat of Passion Manslaughter. [§233]

(1) **An unlawful** (2) **intentional** (3) **killing that** (4) **results from provocation**, i.e., **an (a) actual and (b) objectively reasonable sudden heat of passion**; (5) which is considered **legally adequate**; and (6) which occurred **before** the defendant had a reasonable opportunity to "**cool off**".

(a) **"Legally Adequate" Provocation**: **mere words are not enough to legally provoke**.

(b) The "**Cooling Off Doctrine**" limits the **time** in which a defendant may justifiably respond to a provoking incident. If a **reasonable person would have cooled off** from the provoking event by the time the defendant responded to the provocation, then the defendant is not deserving of a partial excuse, and cannot claim heat of passion.

(2) Imperfect Justification Manslaughter. [§237]

(1) An **unlawful** (2) **intentional** (3) **killing** resulting from an (4) **actual belief** that the use of **lethal force was necessary** under the circumstances, and (5) the **belief was unreasonable**.

(3) Recklessness or Negligence Manslaughter. [§241]

Requires (1) **the unlawful** (2) **reckless or negligent** (3) **killing of another human being**.

(4) Misdemeanor ("Bad Act") Manslaughter. [§243]

Is the **death of a human being during the commission or attempted commission of a specified unlawful act**.

(5) The Model Penal Code on Criminal Homicide. [§244]

Under the MPC:

(a) Criminal homicide is divided into **three** categories: **murder**; **manslaughter**; and **negligent homicide**.

(b) The **mental state terminology** for intent to kill, intent to commit serious bodily harm, and "depraved heart" murder has been slightly **modified** in favor of requiring the defendant to purposely or knowingly kill the victim, or to kill the victim recklessly "under circumstances manifesting extreme indifference to the value of human life."

(c) The category of intent to commit serious bodily harm is not expressly included in the MPC. Intent is treated as gross recklessness, becoming murder if it manifests "extreme indifference to the value of human life."

(d) **Felony murder is preserved**, but evidence can be offered by the defendant to rebut this presumption. If the presumption is rebutted, the prosecutor must prove malice.

(e) Instead of heat of passion manslaughter, the MPC adopts broader terminology, providing a partial defense to persons whose actions result from an "**extreme mental or emotional disturbance**."

2. ASSAULT AND BATTERY. [§245]

Both are misdemeanors with a maximum incarceration of one year in jail. Aggravated assaults and aggravated batteries are often felonies, punishable by more than one year in prison.

a. Assault. [§246]

There are **two types** of assault: (1) an **attempted battery**, or (2) the **intentional creation of the imminent apprehension of a battery** (i.e., intentional scaring). Both types of assault are specific intent crimes.

b. Battery. [§249]

Battery is the (a) **harmful** or (b) **offensive** (2) **touching of another person**. Battery is a **general intent** crime requiring **negligence** at a minimum.

c. The Model Penal Code. [§251]

The MPC **groups** both **assault and battery together** under the label "**assault**." [MPC § 211.1.] Occurs when an individual either (1) **attempts to cause**, or (2) **purposely**, **knowingly**, or **recklessly causes**, the **bodily injury of another**, or (3) **negligently causes** the **bodily injury of another with a deadly weapon**, or (4) **attempts** through **physical menace** to put another person in **fear of imminent serious bodily injury**.

3. ROBBERY. [§253]

The (1) **trespassory** (2) **taking** and **carrying away** (3) of the **personal property of another** (4) with the **intent to deprive the other of the property permanently** (5) from the **other's person or presence** (6) **by force or fear**. Can be viewed as a **larceny accompanied by an assault**.

4. RAPE. [§255]

Rape is defined at common law as (1) the **carnal knowledge** (2) **by a man** (3) **of a woman** (4) **by force or fear and against her will**.

a. Carnal Knowledge. [§256]

Rape requires penetration.

b. By a Man. [§257]

A woman, however, can be charged with aiding and abetting.

c. Of a Woman. [§258]

Modern law permits prosecution when the woman raped is the defendant's wife.

d. "By force or Fear and Against Her Will." [§259]

Without consent.

e. Intent. [§260]

Rape is a **general intent crime**, satisfied by a minimum of **negligence**. Recklessness, knowledge, or a purposeful mental state also will suffice.

5. FALSE IMPRISONMENT. [§262]

A person commits false imprisonment if she: (1) **unlawfully confines the victim**, (2) **against her will**, so that, (3) **the victim does not have the freedom to leave**.

6. KIDNAPPING. [§267]

This crime requires: (1) the **confinement of a person**, (2) **against her will**, (3) who is **transported or secretly confined**. (Note that in some jurisdictions, secret confinement alone is required and transportation is irrelevant.)

In those jurisdictions requiring either transportation or secrecy, secrecy is **presumed** if transportation of the victim is shown. If there is no movement of the victim, a kidnapping charge will be sustained only if it is shown that the victim was, in fact, secretly confined.

7. MAYHEM. [§271]

Mayhem requires: (a) an **intentional act**, (b) to **disfigure, dismember, or disable**, (c) another **human being**.

a. "Intentional." [§272]

Requires that the defendant's act be intentional — purposeful or knowing. Reckless or negligent acts cannot support a mayhem charge.

b. "Disfigure, Dismember, or Disable." [§273]

The defendant must intend to disfigure, dismember, or disable, and must be successful. Must, in fact, permanently disfigure or disable the victim. Mayhem still occurs when the defendant disfigures, disables, or dismembers a body part different than the body part originally intended to be harmed.

D. CRIMES AGAINST PROPERTY

1. ARSON. [§276]

At common law, arson is defined as the (a) **malicious** (b) **burning** of the (c) **dwelling house of another**.

b. Model Penal Code. [§278]

Under the MPC, arson occurs when a person (1) starts a fire or an explosion (2) with the purpose of destroying a building or occupied structure of another or to (3) destroy or damage his own or another's property to collect insurance. [MPC § 220.1(1)(a)(b).] Applies to persons who (1) purposely start a fire or an explosion and (2) recklessly place (a) a person in danger (of death or bodily harm), or (b) a building or occupied structure of another in danger of damage or destruction.

2. LARCENY. [§280]

At common law, larceny is defined as the (a) **trespassory** (b) **taking** and **carrying away** (c) of the **personal property of another** (4) **with the intent to deprive the other person of that property permanently**.

a. Trespassory. [§281]

Property must have been taken **without** the owner's (or rightful possessor's) **permission**. An exception exists, which is called "**larceny by trick**." Involves the use of **trickery** to obtain **custody** of another person's property.

b. Taking and Carrying Away. [§282]

The property must be **physically moved** by the perpetrator.

c. The Personal Property of Another. [§284]

Larceny can occur only if the **tangible personal property of another**, namely goods or chattels, is taken. Larceny questions are not so easily resolved when the property is subject to joint ownership and one of the joint owners is the perpetrator.

d. Intent to Deprive the Other of That Property Permanently. [§286]

Requires an **intent to steal the property**, not just to borrow it. Intent is determined at the time of the taking.

e. Larceny by Trick. [§288]

The perpetrator **obtains possession of the property by fraudulent means**. If the **title** to the property, as opposed to its mere possession, is obtained by fraudulent means, the crime is not larceny by trick, but instead the statutory crime of false pretenses.

3. BURGLARY. [§290]

At common law, burglary is defined as (a) the **breaking and entering** (b) of the **dwelling house of another** (c) at **nighttime** (d) with the **intent to commit a felony therein**.

a. "Breaking and Entering." [§291]

Permission to enter, or entry through an already open door, does not satisfy the "breaking" requirement at common law. An "entering" is considered to occur when any part of the perpetrator's body enters the house.

b. "Dwelling House of Another." [§292]

If someone other than the perpetrator lawfully occupies the premises. Ownership of the dwelling is not controlling on the issue of whether the structure is "of another."

c. "At Nighttime." [§293]

At common law, "nighttime" depended upon whether a person could be seen by natural light.

d. "Intent to Commit a Felony Therein." [§294]

If, at the time of the breaking and entering, the perpetrator was not intending to commit a crime inside, but thereafter changed her mind once inside, a burglary has not occurred. The intent to commit a felony must occur simultaneously with the breaking and entering.

4. MALICIOUS MISCHIEF. [§296]

A defendant is guilty of this crime if she: (a) intentionally (b) destroys or damages (c) the property of another.

E. STATUTORY CRIMES

1. EMBEZZLEMENT. [§297]

The (a) **fraudulent** (b) **conversion** of the (c) **personal property** of another by (d) an individual in **lawful possession** of that property. The **embezzler** already **is in lawful possession** of the property, which is then appropriated for her own use. In comparison, larceny requires that a perpetrator obtain custody of the property by stealth or deceit.

2. FALSE PRETENSES. [§299]

Is a statutory-based crime. It requires a wrongdoer who, with (a) the **intent to defraud another** (b) **knowingly** makes a (c) **false** and (d) **material** (e) **representation of fact**, which results in the perpetrator (f) **obtaining title** to another's property.

a. Comparison with Embezzlement and Larceny by Trick. [§300]

In embezzlement, the defendant already has lawful possession of the property, whereas in larceny by trick, the defendant obtains possession — but not title — by fraud. In false pretenses, the defendant obtains title to the property — not just possession — by fraud.

3. FORGERY. [§301.5]

This crime requires: (a) making or altering (b) a writing with apparent legal significance (e.g. a check or contract) (c) so that ti is false (d) with an intent to defraud.

4. RECEIVING STOLEN PROPERTY. [§302]

The defendant must: (a) **knowingly**, (b) **receive stolen property**, (c) with the **intent to permanently deprive** the true owner of the property.

a. "Knowingly." [§303]

Must actually know that the property received is stolen. Can be inferred from the totality of the circumstances.

b. "Receiving Stolen Property." [§304]

A perpetrator receives stolen property if it is in her **actual** or **constructive possession** or **control**.

c. "Intent to Permanently Deprive the True Owner of the Property." [§305]

The accused intends, either purposefully or knowingly, to **permanently dispose** of the stolen property. The intent to permanently deprive is a **specific intent**. **Legal impossibility**, is a complete defense to the attempt charge.

5. THEFT. [§307]

Requires the: (a) **unlawful**, (b) **appropriation**, (c) of the **property of another**, (d) by a person who **intends to deprive the true property owner** of the property **permanently** or **temporarily**.

6. STATUTORY RAPE. [§308]

This crime requires: (a) **sexual intercourse**, (b) with a **female under the age of consent** (generally under the age of 18).

It is tantamount to a strict liability offense. Accordingly, consent by the female is not a defense to this charge. A minority of courts allow an honest and reasonable mistake as to the age of the female as a valid defense to this crime.

7. INCEST. [§309]

Occurs when the defendant has: (a) **sexual intercourse** with, **or** (b) **is married to**, (c) a **blood relative**. A minority of jurisdictions extend liability to situations in which the defendant marries certain non-blood relatives.

VII. VICARIOUS LIABILITY

> **NOTE:** This form of liability is also known as "COMPLICITY". Defendant can be held liable for the acts of others.

A. VICARIOUS LIABILITY. [§310]

1. COMPARING CONSPIRACY AND ACCOMPLICE LIABILITY. [§310.5]

Conspiracy liability revolves around an **agreement** to commit a crime. **Accomplice liability**, on the other hand, is predicated on a person **actually assisting** another in committing a crime; the formation of an agreement to commit the crime is irrelevant to the existence of accomplice liability.

B. CONSPIRACY LIABILITY. [§311]

A conspirator will be held liable for the **acts of co-conspirators occurring during and in furtherance of the conspiracy**, even if she did nothing more than agree to participate in the conspiracy.

C. ACCOMPLICE LIABILITY. [§311.5]

Accomplice liability arises if a person (1) **knowingly** (2) **aids, abets, or assists** another in committing a crime. Assistance can occur **before**, **during** or **after** the commission of the offense.

1. TYPES OF ACCOMPLICES. [§312]

At common law, those persons who **actually carry out the crime** are called **principals**. Those who **assist before or after** the crime's commission are called **accessories** to the crime.

a. Types of Principals. [§313]

(1) Principal in the First Degree. [§314]

Individuals who actively commit the crime are called principals in the first degree.

A person still will be considered a principal in the first degree even if she uses an **innocent instrumentality**, a person who has been duped or tricked, to commit the actus reus of the crime.

(2) Principal in the Second Degree. [§315]

A person who **intentionally assists** in committing the crime, and is **present at the scene** in a **less than central position**, is called a principal in the second degree.

b. Types of Accessories. [§316]

Accessories generally play a lesser role in the crime than either type of principal.

(1) Accessory Before the Fact. [§317]

Not present at the scene at all, but **intentionally assists** the principals **prior** to the crime's commission.

(2) Accessory After the Fact. [§318]

Not present at the scene, but **intentionally assists** the principals in escaping or avoiding detection **after** the crime has been completed.

c. Significance of Distinctions at Common Law. [§319]

At common law, an accessory to a felony could not be convicted of a crime greater than the crime for which the principal was convicted. Unless a principal was convicted, an accessory could not lawfully be convicted either. For **misdemeanors** or the felony of **treason**, all participants were considered principals at common law.

2. THE SCOPE OF LIABILITY. [§320]

At common law, accessories before the fact, principals in the first degree and principals in the second degree all could be held liable for the commission of the object crime, regardless of the extent of their participation.

a. "Long-Arm" (Vicarious) Accomplice Liability. [§322]

If the object crime is a homicide, in a minority of jurisdictions, the defendant also may be held responsible for the "**natural and probable consequences**" of the acts of other accomplices in committing the object homicide.

3. ACCOMPLICE LIABILITY MENS REA. [§323]

Requires both an act and a mental state. (The act is the actual assistance of another in committing the crime, including encouragement or enticement.) The **mental state** is the **intent to commit, or to assist another in committing**, the object offense. Accomplice liability requires **specific intent**.

4. THE LEGISLATIVE EXEMPTION RULE. [§324]

If an individual is in the **class of persons a criminal statute is designed to protect**, the person **cannot** be prosecuted as an accomplice.

VIII. DEFENSES.

A defense to a criminal charge can **partially or completely negate** liability.

A. DEFENSES TO INCHOATE CRIMES. [§326]

1. DEFENSES TO SOLICITATION. [§326.5]

No clear consensus as to whether **abandonment** serves as a defense to solicitation at common law. Several states, by statute, provide for such a defense when there is a **complete and voluntary renunciation** by the defendant of his **criminal purpose** (in some jurisdictions, the defendant must **thwart** the commission of the crime).

2. DEFENSES TO ATTEMPT. [§327]

a. Impossibility. [§328]

Means that under the particular circumstances of the case, it is impossible for the defendant to complete the crime.

(1) Legal Impossibility — A Valid Defense. [§329]

(1) **Conduct** which, (2) **had it been completed, would not constitute a criminal offense**.

(2) Factual Impossibility. [§330]

(1) **Conduct** which is **impossible to complete** (2) due to some **unforeseen fact or physical condition**. The **central difference** between factual and legal impossibility seems to be their focus: factual impossibility asks whether the failure to complete the crime is due to a fortuity (i.e., an unforeseen fact), and legal impossibility asks whether the attempt, had it been successful, would have constituted a completed criminal offense.

(3) True Legal Impossibility. [§333]

There is **no fact** that prevents the accused's conduct from being a crime, merely the **accused's erroneous belief about what the criminal law prohibits**.

(4) Comparison: Inherent Legal Impossibility. [§335]

Involves persons who intend to achieve a criminal objective through woefully inadequate, **de minimus conduct**. Generally, the actor will **not** be held liable for an attempt if only de minimis conduct occurs. The conduct is not sufficiently dangerous.

Sum & Substance QUICK REVIEW of Criminal Law

b. Abandonment. [§337]

Generally **not available** as a defense to an attempt crime at **common law**.

3. DEFENSES TO CONSPIRACY. [§338]

a. Impossibility. [§338.1]

Generally **not** a defense to a conspiracy charge.

b. Abandonment and Withdrawal. [§338.2]

Abandonment generally is not considered a defense to conspiracy at common law. **Withdrawal** from a **continuing conspiracy** may be significant for several reasons: (1) withdrawal may **toll** the **statute of limitations**; (2) withdrawal may **terminate the use of hearsay statements** against the withdrawing members by co-conspirators in furtherance of and during the conspiracy; and (3) withdrawal from a conspiracy may **terminate the conspirator's vicarious liability** for the subsequent offenses of co-conspirators in furtherance of the conspiracy.

In order to effectively withdraw, a conspirator must **communicate** the fact of withdrawal to all other members of the conspiracy, and the withdrawing member must take **affirmative steps to thwart** the successful completion of the object of the conspiracy.

4. ABANDONMENT OF ACCOMPLICE STATUS. [§339]

An accomplice can abandon her criminal activity and avoid future liability if she **communicates** the fact of abandonment to the other accomplices, and then attempts to **thwart** the criminal purpose.

B. DEFENSES NEGATING AN ELEMENT OF THE CRIME.[§340]

1. MISTAKES. [§340.5]

a. Mistake in Fact. [§341]

Arises when the defendant bases her conduct on an **erroneous factual belief** constituting a misperception of reality.

b. Mistake in Law. [§342]

Occurs when a person is mistaken about the **applicable law** (the person usually believes that the intended conduct is not prohibited, when in actuality it is).

c. Mistake in Justification. [§343]

Occurs when the actor **mistakenly believes** that a **justification defense** is warranted.

d. Analysis of Mistake in Fact. [§344]

Whether a mistake in fact will negate the mens rea of a crime usually depends on whether the crime is a **specific** or **general intent offense**.

(1) Specific Intent Crimes: [§345]

The mens rea in a specific intent crime can be negated by an **honest mistake**, no matter how unreasonable.

(2) General Intent Crimes: [§346]

The mens rea in a general intent crime can be negated only by a mistake that is **both** (1) **honest** and (2) **reasonable**.

e. Analysis of Mistake in Law. [§354]

Ignorance of the law is no excuse.

(1) Exceptions. [§355]

A mistake about the law may serve as a defense if:

(a) A defendant relies on a state Supreme Court **ruling** that is later overruled;

(b) A defendant relies on a **statute** that is later declared void; or

(c) A defendant relies on an **official, but erroneous, interpretation** of a law by an individual or agency holding the power to execute the law.

2. INTOXICATION. [§359]

a. Voluntary Intoxication. [§360]

May serve as a **defense** to a **specific intent crime**, but **not** to a **general intent crime**. The intoxication may **negate** the **purposefulness** or **knowledge** required to commit the crime. Not a defense to a strict liability crime.

b. Involuntary Intoxication. [§365]

If a person becomes intoxicated **involuntarily** through **no fault** of her own, the intoxication **may serve as a defense** to any crimes committed under the influence of the intoxicant. Can serve as a defense to **all** crimes, including general intent offenses.

c. The Model Penal Code. [§367]

Recognizes three forms of intoxication: (1) **voluntary**, (2) **pathological**, and (3) **involuntary**. **Voluntary intoxication** under the Code **is a defense** to a **specific intent** crime. **Pathological intoxication**, occurs in very limited situations in which a person, who is generally suffering from a previous brain injury, has a **severe reaction to the voluntary ingestion of small amounts of intoxicants** such as alcohol. **Involuntary intoxication**, by comparison, is **not** self-induced, and is caused by substances which the actor does not knowingly introduce into her body. Involuntary intoxication is a defense to all crimes.

C. AFFIRMATIVE DEFENSES. [§369]

(1) **Justification** and (2) **excuse**.

1. JUSTIFICATION AND EXCUSE COMPARED. [§370]

When a person acts from justification, as in self-defense, society agrees that the **benefits** from avoiding potential harm to an innocent person **outweigh** the **costs** of the actor's conduct. With an **excuse**, society **abhors the result** that occurs, but due to some defect in or coercion of the actor, such as duress or insanity, finds that the actor is **not morally blameworthy**.

Features shared by both types of defenses are:

a. Coercion. [§371]

b. Efficient Harm Avoidance. [§372]

2. JUSTIFICATION. [§374]

Permits the **acquittal** of a defendant who otherwise meets all of the elements of a crime. Justifications generally occur when a person defends him or herself, either from an attack by another person, or a natural calamity.

a. Self-Defense. [§375]

Arises when a person uses physical force to repel what the person reasonably believes is the imminent infliction of bodily harm. Requires (1) an **actual**; (2) and **reasonable belief** of **imminent bodily harm**; (3) a **proportional response**; and (4) a defendant who is **not** considered to be the **aggressor**. The use of **lethal force** in self defense requires that the defendant **reasonably fear** the **imminent infliction** of **serious bodily harm or death**.

(1) Actual and Reasonable Belief. [§376]

With respect to reasonableness, the operative question is whether the average prudent person would believe, under the same circumstances, that bodily harm was imminent.

(2) Proportional Response. [§377]

The amount of force considered proportional depends on how much force is being resisted. Must be **equivalent** to the harm avoided.

(3) Non-Aggressor. [§379]

The **aggressor** is the person who **initiates** or **escalates** a **conflict**.

A defendant who initiates an altercation can completely **withdraw** or **terminate participation** in the affray.

(4) Imminence. [§383]

Self-defense can only be raised when an attack is **either occurring or is imminent**.

(5) Use of Lethal Force in Self-Defense. [§385]

A person may lawfully use lethal force in self-defense if: she (1) **actually** and (2) **reasonably believes** that **lethal force** is (3) **necessary** to repel the **apparent imminent application** of **lethal force** by another, which would cause either **death** or **serious bodily harm** and (4) she is **not the aggressor**.

In a **minority** of jurisdictions, a fifth requirement exists: (5) a **duty to retreat**. A person who is outside of her own residence must refrain from using lethal force if she **knowingly can retreat in complete safety**.

(6) The Castle Doctrine. [§386]

The exception to the duty to retreat requirement is known as the "castle doctrine," because if a person is **in her own residence**, it is as if it is her castle; **she need not retreat** even if she could do so safely. In some jurisdictions, however, if both the victim and the defendant are lawful occupants of the same home, the duty to retreat still applies.

(7) The Model Penal Code. [§388]

An individual may use **non-deadly force** in self-defense under the MPC if the defendant believes it is **immediately necessary** to use such force to defend against the use of unlawful force by another. This test is completely **subjective**; the belief by the defendant as to the need for force need not be reasonable. The defendant must only believe that the use of force is immediately necessary, not that an attack is imminent.

(8) Lethal Force Under the MPC. [§389]

Allows the use of **lethal force** in self-defense **only** if a person believes such force is **necessary** to protect against one of four things: (1) **death**; (2) **serious bodily harm**; (3) **kidnapping**; or (4) **rape**. MPC does not permit the use of deadly force if the accused is the aggressor. The Code also adopts the **minority retreat rule** — if a person knowingly can retreat in complete safety, she must do so. **"Castle" exception also exists** — a defendant has no duty to retreat in her own home.

b. Mistake in Justification. [§390]

A person is mistaken when believing that the use of force is necessary to repel another, if the **mistaken belief** is both (1) **honest** and (2) **reasonable**. The **reasonableness** of a mistake, however, is judged by an **objective standard**.

c. The Battered Woman's Syndrome. [§392]

Applicable when a **defendant kills while experiencing** the battered woman's syndrome.

d. The Defense of Law Enforcement. [§394]

At common law, a police officer is entitled to use **non-deadly force** to effectuate an arrest for what the officer reasonably believes is the commission of, or the prevention of: (1) either a **felony**, or (2) a **misdemeanor** involving a **breach of the peace**. **Deadly force** is permitted in the **prevention of a felony**, but not to prevent a misdemeanor. Most jurisdictions limit it to **dangerous felonies** such as murder, robbery, arson, burglary, and rape, and not just any felony.

(2) Resisting an Unlawful Arrest. [§396]

A defendant is permitted to **resist** an unlawful arrest with **reasonable, non-deadly force**.

e. Defense of Others. [§397]

(1) The "Family/Employment Rule." [§398]

Early English rule which permitted a defendant to **protect only** those with whom he had **a specially recognized relationship**, such as a member of the **defendant's family**, or an **employer and employee**.

(2) The "Alter Ego" Rule. [§399]

Some common law jurisdictions still impose an "alter ego" limitation so that a defendant is placed **in the shoes** of the individual(s) being **attacked**.

(3) The Model Penal Code. [§401]

Permits individuals to protect others **without** any limitations regarding familial, employment status, or other restrictions depending on the defendant's relationship to the person(s) helped.

f. Defense of Property. [§402]

A person may use **non-lethal force** to protect her property from another person if she has a **reasonable belief** that force is **necessary** to protect that property from **imminent unlawful action**. A request to cease must occur prior to the use of such force.

Cannot use lethal force to do so. **Exception** that involves **defending one's home**.

(1) Defense of Habitation. [§403]

Deadly force can be used to defend one's habitation, when: (1) there was **reasonable apprehension** that **deadly force** was **necessary to prevent** an **attempted forcible entry**, which created (2) a **reasonable apprehension** that the assailant would (a) **commit a felony** once inside, or (b) **commit bodily harm** to an **occupant** of the dwelling.

(2) Defense of Property with Mechanical Devices. [§406]

Highly **disfavored** method of "**self-help**" at common law, not completely banned. Permitted if, under the circumstances, the dweller of the house would have been privileged to use the gun in defense of habitation **had the dweller been present.**

(3) The Model Penal Code. [§408]

Permits a person to use **non-deadly force** to protect his property against aggression so long as the person believes that: (1) the intruder's conduct is **unlawful**; (2) the intruder's conduct **affects property** the person possesses or is in his care; and (3) the **imminent use of force is necessary** to prevent or terminate the unlawful entry or the dispossession of personal property.

Does not allow the use of **deadly force to protect** property except against (1) **an intruder** who is believed to be either (a) **attempting to dispossess** the defendant of the **dwelling house**, or (b) **attempting** to commit a **dangerous felony** on the property.

Mechanical devices, permitted only if: (1) that device is **not** known to cause a substantial risk of **serious bodily harm**; (2) the protective device is **reasonable** under the circumstances; and (3) the device is **customarily used** for such a protective purpose.

g. The Necessity or "Choice of Evils" Defense. [§410]

May be raised if: (1) an **emergency** occurs; (2) the emergency is **not** the **defendant's fault**; (3) the emergency creates a **reasonable expectation of imminent harm**; (4) there is **no reasonable opportunity to avoid the injury except** by doing the **criminal act**; and (5) the **harm** from the injury **avoided outweighs** the **harm** from the **criminal offense committed**.

At common law, the necessity defense was **not available** (1) as a **defense to homicide**; (2) to justify stealing food or for other **economic reasons**; or (3) if the **legislature** has deliberately **decided** that the activity allegedly causing harm is more beneficial than the potential harm it may cause.

(1) Mistake in Necessity. [§411]

If a mistake about the need for acting occurs, the mistake must be **both honest and reasonable** to warrant an acquittal.

(2) The Model Penal Code. [§413]

Similar to the common law.

3. EXCUSE. [§415]

"Excuse" includes **insanity**, **duress**, and **entrapment**. It exonerates conduct that otherwise would be criminal.

a. Insanity. [§416]

Raised by a defendant who **admits to committing the offense**, but claims to have done so **as a result of a mental disease or defect**.

(1) Time at which Insanity is Determined. [§417]

The relevant time for assessing whether the defendant is insane is when the crime allegedly occurred, not the time of trial.

(2) Waiver. [§418]

Insanity is raised as an **affirmative defense** at trial. **It can be waived**.

(3) Punishment/Treatment. [§419]

An accused who is excused by insanity is **not punished**. They can be **involuntarily committed** to a psychiatric hospital for treatment until such time as they are no longer dangerous as a result of their mental illness. A criminally committed defendant has the **burden of proof** in a release hearing to show she is no longer dangerous as a result of the mental disease or defect.

(4) The M'Naghten Test. [§421]

The defendant will be found not guilty by reason of insanity if: (1) as a result of a **mental disease or defect** (generally a psychosis), the defendant (2) either (a) **did not understand the nature or quality of his actions, or** (b) **did not know right from wrong.**

(5) The "Irresistible Impulse" Test. [§423]

Other than M'Naghten, the "irresistible impulse" formulation is the most popular common law test. A defendant will be found not guilty by reason of insanity under this test if: (1) as a result of a **mental disease or defect**, (2) she had an **irresistible impulse preventing** her from **complying** with the **requirements of the law**.

(6) Model Penal Code. [§425]

Combines and broadens the irresistible impulse and M'Naghten tests. Permits an insanity defense if, (1) as a **result** of a **mental disease or defect**, a person lacks (2) **substantial capacity** (3) either to **appreciate the criminality** [wrongfulness] of the **conduct** or to **conform the conduct to the requirements of law.**

(7) Guilty but Mentally III. [§427]

Automatically offers **psychiatric treatment** to the convicted defendant.

(8) Insanity Versus Incompetency to Proceed. [§428]

(a) Insanity. [§428.1]

(1) **Affirmative defense** raised at trial that can be waived.

(2) If successful, may be **confined indefinitely** for treatment in a psychiatric hospital.

(3) The insanity is measured only at the **time** of the **alleged incident** in question.

(4) Requires a **mental disease** or **defect**.

(b) Incompetency to Proceed. [§428.2]

(1) **Applies to any significant stage of the proceedings. Incompetency** to proceed **cannot be waived.**

(2) If the defendant is found incompetent she **cannot be detained indefinitely**.

(3) The competency is measured as of the **time of the pre-trial**, **trial** and **post-trial proceedings**.

(4) **Does not require** that the defendant have a **mental disease or defect**. A defendant is incompetent if: (1) she is **unable to understand the nature of the proceedings** against her; or (2) she is **unable** to **assist counsel with the defense**.

b. Duress. [§429]

There must be (1) a **threat of imminent death or serious bodily harm to the defendant or to a member of the defendant's family**; (2) the coercion must be **by another human being**; (3) the **response** to such threats must be **reasonable**; and (4) the **situation** creating the coercion must **not be** the **defendant's fault**.

(1) The Model Penal Code. [§431]

Duress occurs if the defendant is: (1) coerced to commit an offense; (2) by the use or threat of unlawful force against the defendant or any other person; and (3) a person of reasonable fairness in that situation would have been unable to resist.

c. Entrapment. [§433]

The essence of entrapment is that the police used unfair tactics to coerce a defendant into committing a crime.

(1) Tests for Entrapment. [§434]

(a) The Subjective Test. [§435]

Met if: (1) the **police**, or an **agent** of the police, such as a confidential informant, **originated** and **created** (i.e., **induced**) the crime; and (2) the **defendant** was **not predisposed** to committing such a crime.

(b) The Objective Test. [§436]

This test asks whether (1) the offense is **created**, **originated** and **induced by the government** or its **agents**, creating a substantial risk that (2) a **reasonable law-abiding person** would have committed the crime.

(c) The Model Penal Code. [§439]

The MPC adopts an **objective test** for entrapment.

d. Infancy or Immaturity. [§440]

(1) A **child under seven years** of age is **conclusively presumed** to be **unable** to commit a crime. (2) **Children between** the **ages of seven** and **fourteen** also are **presumed incapable** of committing a crime. However, such a presumption is **rebuttable**. (3) **No presumption of incapacity** to commit a crime exists for **children age 14 and over**.

(2) The Model Penal Code. [§442]

Uses the age of 16 as the minimum age for treating a person as an adult capable of committing a crime.

e. Diminished Capacity. [§443]

Refers to a **mental disease, defect,** or **abnormality that is not as severe as insanity**, but one that still affects a person's conduct. Some jurisdictions use it to negate the mens rea for a crime. Some jurisdictions allow it as a defense, for example, but only to certain types of crimes.

(1) The Model Penal Code. [§444]

Permits this defense for all crimes.

With special thanks and appreciation to Leslie Deckelbaum, Betty Branyon, Janet Corso, Diana Ho-Yen Williams, Kelly Romano and my wife, Jennifer.

I. INTRODUCTION

About the Author —

Since graduating with honors from Harvard Law School in 1981, Professor Steven Friedland has served as an Assistant United States Attorney in Washington, D.C. and taught at several law schools. These include the University of Miami, the University of Georgia, the University of Florida, and Nova Southeastern University, where he is a full-time professor. He also has been a Dollard Fellow at Columbia Medical School in Law, Medicine, and Psychiatry, and holds L.L.M. and J.S.D. degrees from Columbia University School of Law. He has received teaching awards at several schools and has published a variety of articles on criminal law, as well as an Evidence textbook. In addition to teaching and publishing, Professor Friedland helped create a Guardian Ad Litem program dedicated to representing the interests of abused, abandoned, and neglected children.

From the Author —

A. WHAT IS CRIMINAL LAW?

Substantive criminal law concerns the scope and nature of crimes. More specifically, a first year course in substantive criminal law defines and examines: (1) the **elements of crimes** and their **defenses**; and (2) why certain **conduct is** deemed **criminal**. In many law schools, **substantive criminal law** is separated from **criminal procedure**. "Criminal Law" focuses on the rights set forth in the Amendments to the United States Constitution, particularly the Fourth Amendment right to be free from unreasonable searches and seizures, the Fifth Amendment privilege against self-incrimination and the Sixth Amendment right to counsel. The subject matter of criminal procedure will not be discussed in this book, except tangentially.

The purpose of this Quick Review is to make substantive criminal law easier to understand. The Quick Review does this by reorganizing and simplifying the various components of a criminal law course. It does not "hide the ball," but attempts to be "user-friendly" instead. Special attention is given to the important details and subtleties of the law as well as to its larger themes.

The information provided is not presented in a vacuum to students who enjoy the subject matter. To the contrary, the Quick Review is specifically designed and packaged to help students prepare for a criminal law examination.

While this guide provides a comprehensive review of the criminal law subject matter, it is intended as a supplement to, and not as a substitute for, other important preparatory examination tools — particularly the review of class notes, assigned course readings, and old examinations given by the professor. This guide, however, can be relied on as a criminal law "**organizer**" throughout the semester, helping to clarify relevant rules and principles.

No matter how clear the rules seem when they are in one's head, they are of little use if they emerge from one's mouth or pen garbled. Because there often is a huge gulf between reading criminal law rules in class and understanding what they mean, this Quick Review uses various mnemonic devices and acronyms to allow you to visualize the criminal law rules for better comprehension and application.

It is important to note that the early criminal law was **common-law** based, meaning judge-made. Over time, due in large part to the influence of the **Model Penal Code** (an **advisory** criminal law statute, drafted by lawyers, law professors, and judges), many legislatures adopted **penal codes** and revamped their criminal laws. Consequently, while this book focuses on the common law rules, it often refers to the Model Penal Code (**MPC**), which is representative of the codes of many states. Criminal law courses may use the common law, the Model Penal Code, state or federal laws, or a combination of these sources of law.

B. STUDYING: THE FOREST AND THE TREES.

For a first year law student, information overload is common. Many students do not know what really "counts." Consequently, there is an attempt to digest everything offered in a course in a non-discriminating fashion, from the textbook to other secondary resources. Moreover, the level of confusion is exacerbated when no clear, concrete answers are offered to the many questions asked in class.

Sadly, memorizing the textbook and other such heroic acts cannot overcome the ambiguity of the law. Instead, it is important to recognize that some information is more important than other information. Thus, the "**highlight**" approach requires an initial question before studying: Is this point important in the larger scheme of things in the substantive criminal law? That is, "Where does this information fit into the grand puzzle?" Asking on a regular basis about what the forest looks like, and not solely about every individual "tree" the course passes by, is the best way to keep from getting lost.

The forest in criminal law often centers on two areas — mental state and defenses. Those often dominate class discussion, exams and the "real world."

C. THE CRIMINAL LAW HIGHWAY.

The criminal law highway is a **concept map** of the criminal law course. It is one way of depicting the criminal law "forest" or the "big picture." The visual image of a "criminal law highway," complete with detours and defenses, provides structural guidance to meet organizational needs on an examination.

Sum & Substance QUICK REVIEW of Criminal Law

The benefits from using the "highway" to organize the "forest" are many: It forces a student to be methodical, and to avoid the "rushes to judgment" so anathema to professors. The student develops the habit of asking all of the necessary questions about the issues. The highway is fairly straightforward. Completed travel results in a crime. First, however, several checkpoints must be passed successfully. In equation form, the main road of the highway looks like: "**A (+ R) + M = C - D**," meaning, **Act (+ Result) + Mental State = Crime, unless Defense**. The "result" portion of the highway is in parentheses because not all crimes demand results, so it does not always apply. This highway is particularly useful on an examination in analyzing and writing out answers to "**issue spotter**" questions that ask about the potential crimes committed in the fact pattern presented. In addition to providing an answer format for questions about the elements of crimes and their defenses, the highway contains a preliminary structure focusing on constitutionally-based challenges to the overall validity of the criminal laws, involving such areas as due process and freedom of speech.

This chart provides an overview of the contents of many criminal law courses. It can be used as a "super quick" reference and reminder about the larger scheme of Criminal Law. Here is what it means:

Pass the check-points on the highway to reach the completed crime.

"A (+ R) + M = C - D"

Act (+ Result) + Mental State = Crime, unless Defense

THE CRIMINAL LAW HIGHWAY
I. ACT

    1. Voluntary act requirement

    2. Omissions

      a. Legal Duty to Act

      b. Prerequisites to Legal Duty:

        (1) Capacity to Assist

        (2) No danger to actor

      c. Five Legal Duty Situations: ("SCRAP")

        (1) **S**tatute

        (2) **C**ontract

        (3) **R**elationship (special types only)

        (4) **A**ssumption of care and seclusion

        (5) **P**eril wrongfully created

II. RESULT

    A. Concurrence (of act and mental state)

    B. Causation

      1. Actual ("but for") causation

2. Proximate (legal) causation

III. MENTAL STATE: types of Mens Rea —
the mental state pyramid, with the first

  A. Purpose

  B. Knowledge

  C. Reckless

  D. Negligence

IV. CRIMES

  A. Inchoate Crimes

    1. Solicitation

    2. Attempt

    3. Conspiracy

    4. Possession

  B. Crimes Against the **Person**

    1. Homicide

      a. **Murder** (4 types)

        (1) Intent to Kill

        (2) Intent to commit serious bodily harm

        (3) Gross recklessness (depraved heart)

        (4) Felony murder

          i) "DIDI" limitations (**D**irect death, **I**nherently **D**angerous felony
or "attempted" felony, **I**ndependent felony or attempted felony)

          ii) when a non-felon kills

            a) proximate cause approach

            b) limited proximate cause approach

            c) agency approach

      b. **Manslaughter** (4 types)

        (1) Heat of passion (i.e., provocation)

        (2) Imperfect justification

        (3) Recklessness, negligence

        (4) Bad act manslaughter

    2. Assault and Battery

    3. Robbery

    4. Rape

    5. False Imprisonment

6. Kidnapping

7. Mayhem

C. Crimes Against Property

1. Burglary

2. Larceny

3. Arson

4. Malicious Mischief

D. **Statutory Crimes**

1. Embezzlement

2. False Pretenses

3. Receiving Stolen Property

4. Theft

5. Statutory Rape

6. Incest

V. DEFENSES

A. Negating the Mens Rea:

1. Mistake of fact

a. specific intent

b. general intent

2. Intoxication:

a. voluntary (valid against specific intent crimes only)

b. involuntary (potentially valid against all crimes)

B. Affirmative Defenses:

1. **Impossibility** (of completion of the offense)

a. factual

b. legal

2. **Necessity** (coercion by nature)

3. **Duress** (coercion by another human being)

4. **Entrapment** (coercion by the police or government agent)

a. objective (focus on police tactics)

b. subjective (predisposition of the defendant to commit a crime is relevant)

5. **Mistake**

a. in law

II. 10 - 5 - 2 HOUR STUDY GUIDE FOR CRIMINAL LAW

To get an **edge** on preparing for final examinations, three different preliminary areas are worth considering: (1) **Perspectives**; (2) **Time Management**; and (3) **Organization of an Examination Answer**.

Perspectives.

Before studying for the final examination, keep in mind that all criminal law courses are not the same. Professors structure their courses **differently**, presenting distinct emphases and different coverage. One teacher may focus on criminal homicide, for example, while another may spend numerous hours on the death penalty. Professors also have vastly different ideas about evaluating and grading final examinations. Thus, make sure that when you prepare for your criminal law exam you are preparing for **your** particular professor's exam, and not what you think a criminal law exam should look like, or what a different professor finds important. It is worth your while to ask yourself (before you even begin to study), questions about the teacher's perspective, such as: what topics did the professor **emphasize** in the course?; which topics did the professor find particularly **interesting**?; and what was **important** to the professor in discussing these topics? The answer to these questions should influence what you study and how you prepare for the exam.

Time Management.

Prior to an examination it may be helpful to write out a **detailed study schedule** that explains which parts of criminal law you will study at what time. The greater the degree of scheduling detail, the better the chance for an efficient use of time. The analogue of this game-plan is **business planning** — if successful business managers make elaborate plans, why not make a plan in managing your exam preparation? The **Capsule Outline** in this Quick Review can assist in organizing study schedules.

In the interest of scheduling efficiently, here are some suggestions often made by time management consultants. (1) **Establish priorities**. This is another way of saying do the most important things first. Do not "save the best for last." If there is trepidation about attacking the important areas because they appear to be imposing and obfuscatory (confusing), break the areas down into bite-size chunks. (2) Focus only on **one area of criminal law at a time**, and learn that area thoroughly. When students say they "know" a subject, they often mean they have memorized the rules and have a general familiarity with the area. This is a far cry from truly understanding how and when criminal law concepts apply in subtle or factually specific contexts. (3) **Sub-divide** your **review** of crimes by their elements. Do the same for the defenses. For example, instead of studying defenses, study self-defense. Instead of studying self-defense, study the concept of "imminent harm;" taking "**baby steps**" in studying will be good practice for doing the same on examinations. (4) Schedule **active** studying exercises. "Active" studying means **practicing exam-taking skills**. Treat studying as "spring training," and practice answering essays and multiple

OUTLINE

choice questions (which can provide feedback on whether you really understand the "black letter" rules). Make this a significant part of the preparation regimen. To augment the utility of these techniques, practice under simulated examination conditions (i.e., practice under time pressure).

Organization of An Examination Answer.

As important as it is to organize studying time, it is equally as important to organize examination answers. During an examination, use a **predetermined framework**. (One option is to follow the criminal law highway, unless this method is inconsistent with your professor's approach.) Know what sub-headings, if any, you will use; whether you will divide up your answer based on all crimes committed by a single perpetrator or by all crimes pertaining to a factual event; whether you will evaluate defenses following a discussion of a particular crime or at the end of a discussion about a factual event; whether you will offer a brief conclusion at the beginning of each answer or only at the end; and the like.

10 HOURS OF STUDY TIME BEFORE THE FINAL EXAM

___ Review class notes. Focus on the areas highlighted by the professor, particularly any statements made about the rules of law and their justifications.

___ Read the **Quick Review** outline to clarify or enhance an understanding of the rules and principles of criminal law.

___ Answer several multiple choice or essay practice questions to grasp how the rules and principles apply to particular situations. The questions at the end of this **Quick Review** offer a good place to start.

___ Review each of the major cases discussed in your class for its central proposition. It helps to state the proposition out loud (assuming one is in an appropriate place). Determine what was the professor's purpose in assigning that case and what point(s) the case added to the criminal law rules and principles that you learned. Review the **Case Squibs** in this book to assist you in quickly referencing the important cases.

___ Practice answering essay questions to test your essay writing skills. (Each answer need not take more than one half hour to complete in order to achieve the desired result.) Read your answer out loud after it is completed to see whether it communicates what you intended. Do you say what you mean? Answers can be written to the practice essay questions in the rear of the **Quick Review**.

___ Have a friend, relative, or other person use the **Quick Review** to quiz you on the precise definitions of the criminal law rules and principles. It should take only five to ten minutes to recite at least ten different rules and principles. Do this twice a day.

___ Boil down the course into "**buzz words**" — those meaningful words that describe or trigger (for you and the professor) criminal law rules and principles (e.g., "legal duty," "overt act," "gross recklessness," "inherently dangerous felony," etc.). Use the buzz words as well as the mnemonic devices and acronyms listed in this **Quick Review** (as well as your own mnemonic devices), for quick memory recall during the examination.

Sum & Substance QUICK REVIEW of Criminal Law

5 HOURS OF STUDY TIME BEFORE THE FINAL EXAMINATION

___ Review the **Capsule Outline** in the **Quick Review**.

___ Carefully review any area of criminal law that you still do not understand.

___ Review the "Criminal Law Highway."

___ Skim quickly through your class notes to remember areas highlighted by the professor.

2 HOURS OF STUDY TIME BEFORE THE FINAL EXAM

___ Review the capsule summary in **Quick Review** and the Criminal Law Highway once again.

___ Review the "analytical and exam approach" sections in **Quick Review**.

___ Boil down your "buzz words" and acronym list into a final checklist of the most important words in each subject area, making sure the list is no more than ten to fifteen words total. These words can fall under such headings as "Act," "Result," "Mental State," "Defenses," and "Crime Definitions." The words should be reminders of or clues to the rest of the legal rules and principles in each of the areas mentioned.

___ Remind yourself right before the exam of the following thought: one hundred years from now, who will know about your criminal law exam? Relax and go into the exam with enthusiasm; create your own momentum.

III. ANALYTICAL AND EXAM APPROACH

A. THE COMMON LAW AND THE MODEL PENAL CODE. [§1]

As noted previously, many criminal law courses focus exclusively on the common law. Other criminal law courses combine the common law with the Model Penal Code. Still other courses refer to the state's own penal code, or a combination of the above. This Quick Review includes Model Penal Code provisions, but focuses primarily on the common law, which is the source or basis for many state criminal laws. In answering examination questions, it is necessary to first determine what the **applicable law is** — common law, Model Penal Code, or state criminal code? If it is debatable as to which law is applicable, briefly mention the source of law you are relying on when answering an essay question.

B. TYPES OF EXAM QUESTIONS. [§2]

There are **three types** of questions that dominate criminal law examinations:

Type # 1: [§3]

The first and most common type of question is the "**issue spotter**." This question type involves long fact patterns in which students are asked to identify and then explain the potential criminal conduct of the participants. Usually, the fact pattern involves several potential defendants who commit a multitude of apparent crimes.

Type # 2: [§4]

The second question type asks the student to critique criminal law **theory**, **norms** or **morality**. These questions often ask what the law **ought to** look like, and includes topics such as the death penalty, "victimless" crimes like prostitution, battered women's syndrome, and other important topics.

Type # 3: [§5]

The third type of question invites **challenges to the law itself**. Most of these attacks are **constitutionally based**. They include the due process "void for vagueness doctrine," and the substantial overbreadth doctrine of the First Amendment.

C. ANSWERING THE THREE QUESTION TYPES ON CRIMINAL LAW EXAMINATIONS. [§6]

Each of the three question types requires a different approach on an examination.

Type # 1: [§7]

The **issue spotter** question requires a discussion of the elements of crimes and any applicable defenses. The act, mental state, and result components, followed by possible defenses, are all relevant, with mental state and defense issues usually dominating.

OUTLINE

Type # 2: [§8]

Questions asking what the criminal law ought to look like often call for **policy** discussions, including analyses based on considerations of **efficiency**, **deterrence**, whether the rules can be implemented **feasibly**, the **competence** of courts to answer the question, and **morality**. A common mistake made in answering this kind of question is for the test taker to merely restate the applicable legal rules and principles. This reiteration is not responsive to the question asked and consequently is not useful.

Type # 3: [§9]

Questions that ask about a law's validity either require a **constitutional analysis** of the void for vagueness or substantial overbreadth doctrines, or a discussion of the principle of legality. Sometimes, this third type of question may be mixed in with the other two types.

IV. THE PURPOSES AND GENERAL REQUIREMENTS OF THE CRIMINAL LAW

A. PURPOSES. [§10]

(1) A primary purpose of the criminal law is to **punish** those people who, by their behavior, should be **morally condemned**. Punishment is far from the law's only purpose, however; (2) Another purpose is **deterrence**, which functions to promote a minimum level of acceptable behavior as well as to protect society from harmful conduct and dangerous people; ("Harmful conduct" includes conduct that harms society as a whole; it does not necessarily mean physical injury to a particular person or persons. For example, conduct that undermines society's moral standards may be criminalized.) (3) The criminal law also is designed to **rehabilitate** offenders; and (4) **promote a safer society**.

1. PUNISHMENT (RETRIBUTION). [§11]

If an individual has committed a crime, a criminal conviction declares that the individual is to be morally condemned for the conduct. Further, the criminal law can impose **sanctions** and exact retribution for the harm caused. These sanctions can take several forms, from the death penalty, to incarceration, to fines, to other forms of behavioral limitations on work and association. Retribution is the defendant's payment to society for the criminal activity. There are two major reasons advanced as to why punishment is appropriate for someone who violates the criminal law. The first reason is based on utility — punishment will create a greater good compared to a lack of punishment. The second reason involves morality — someone who commits a crime deserves to be punished, regardless of whether that result leads to a greater good.

Typically, misdemeanors are those crimes punishable by a year or less in the county jail while felonies are more serious crimes punishable for a year or more in prison.

2. DETERRENCE. [§12]

By threatening sanctions such as incarceration, restitution, and death, the criminal law deters individuals from engaging in criminal conduct and encourages lawful behavior. There are two types of deterrence. One involves deterring the individual who committed the crime by removing that person from society (see Safety, §14 below). There is also the deterrence of the general public which is a significant goal of criminal law. General deterrence insures a minimum level of acceptable conduct.

3. REHABILITATION. [§13]

If an individual has committed a crime, the government, through coercive measures, can serve to encourage the individual to **reform** and learn how to become a more productive, law-abiding citizen.

4. SAFETY. [§14]

An individual who has committed a crime can be removed from society through **incarceration**, or even **capital punishment**, thereby making society safer for law-abiding citizens.

> **a. Example of Criminal Law Purposes.** Ted gets drunk in a not-so-excellent adventure in his car and smashes into the Simpsons' living room. Ted has committed a wrong against society because he has unacceptably endangered others and their property by not complying with a minimum threshold of acceptable conduct. Consequently, he may be charged with committing a crime. (He also may have committed a civil wrong against the Simpsons by damaging their property. They could bring suit in tort for monetary compensation.)

5. COMPARISON WITH CIVIL LAW. [§16]

In several salient respects, criminal law is different than civil law. A central distinction is that the **criminal law**, unlike civil law areas such as torts and contracts, is designed to **morally condemn** and **punish** violators through incarceration or death. **Civil law** is primarily intended to **compensate** an injured party through damages or other remedies, and generally does not involve punishment. While criminal law penalties also can be compensatory and require payment of restitution to a victim, that is not the criminal law's primary function.

Illustration: A prosecutor can press criminal charges against a batterer on behalf of the public even if the victim does not want to prosecute or seek monetary damages in a civil suit. (Victims of domestic violence, for example, are particularly reluctant to pursue criminal charges.)

Because the stakes are so much higher in criminal cases, the rules of criminal law are also different than the rules in civil cases. Unlike civil cases (which often permit a finding of liability based on a preponderance of the evidence), **criminal cases** require **proof beyond a reasonable doubt** of all of the elements of the crime for a conviction to occur. (See §31.) Various constitutional safeguards such as due process rights and the privilege against self-incrimination also attach before, during, and after a criminal trial.

B. FORMS OF CRIMINAL LAW. [§17]

There are **two major types** of criminal laws: **common law** and **statutory law**. The American law has a "common law" origin, meaning that at one time it was judge-made. The American common law owes much of its form and history to English law. In recent years, the enactment of criminal law codes by state legislatures has been widespread. In almost all states, criminal laws stem from statutes. The primary role of the judiciary, is to interpret those statutes and to measure the statutes constitutionality.

While most states have codified their criminal laws, judge-made interpretations of these laws are still prevalent and important. In a criminal law class, judge-made laws, as well as judicial interpretations, likely will be discussed. In addition, many criminal law courses rely on the **Model Penal Code**. This mock statute was created by a group of law professors, judges, and lawyers to offer states a comprehensive revision of the criminal law. The Model Penal Code is not law and has no binding effect. But, it has been the model for many state criminal codes and has been very influential on state and local legislators. This book will reference many of the Model Penal Code sections because of its widespread use in criminal law classes.

C. "THE PRINCIPLE OF LEGALITY." [§18]

This common law principle sets forth **limitations** on the formation, creation, and interpretation of the criminal law. It is important to emphasize that this principle is not so much a rule of law, but a guide for judges who, in earlier times, were the creators and overseers of the criminal law. The principle reached its zenith in the 17th and 18th centuries in both America and Europe.

The principle promotes the concept "**nullum crimin sine lege**," or "**no crime without law**." The principle thus embodies civility in the law, moving the operation of law further away from historical barbarism. To achieve this end, the principle requires **advance notice** and **fair warning** of what is criminal; **retroactive crime creation** is **unacceptable**. The principle minimizes excessive discretion — and an invitation to the abuse of power by government officials, namely the police, prosecutors, and the courts. If the principle did not exist, police, prosecutors, and the courts would have an incentive to prosecute individuals engaging in what appeared to be lawful conduct at the time, with the hope that a court or jury will decide later, after the fact, to make such conduct criminal.

The principle that criminal laws must be prospective or forward-looking suggests that the legislature, with all of its resources, and not the courts, is the best-equipped branch to handle the responsibility of fashioning the criminal law. The legislative creation of criminal law further advances the democratic nature of the law, and makes its formation more consistent with the American representative democracy (i.e., "of the people, by the people ...").

1. THE PROBLEM OF JUDGE-MADE CRIMINAL LAW: RETROACTIVITY AN EXAMPLE. [§19]

Farhquar Jones decides to water his garden in his underwear. He is charged with and convicted of a common law crime, defined only as "committing a public mischief." His conviction violates the principle of legality because there appears to have been no fair warning or notice that watering a garden in one's underwear constituted a public mischief. The court thus can be seen to have acted retroactively, deciding what constitutes a "public mischief" on a case-by-case basis without notice or fair warning to potential violators. *Shaw v. Director of Public Prosecutions*, 2 All E.R. 446 (1961).

The principle of legality also requires that criminal laws have a general as well as prospective application. This requirement of generality in the law is based in large part on necessity. It would be impossible to state with specificity all of the possible applications of the law. One significant limitation exists, however. The generality of the laws must not become so great that a law becomes unduly vague, encouraging arbitrary enforcement by the government and resulting in a lack of adequate notice to prospective "law-violators."

D. CONSTITUTIONAL LIMITATIONS ON THE CREATION AND APPLICATION OF THE CRIMINAL LAW. [§20]

While the principle of legality traces its formation and history to England, the principle largely has been subsumed and embodied in several constitutional limitations. These constitutional protections exist to ensure fairness in the criminal process and to minimize the risk of erroneous convictions.

1. NO EX POST FACTO LAWS — A Limitation on the Creation of Criminal Law. [§21]

The United States Constitution, Art. 1, § 9, and § 10, prohibit the federal and state legislatures, respectively, from enacting **ex post facto** laws (laws which look backward or are retroactive). These constitutional provisions reflect the principle of legality — laws must be **prospective** in application only. *State v. Holloway*, 144 Conn. 295, 130 A.2d 562 (1957).

> **a. EXAMPLE.** After a huge savings and loan scandal involving questionable but legal loans, Congress passes a law which criminalizes making such loans within the past two years. Is this law permissible? No. The law retroactively criminalizes what at the time was lawful conduct. (If the law had stated that all such loans in the future would be subject to criminal sanctions, it would have passed constitutional muster.)

2. NO BILLS OF ATTAINDER — Another Limitation on the Creation of the Criminal Law. [§23]

The United States Constitution, Article 1, §§ 9 and 10, prohibit bills of attainder, which are essentially laws that **punish** specific individuals or members of a group without the benefit of a judicial trial. "Punishment" includes much more than just incarceration, and extends to other deprivations as well. *Cummings v. Missouri*, 71 U.S. (4 Wall.) 277, 325 (1867).

> **a. Example of "Punishment".** An ordinance states that any city official who is found to have violated city laws, after a two-thirds vote by the city council, will be fined and/or imprisoned, and removed from office. This law is an unconstitutional bill of attainder because it punishes city council members without a judicial trial.

> **b. Example of "Punishment".** A state statute in the 1960's requires all members of the clergy to take an oath, prior to being permitted to practice their profession in the state, that they do not oppose the United States involvement in the Vietnam War. This law is an unconstitutional bill of attainder, since it imposes the punishment of "swearing" on a group of people without a judicial trial.

3. DUE PROCESS. [§26]

The due process clauses of the **Fifth** and **Fourteenth Amendments** to the United States Constitution restrict the states and the federal government, respectively, in the way in which criminal laws are created and applied. The **Bill of Rights**, which comprises the first ten amendments, directly limits only the federal government (*Barron v. Baltimore*, 32 U.S. (7 Pet.) 243 (1833)), and the Fourteenth Amendment due process clause has been interpreted to selectively apply the Bill of Rights to the states. *Duncan v. Louisiana*, 391 U.S. 145 (1968). This selective application is known as the "incorporation" doctrine.

a. The Incorporation Doctrine. [§27]

It has long been established that the Bill of Rights do not directly apply to the states. *Barron v. Baltimore*, 32 U.S. (7 Pet.) 243 (1833) (Marshall, C.J.). However, the Supreme Court has held that the due process clause of the Fourteenth Amendment selectively "**incorporates**" most of the Bill of Rights as limitations on the states. *Duncan v. Louisiana*, 391 U.S. 145 (1968). The rights which have been incorporated that relate to criminal law include the Fourth Amendment **protection against unreasonable searches** and **seizures**, the Fifth Amendment **privilege against self- incrimination**, the Sixth Amendment **right to a jury trial** in criminal cases, and the Eighth Amendment **prohibition against cruel and unusual punishment**, among others.

> **(1) EXAMPLE.** The State of California enacts a law permitting prosecutors to comment on a defendant's failure to testify. This law is unconstitutional. The Fifth Amendment privilege against self-incrimination, applied to the states through the Fourteenth Amendment due process clause, prohibits the State of California from passing such a law. *Griffin v. California*, 380 U.S. 609 (1965).

b. Basic Due Process — Fundamental Fairness. [§29]

The due process clauses of the Fifth and Fourteenth Amendments also impose direct limitations on federal and state governments. Criminal laws must be, at a minimum, "fundamentally fair" to be properly applied. "Fundamental fairness" requires that all laws, at a minimum, be reasonable. This includes the procedures used to charge, prosecute, and sentence an individual as well.

> **(1) EXAMPLE.** Montana passes a law prohibiting the wearing of red clothing on Wednesday. Is this law constitutional? No. The law is fundamentally unfair because it is an unreasonable exercise of state power. There is no legitimate government objective. The law consequently violates the due process clause.

c. Procedural Due Process e.g., Burden of Proof. [§31]

Because of the high stakes of criminal trials, the due process clauses require that all elements of a crime be proven by the government "**beyond a reasonable doubt**." *In re Winship*, 397 U.S. 358 (1970) (see Case Squibs section). This high standard reduces the risk of erroneous convictions. It also satisfies the proposition that "it is far worse to convict an innocent person than to let ten guilty persons go free." In civil cases, although a great deal of money may be involved, the stakes are not considered to be as high, and the burden of proof is consequently lower. The requisite proof in civil matters is either "by a preponderance of the evidence" or "by clear and convincing evidence." The burden of proof illustrates the "procedural fairness" requirement of the due process clauses.

There are two different types of burdens of proof. The burden of production, also known as the burden of going forward, is the initial burden of offering evidence on an element of the crime or defense. This burden of producing some evidence requires the party to make a "prima facie" case. If this burden is not satisfied, upon proper motion the judge will not let the case go to the trier of fact, generally the jury. Instead, the court will dismiss the action.

If the burden of going forward is satisfied, however, then the second and greater burden becomes relevant — the burden of persuasion. This burden is the one which requires the party to offer a sufficient amount of evidence to persuade the jury that the elements of which the crime or defense exist. Generally, but not always, the burden of persuasion is placed on the same party which had the production burden. As noted above, the burden of persuasion in a criminal case is "beyond a reasonable doubt."

---

(1) EXAMPLE. Arkansas adopts a law permitting juveniles to be adjudicated delinquent based on a "preponderance of the evidence" standard. Is the Arkansas law constitutional? No. While a juvenile delinquency adjudication is labeled civil, it is so functionally similar to a criminal case that the "beyond a reasonable doubt" safeguard is required in such proceedings as well. Calling such a proceeding civil is merely a "label of convenience and should not be permitted to mask the functional similarities to criminal cases." *In re Winship*, 397 U.S. 358, 373 (1970).

---

d. What the Prosecutor Must Prove. [§33]

The principle that all elements of a crime must be proven beyond a reasonable doubt by the prosecution leaves open the subsidiary question of what elements actually must be proven by the State. For example, does the prosecution have to prove that the defendant is sane, or that there was no duress, entrapment or self-defense involved? The answer given by the United States Supreme Court appears to be that the State must prove only that which it says in the law it will prove. If the pertinent law lists an element as part of the crime, that element must be proven beyond a reasonable doubt. If the law does not include an element as part of the crime definition, then it appears the State need not prove the issue at all. (See Case Squibs Section, *Patterson v. New York*.)

---

(1) EXAMPLE. The State of Maine defines murder as "the unlawful and unexcused intentional killing of another human being without heat of passion." Since "without heat of passion" is one of the elements included by the State in its definition of murder, it must be proven beyond a reasonable doubt by the prosecution. *Mullaney v. Wilber*, 421 U.S. 684 (1975).

---

4. VOID FOR VAGUENESS — A LIMIT ON THE CREATION AND APPLICATION OF THE CRIMINAL LAW. [§35]

This constitutional doctrine stems from due process. It prohibits criminal laws from being **so vague** that **reasonable people must necessarily guess** as to the **meaning** of the law and its **application**. Thus, laws must provide fair notice or warning to potential violators and have ascertainable standards by which to determine guilt or innocence. *Papachristou v. City of Jacksonville*, 405 U.S. 156 (1972). *Lanzetta v. New Jersey*, 306 U.S. 451 (1939). The doctrine is often used as a defense against laws that criminalize speech allgedly protected by the first amendment

Note, however, that the void for vagueness doctrine is based on the belief that most criminal laws must necessarily be vague. Vagueness comes with generality, a significant attribute of the criminal law. Hence, it is important to emphasize that the void for vagueness limitation is triggered only when laws become so vague that reasonable people must necessarily guess as to their meaning and application; the criminal laws are meant to protect reasonable, law-abiding people; not put them at risk of prosecution.

> **(1) EXAMPLE.** A Texas law forbids all "raunchy bumper stickers." This law is void for vagueness because reasonable people must necessarily guess as to the meaning and application of "raunchy." It does not provide fair notice or warning to potential violators or ascertainable standards for courts to decide where to draw the line.

> **(2) EXAMPLE.** Mean Gene, "the Obscene Machine," wishes to film a pornographic reenactment of the Bible called "Begat." He realizes obscenity is a form of speech unprotected by the First Amendment to the Constitution, but is unsure whether his film meets the obscenity definition. Mean Gene will be risking prosecution if he markets the film because the Supreme Court's standard for obscenity, while arguably vague, is not considered by the Court to be so vague that it is void for vagueness. The significance of this conclusion is that obscenity, like so many other laws, has a hazy boundary which places people at risk of violation when their conduct gets close to that boundary.

5. HOW A CONSTITUTIONALLY VAGUE STATUTE MAY SURVIVE A VOID FOR VAGUE CHALLENGE. [§38]

A law that is excessively vague on its face can be interpreted narrowly by courts, legislatures, or appropriate administrative bodies to create **"tolerable vagueness."** The law will then meet constitutional requirements.

> **a. EXAMPLE.** A military law requires that all soldiers conduct themselves as "officers and gentlemen," or else be subject to discipline. This law is not void for vagueness if a court or administrative body has minimized the facial vagueness of the law by narrowing its application. (See Case Squibs Section, *Parker v. Levy.*)

6. CRUEL AND UNUSUAL PUNISHMENT. [§40] (THE EIGHTH AMENDMENT'S PROHIBITION OF)

This **Eighth Amendment** provision has been interpreted to prohibit punishment grossly **disproportionate** to the crime charged. In other words, this limitation requires that the punishment fit the crime. *Gregg v. Georgia*, 428 U.S. 153 (1976).

> **a. EXAMPLE.** John Doe is convicted of rape and sentenced to death. The sentence is unconstitutional because it violates the prohibition against cruel and unusual punishment. The death penalty is disproportionate to the crime of rape. *Coker v. Georgia*, 433 U.S. 584 (1977).

PROBLEM 1. "Wrasslin." Rowdy Robby, a professional wrestler, is charged with "creating a pubic mischief," a judge-made crime, not statutory. Rowdy is alleged to have sneered at a passerby while standing on a street corner. If a judge decides that this is a public mischief and convicts Rowdy, will the conviction stand?

Answer: No. Rowdy had no notice or fair warning that sneering in public constituted the crime of "public mischief." The conviction violates due process and the principle of legality, which require that the criminal law provide fair notice and warning of what is criminal.

PROBLEM 2. "Annoying." If the legislature had enacted a law prohibiting "anyone from standing on street corners annoying passers-by," could Rowdy be properly prosecuted?

Answer: No. Such a law likely would be unconstitutional in violation of the void for vagueness doctrine of the due process clause. The test for determining void for vagueness is whether reasonable people must necessarily guess as to the meaning and application of the law. In this case, reasonable people must necessarily guess as to the meaning of the word "annoying." The definition of "annoying" depends completely on the sensitivity of the hearer, and varies considerably from individual to individual. The consequence is that the law is unduly vague and fails to provide fair notice or warning as to what constitutes a violation of it. Furthermore, there exist no ascertainable standards by which to judge if the law has been violated. *Coates v. Cincinnati*, 402 U.S. 611 (1971).

PROBLEM 3. "Preacher Jones." Congress enacts a law which states, "All preachers named Jones must carry $5 million in special bodily injury insurance." Is this law constitutional?

Answer: Not likely. This law appears to be a bill of attainder, which occurs when a governmental body imposes some form of punishment prior to a judicial trial. Here, the burden of carrying "special insurance," particularly non-functional bodily injury insurance, is likely a penalty within the meaning of punishment. Significantly, the penalty is applied prior to a judicial trial.

PROBLEM 4. "Unusual." A Delaware law prohibits "unusual sexual intercourse in the State of Delaware." Is this law constitutional?

Answer: Probably not. On its face, the word "unusual" appears to be in violation of the void for vagueness doctrine. Reasonable people must necessarily guess as to the meaning and application of the word "unusual." However, if a narrowing construction of the word "unusual" has been issued by the courts, legislature, or appropriate administrative body, explaining with greater clarity what the word means, the law may become tolerably vague and survive due process scrutiny.

V. CRIME COMPONENTS

A. BASIC PRINCIPLES. [§42]

All crimes require an act, also called an **actus reus**. With many crimes, the act must be committed under certain **circumstances**, such as in common law burglary, where the breaking and entering must occur at nighttime. The large majority of crimes further require a concurrent mental state or **mens rea** with the act. It is the existence of the mens rea that makes the act culpable or "bad," warranting prohibition and moral condemnation of the actor (i.e., the person doing the act). Many crimes also require a **result**, such as homicide, which requires the death of a human being. When a result is required, whether the defendant **proximately** and **in fact caused** the result to occur is a relevant issue.

An easy way of remembering these essential elements is the acronym "**ARM**," which stands for Act, Result (causation), and Mental State. The basic crime components of the act, result, and mental state will be discussed below.

In the criminal law, the mental state of the alleged perpetrator is extremely important. It determines (1) whether a crime has been committed, and (2) the degree of culpability of the actor. Thus, depending on the actor's mental state, if someone is killed by another person, the killing may be a non- criminal accident, attributable to culpable negligence, or a "cold-blooded" intentional and unexcused killing. The individual's mental state is extremely important if not dispositive concerning the way society looks at the conduct.

B. BRIEF OVERVIEW

1. THE ACTUS REUS. [§43]

A **voluntary** act is required. It must be performed in concurrence with the required mental state. An incomplete or failed act may still produce a crime (i.e., inchoate crimes).

2. MENS REA. [§45]

The mental state of an actor determines her culpability and what kind of crime has occurred, if at all. Mental states can be objective, (based on a reasonable person), or subjective.

3. RESULT. [§47]

Some crimes require a particular result. An important example is the crime of homicide, which exists only if a human being is killed. The requirement of a result **raises issues of causation**, particularly if there is more than one cause of the particular result, or the actor played only an incidental role in the result.

4. CONCURRENCE. [§49]

The **act** and the **mental state** must be concurrent for a crime to occur. If either one precedes the other, the precise requirements of the criminal law will not be met.

C. THE ACTUS REUS REQUIREMENT. [§51]

The act requirement includes all types of **conduct**, from physical movements, to words inciting other people to act, to the use of mechanical objects, and to the manipulation and use of other people to do one's bidding. There are relatively few limitations on the act requirement, but they are important to know.

Thoughts alone are an **insufficient** basis for a criminal conviction. There are several reasons for this rule.

(a) Everyone has bad thoughts, including most law-abiding citizens who do not act on those thoughts. Thus, if such thoughts could be detected, almost if not everyone would be subject to prosecution.

(b) Unlawful thoughts are not dangerous in and of themselves, but only become dangerous when acted upon.

(c) Prosecutions based on thoughts could be fabricated all too easily by the government.

> **a. EXAMPLE.** A former president has "lust in his heart." Can he be prosecuted for such thoughts? No. His thoughts alone would provide an insufficient basis for prosecution. There is no real harm in such thoughts, and to bring charges would lead police and prosecutors down the slippery slope to a wide variety of other charges for "bad thoughts."

1. THE VOLUNTARY ACT REQUIREMENT. [§52]

The key question: "Did the actor have a choice?" There are **two categories** of **acts**: **voluntary** and **involuntary**. Only voluntary acts can be criminal. The word "voluntary" defines an act that involves **choice** or **volition** on the part of the actor. An act that is not by choice, and does not involve any **mind-body connection**, (such as a reflex, a cough or an unconscious movement like a seizure or sleep-walking), is considered involuntary. Unfortunately, the distinction between "voluntary" and "involuntary" often defies precise definition. [MPC §2.01.] The dividing line between the two is perhaps not as helpful as learning which acts (they are few in number) are considered involuntary.

a. "Voluntariness" Does Not Equal "Blameworthiness". [§53]

Just because an act is voluntary does not mean it is blameworthy. The question of blameworthiness is completely distinct. Blameworthiness or culpability depends on the person's **mental state** at the time of the act. The doctrine of **voluntariness** is limited to the volitional nature of the act; whether it is committed **by choice**. Keep the issues of voluntariness and blameworthiness separate.

> **(1) Example of Voluntary Act — Duress.** Fred Schmerd feels a gun at the back of his head after withdrawing money from the bank, and hears a voice saying "Help me rob the bank or I'll kill you." Fred assists in robbing the bank. Did he commit a voluntary act? The answer is yes, even though it appears that Fred did not have much of a choice in his conduct. The significant factor is that Fred **did have a choice**, and that it was his mind telling his body to help the robber. This mind-body link appears crucial to the determination that a voluntary act occurred.

> **(2) Example of a Voluntary but Inadvertent Act.** Susan Snora drives home from her boyfriend Eddie's house late one night. Susan left after a huge fight, and she was so preoccupied on the way home that she did not have any conscious memory of the drive. Even so, Susan is considered to have acted voluntarily, since her mind was in fact telling her body what to do while she operated the car.

(3) Example of Voluntary Conduct. One morning Amy poured coffee into her coffee mug almost reflexively, as she had done every morning for years. She didn't realize that there was a hole in the cup, and the dripping coffee had burned her friend Nate. Amy's act of pouring the coffee was voluntary, because, while she could have been more careful, her mind was telling her body what do so, meeting the requisite mind-body connection.

(4) Example of Voluntary Blameworthy Conduct. If Amy had poured the coffee into the mug in the preceding example without looking, her action may not only be voluntary, but also unreasonable, in that it failed to meet a minimum acceptable standard of care. Amy's conduct therefore would be both voluntary and blameworthy.

(5) Example of Involuntary Conduct. While driving home, Franny O'Schwartz suffered an epileptic seizure. Her car careened out of control, causing an accident. Franny's actions in suffering the seizure are involuntary, and therefore she does not meet the voluntary act requirement for criminal liability.

b. Exception: When There is a Voluntary Act in the Course of Involuntary Conduct. [§59]

Some courts still will hold Franny responsible in the example above **if the involuntary conduct occurs during the course of voluntary, culpable conduct**. If Franny had begun to drive the car knowing she was an epileptic and susceptible to a seizure, her decision to drive under those circumstances was by choice, and therefore voluntary. Consequently, if Franny was also blameworthy in making such a choice, she may be held responsible for harm caused by subsequent involuntary conduct, such as an epileptic seizure, even though she had absolutely no control over the conduct that directly led to the crash. *People v. Decina*, 2 N.Y.2d 133, 138 N.E.2d 799 (1956).

c. The Model Penal Code. [§60]

The MPC, §2.01, states that "a person is not guilty of an offense unless his liability is based on conduct which includes a voluntary act ... [Examples of involuntary acts are] a reflex or convulsion; ... a bodily movement during unconsciousness or sleep; ... conduct during hypnosis or resulting from hypnotic suggestion ... a bodily movement that otherwise is not a product of the effort or determination of the actor, either conscious or habitual." Thus, the MPC also uses illustrations to help draw what remains a fuzzy line between voluntary and involuntary conduct.

(1) Model Penal Code Example. [§61]

Dr. Von Ruth hypnotizes the defendant, and suggests that the defendant kill Dr. Von Ruth's enemy. If the defendant subsequently kills Dr. Von Ruth's enemy, has he committed a voluntary act? Pursuant to the MPC, the defendant acted under hypnosis and did not commit a voluntary act. (However, some jurisdictions do not consider hypnosis to be sufficient to negate an individual's freedom to choose. These jurisdictions argue that one's willingness to be hypnotized is evidence of a voluntary act. Thus, like duress, hypnosis is a voluntary act which may be excusable.)

d. Constitutional Requirement. [§62]

The United States Constitution requires that crimes be based on a **voluntary act**, and not on the status of a person or a sickness over which a person has no control.

> **(1) EXAMPLE.** The State of California enacts a law making it a crime for any person to "be addicted to the use of narcotics." The law is unconstitutional because it prosecutes a person for his status as a drug addict, which often is considered an illness, without requiring that an act be committed within the jurisdiction. This law constitutes cruel and unusual punishment in that it is similar to punishing a person for being mentally ill, a leper, or for suffering from a venereal disease. *Robinson v. California*, 370 U.S. 660 (1962).

> **(2) EXAMPLE.** The State of Texas makes it a crime for a person to "appear drunk in a public place." Is this law constitutional? The answer is yes, because the voluntary act of appearing drunk in public is included. Consequently, this law does not punish a person for the status of being an alcoholic, but for the voluntary act of appearing in public. *Powell v. Texas*, 392 U.S. 514 (1968).

2. OMISSIONS. [§65]

Unless there is a **legal duty to act**, an individual will not be subject to criminal penalties for omitting or failing to act. While it may be morally appropriate to act, and a "good samaritan" would have acted under the circumstances, unless there was an affirmative legal duty to act, the mere existence of a moral obligation is insufficient to create criminal liability. *State v. Ulvinen*, 313 N.W.2d 425 (Minn. 1981).

> **a. EXAMPLE.** Boris Goodenough observes his archenemy lying face down in a puddle. Boris, an Olympic swimmer and well-known strong man, could easily lift his enemy's face out of the puddle, saving his life. Instead, Boris, notorious for his nefarious deeds, steps calmly over his enemy and watches him drown. Boris is not criminally liable for his conduct, since he did not have a legal duty to assist or aid his enemy. While a Good Samaritan in similar circumstances would have lifted his enemy's head out of the puddle, Boris was not required to do so.

b. A Legal Duty to Act. [§67]

There are **five** general situations in which a legal duty to act exists. In these situations, an omission to act serves as an "**act substitute**." Criminal liability still depends on whether the other elements of the crime, namely the mental state and result, exist, but a prosecution will not be prevented because the defendant did not act. Thus, when analyzing omissions, be aware that the violation of a legal duty to act does not in itself create criminal liability.

The five situations in which a legal duty arises can be remembered by the acronym "**SCRAP**."

S = **S**tatutory creation of the duty.

C = **C**ontractual creation of the duty.

R = **R**elationship of a special nature that creates the duty.

A = **A**ssumption of voluntary care and seclusion of an injured person to create the duty.

P = **P**eril to another wrongfully caused by the actor, creating a duty.

OUTLINE

(1) Statute. [§68]

The legislature, by statute, may require people to act on certain occasions. Failure to act in these situations may result in a crime, provided that the requisite mental state also exists. The legislature does not often demand an act, but the statutory creation of a duty is certainly not extraordinary. *Craig v. State*, 220 Md. 590, 155 A.2d 684 (1959).

> **(a) EXAMPLE.** Federal law requires people to file income tax returns each year. The knowing failure to file a tax return is a violation of the federal law.

> **(b) EXAMPLE.** Many state statutes require individuals to stop and identify themselves if they have been involved in an automobile accident. Failure to do so may give rise to criminal liability.

(2) Contract. [§71]

An individual may create a legal duty to act by entering into a contract. The creation of a contractual duty, in contrast to a duty created by statute, results from a voluntary agreement by the person to be bound. *Rex v. Ellen Jones*, 19 Cox Crim. Cas. 678 (1901).

> **(a) EXAMPLE.** Paula agrees to be a part-time lifeguard during college. She has created a legal obligation to watch and attempt to rescue swimmers while she is on duty.

> **(b) EXAMPLE.** An individual who agrees to serve as a baby sitter incurs a contractual obligation to assist and aid the children for whom she is baby-sitting.

> **(c) EXAMPLE.** Dr. O agrees to provide medical care to a patient with gout, but thereafter refuses to treat the patient at an agreed upon time because of an important tennis match in which he is participating. Dr. O may be held liable for any harm that results from a violation of a contractual duty to act.

(3) Relationship. [§75]

In some instances a special non-contractual relationship creates a legal duty to act. The relationship depends on the **status** of the individuals involved. Special relationships are quite limited, but include the husband-wife, parent-child, employer-employee, and land owner-invitee. No such legal duty arises for good friends, lovers, or roommates, regardless of how close the relationship is. *State v. Williquette*, 385 N.W.2d 145 (Wis. 1986).

(a) EXAMPLE. (Family Relationships) Husband and Wife go boating with Daughter and Son. A parent falls overboard. Husband and Wife have a duty to aid or assist each other because of their status as husband and wife. If Son or Daughter falls overboard, both parents also have a legal duty to act on their child's behalf.

(b) EXAMPLE. (Employer-Employee) Employer Edna leaves debris lying around the woodshop and Employee Ed slips and falls. Edna may have a duty to Ed to provide aid or assistance.

(c) EXAMPLE. (Land Owner-Invitee) Harry asks Peter Plumber to repair his sink, but neglects to warn him about the hidden sinkhole next to the driveway. If Peter falls in, Harry may have a duty to aid.

---

(4) Assumption of Voluntary Care and Seclusion. [§79]

An individual who voluntarily assumes the care of another, and then secludes that person from assistance by others, has a duty to continue assisting the person in need, provided that abandonment of care would leave the person worse off. *Regina v. Nicholls*, 13 Cox Crim. Cas. 75 (1874).

(a) EXAMPLE. After an auto accident, bystander Joe Bob Johnson agrees to assist a man who appears to be mildly dazed. Consequently, everyone else leaves the scene. Joe has a duty to continue care if failure to do so would place the victim in a worse position than that in which Joe found him. In effect, this is a Good Samaritan rule with strings attached — if a person agrees to help, the helper cannot abandon assistance and make matters worse.

---

(5) Peril. [§81]

If an individual **wrongfully creates another's peril**, an obligation may arise to assist the person in danger and to minimize further harm. *Jones v. State*, 220 Ind. 384, 43 N.E.2d 1017 (1942). But see, *Commonwealth v. Calj*, 247 Mass. 30, 141 N.E. 510 (1923) (defendant had a duty to act even though peril was innocently created). (Note: The duty to mitigate harm can be viewed as falling within the doctrine of proximate causation, where a person who wrongfully harms another can be held liable for all reasonably foreseeable harm resulting from the wrongful conduct.)

(a) EXAMPLE. Mr. MaGoo recklessly drives on a sidewalk during rush hour. He strikes Patti, a pedestrian, knocking her to the ground. MaGoo has a duty to render assistance to Patti since he wrongfully created Patti's perilous situation.

(b) Prerequisites to Liability for Failure to Comply with a Legal Duty to Act. [§83]

Even if one of the five legal duty categories in "SCRAP" exists, liability may occur only if two prerequisites also are met: (1) there must be **capacity to assist**; and (2) there must be **no substantial danger to the person assisting.**

(i) Capacity to Assist. [§84]

A person who, through no fault of his or her own, lacks the capacity to render assistance, will not be held responsible despite a legal duty to act.

(A) EXAMPLE. A lifeguard notices two swimmers drowning in opposite ends of the swimming area. The lifeguard must make a choice as to which of the two to save, and does so. The lifeguard will not be held responsible for the person who drowned because the lifeguard, through no fault of her own, had no capacity to assist at that time.

If an incapacity to assist is caused by the lifeguard's own culpability, however, then she may be held criminally responsible. If the lifeguard had fallen asleep and did not see a person drowning, she might be held liable because the standard for determining capacity to assist is whether she **should have been** able to provide assistance, not whether she was, in fact, in a position to do so.

(ii) No Substantial Danger to the Person Assisting. [§86]

A person will not be held responsible for failing to assist another if compliance with a legal duty to act places the person in substantial danger.

(a) Examples of "Substantial Danger." (1) A lifeguard who would face a serious risk of bodily harm attempting to rescue a drowning person during a hurricane; (2) a fire fighter who likely would be killed upon trying a certain rescue; and (3) a babysitter who would be at great risk of bodily harm in trying to rescue a child who climbed up a tree, would not be required to jeopardize their own lives to fulfill the duty to act. Other less dangerous actions, such as (1) throwing the drowning person a rope, (2) spraying water at the burning building, or (3) calling for help to assist with the child in the tree, respectively, may be minimally required in these situations.

---

(8) The Model Penal Code. [§88]

The MPC is substantially similar to the common law in this area. It provides for liability if the omission is "expressly made sufficient by the law defining the offense; or ... a duty to perform the omitted act is otherwise imposed by law." The actor also must be physically capable of performing the act in question, or no liability will result. [**MPC** §2.01(3).]

PROBLEM 1. "Don't Drink and Drive." Susan O'Shanter decides to go out drinking on a Friday night with her friends. They drive to a bar about fifteen miles from their homes, dance, drink, have a good time, and then get into their cars to return home. Susan claims to have no memory of what happened after she entered the car for her return trip home. During that trip, Susan crosses the yellow dividing line of the road and ends up in a head-on collision with another car, seriously injuring three individuals in the other car. Susan claims in a subsequent prosecution for battery that she was on "automatic pilot," and was "so drunk, I did not know what I was doing." Did Susan commit a voluntary act?

> **Answer:** Susan committed a voluntary act when she chose to drive home. Her choice to drive home was volitional. The fact that she cannot remember the events due to intoxication does not indicate that the choice to drive was an involuntary act under the law. There appears to have been a "mind-body" connection during the sequence of events; the intoxication likely affected the mind-body connection, but did not sever it. Furthermore, as in the case of *People v. Decina* (see Case Squibs Section), if the voluntary act is measured at the time of the decision to drive, Susan's decision to drive after becoming intoxicated was still a voluntary one. If Susan had a culpable mental state at the time she commenced driving, she could be prosecuted for that act and her concurrent mental state which led to the collision.

PROBLEM 2. "Inside Story." Gomer and Alicia May were two well-intentioned but misguided parents. Their one-year-old baby, G. Williker, was suffering from a bad fever. Gomer remembered reading somewhere that one should "feed a cold and starve a fever" to overcome such maladies. So Gomer and Alicia May decided to starve G. Williker. The cure worked and the fever went away, but G. Williker died from a lack of nourishment. Did Gomer and Alicia May violate a legal duty to act?

> **Answer:** Yes. A legal duty to act was created by the special status relationship of the parents to the child. Consequently, it was the parents' responsibility to act and obtain medical assistance for their child. Whether they can be held criminally liable presents a separate question than whether they had a legal duty to act. Even if the parents' omission violated the legal duty to act, there still remains the question of whether they had a culpable mental state.

PROBLEM 3. "Bubba." The Boy Scouts decided to create a program to help elderly individuals across busy intersections. Bubba, a real joker, decided he would impersonate a boy scout and help an elderly citizen named Bud across the street. As Bubba did so, he stopped in the middle of the intersection and said to Bud, who was nearly blind, "See you around!" Bubba then left Bud to fend for himself. Bud was hit by a car and seriously injured. Did Bubba violate a legal duty to act?

Answer: Yes. A legal duty to act arises when the **peril is wrongfully created**. (It falls within the acronym "SCRAP.") Here, Bubba wrongfully created peril by walking Bud only half-way across the busy intersection. By leaving Bud in a position of danger, Bubba created a legal duty to minimize the likelihood of harm. Bubba also may have had a legal duty to act because he voluntarily assumed the care of the elderly pedestrian by commencing to walk Bud across the street, and in a sense secluded Bud from further assistance. The better theory, however, is the wrongful creation of peril.

PROBLEM 4. "Jack and Jill." Jack and Jill went up the hill to fetch a pail of water. Jack fell down and broke his crown, and Jill left town with Johnny without providing aid to Jack. Was Jill required to assist Jack?

Answer: It depends. Whether Jill had a legal duty to assist Jack depended on whether the situation fell within the acronym "SCRAP." There were no facts given which indicated that one of the components of "SCRAP" was triggered. Even if Jack and Jill were the best of friends, or often had relied on each other in the past, no duty to render assistance would have arisen in the criminal law unless they had a special relationship such as husband and wife, had an agreement (i.e., contract) to assist each other, or fell within one of the other categories.

Oliver Wendell Holmes, Jr. aptly summarized the importance of the mens rea requirement in determining culpability when he said "Even a dog distinguishes between being stumbled over and being kicked."

The determination of what constitutes a crime, and how severe that crime is, generally depends on the mental state of the actor at the time the act was committed. Some actors are more **blameworthy** or **culpable** because of their mental state — or lack thereof. The degree of culpability often determines not only whether punishment is appropriate, but the severity of that punishment as well.

The mens rea is the name given to the **actor's mental state** at the time the actor is performing the behavior in question. A person has a mental state even if the act is committed inadvertently or carelessly. Depending on the mental state, the very same act may be subject to different criminal penalties, or no penalty at all. It is the mental state of the individual, therefore, that determines the level of a person's **culpability** or **blameworthiness**, and consequently, the extent to which punishment is appropriate, if at all.

The different mental states that exist are difficult to define with any sort of precision. A broad array of terminology has been used by courts and legislatures, and sometimes a single term has been given multiple meanings. Yet comparisons can help to clarify matters. There are **two** major **types** of criminal mental state: **subjective** (what is **in the actor's mind**) and **objective** (what should have been in the actor's mind had she been a **reasonable person**).

Mens Rea does **not** equal Motive. Mental state does not refer to the actor's motive for acting. A **motive** offers an explanation of why the actor has a particular mental state (e.g., the defendant may have intended to kill the victim (mental state) because the defendant was in love with the victim's wife (motivation)).

> **a. EXAMPLE.** Z kills another person in an automobile collision. Whether Z committed a crime depends on the nature of Z's driving was it careless, reckless, intentional, or non-negligent? Z's act must be accompanied by a culpable or blameworthy mental state — at the very least, negligence — to be successfully prosecuted.

1. TYPES OF MENS REA. [§90]

There are essentially four different criminal mental states: "**purpose**," "**knowledge**," "**recklessness**," and "**negligence**" (mnemonic: "**PKRN**"). These four mental states descend in degree of culpability, (much like a pyramid of culpability) from purpose, the most heinous criminal mental state, to negligence, the least heinous. There are also non-criminal mental states. For example, when an accident occurs, it does not always mean that the individual was negligent or otherwise culpable at that particular time. As noted above, mental states may be subjective or objective. A subjective mental state embraces the thoughts or beliefs of the person in question. An objective mental state ignores the thoughts and beliefs of the person in question and looks solely to the reasonably prudent person as a reference. Some of the mental states in the mens rea pyramid of culpability are completely subjective, some are completely objective, and some are a combination of both. The more heinous the mental state, the more subjective it is. "Purpose" and "knowledge" are completely subjective, for example, "recklessness" combines both subjective and objective elements, and "negligence" is completely objective.

a. Purpose. [§91]

Purposeful behavior occurs when the actor desires that certain consequences occur. Statutes often use many different words to describe purposeful behavior, including "with design," "intentionally," and "with intent." Note that at common law and under many statutes, "intentional" meant either purposeful conduct or behavior with knowledge.

> **(1) EXAMPLE.** George hates his neighbor with a passion. One day he decides to run his neighbor over with a car. If George acts to run his neighbor over with the objective of doing so, he has acted purposefully.

b. Knowledge. [§93]

Knowledge exists when the actor is **consciously aware** that the **results** will be **practically certain to occur**. The results that actually occur, however, need not be desired.

People v. Nash, 669 N.E. 2d 353, 1996 Appellate Court of Ill

D was charged with knowingly appropriating timber without the owner, M's consent. D had purchased timber from M's neighbor, W, who informed D that she owned up to the fence. However, 77 feet of the land on W's side of the fence was owned by M. D took the timber from this area. The State argued and the judge applied the standard that knowledge means knew or should have known. D was found guilty.

A person acts knowingly or with knowledge when he is "consciously aware that his conduct is of such nature or that such circumstances exist. Knowledge of a material fact includes awareness of the substantial probability that such fact exists." 720 ILCS 5/4-5(a) (West 1992). "Substantial" is defined as "having a solid or firm foundation: soundly based: carrying weight" (Webster's Third New International Dictionary 2280 (1976)), and "probability" is defined as [*986] "likelihood; appearance of reality or truth" (Black's Law Dictionary 1081 (5th ed. 1979)). In contrast, a "possibility" is merely an "uncertain thing which may happen." Black's Law Dictionary 1049 (5th ed. 1979). Here, the State was required to prove that the defendants were consciously aware that they were cutting Diane Meyers' trees or that this was a substantial probability.

The term "knew or should have known" is commonly used in civil cases; however, it should not be equated with the requisite mental state of "knowledge" in criminal prosecutions. "Knowledge" is not the same as "should have known." "Knowledge" involves conscious awareness (720 ILCS 5/4-5 (West 1992)), while "should have [***10] known" implicates "the standard of care which a reasonable person would exercise" and therefore pertains to the lesser mental states of "recklessness" and "negligence."

Reversed.

> **(1) EXAMPLE.** George hates his neighbor and he desires to kill him. To achieve this end, he purposely puts a bomb in his neighbor's car. George knows that his neighbor's in-laws always travel with his neighbor in the car, and would be killed by such a bomb as well. George's conduct in killing his neighbor's in-laws was knowing, because he did not want to kill the in-laws, but he was consciously aware that as a result of the bomb blast, the death of the in-laws was practically certain to occur. For example, in *People v. Nash*, 669 N.E. 2d 353 (App. Ill. 1996), the court stated: "A person acts knowingly or with knowledge when he is 'consciously aware that his conduct is of such nature or that such circumstances exist. Knowledge of a material fact includes awareness of the substantial probability that such fact exists.'"

c. Recklessness. [§95]

Recklessness exists when a person **consciously disregards** a **substantial and unjustifiable risk** of harm. The requirement that the individual "consciously disregard a risk" is **subjective**, and depends solely on whether the individual is in fact aware of the risk. Whether the risk of harm is substantial and unjustifiable, however, is measured **objectively** and based on a reasonable person standard. This part of the test depends on whether a reasonable person would find the risk to be substantial and unjustifiable. *DeVaughn v. District of Columbia*, 628 F.2d 205, 207 (D.C. Cir. 1980). (Note that some jurisdictions distinguish gross recklessness from mere recklessness.)

> **(1) EXAMPLE.** Art decides to drag race Barbara. He sweeps across the yellow median line of a two lane road on a curve to pass Barbara. When he does so, Art realizes that such an action could be dangerous. Art has acted recklessly if he was consciously aware of the risk of crossing the yellow median line, which to a reasonable person would be substantial and unjustifiable. In other words, Art consciously took a "bad" risk — crossing the median on a curve — one that a reasonable person would find to be substantial and unjustifiable.

d. Negligence. [§97]

Negligence occurs when a **person acts unreasonably**, in disregard of a **substantial** and **unjustifiable** risk of harm to others. Negligence is different than either recklessness, knowledge, or purposefulness in that it is based solely on **objective** criteria — specifically, a "reasonable person" standard. *Walker v. Superior Ct.*, 47 Cal. 3d 112, 139, 763 P.2d 852, 869-870 (1988).

Even if people have no conscious awareness that their conduct involves taking an unjustifiable and substantial risk, that is they are empty headed, they are still deemed negligent if they **should have known** that the risk created was unjustifiable and substantial. This standard encourages a minimum level of acceptable conduct in society. If a person cannot comply with this threshold level of competence, such as driving a car in a reasonably safe manner, the person is expected not to engage in the conduct at all. Violation of this standard warrants moral condemnation and may expose the actor to criminal liability. See *State v. Jenkins*, 294 S.E.2d 44 (S.C. 1982).

(1) The Defendant's Empty Head. [§98]

One way to think of negligence is in terms of a person with an empty head. Even though a person acts in an inadvertent, empty-headed fashion, and is **completely unaware** of the significance or consequences of his or her conduct, that person is still considered to have a mental state. The message to empty-headed people in criminalizing negligence is, "You will be held responsible if you act empty-headed, so either fill up your head with reasonable thoughts or don't do the act. If you drive a car, throw a ball, swing a bat, or shoot off fireworks, society will expect you to act reasonably and take reasonable precautions."

---

(2) EXAMPLE. Defendant decides to paint his balcony. He attempts to balance six jars of paint on the balcony railing, not realizing that putting all of those jars on the balcony created a substantial and unjustifiable risk that one of the paint jars would fall, seriously hurting someone down below. Unbeknownst to defendant, a jar falls, injuring a passerby. The lack of actual knowledge on the part of the defendant is irrelevant to whether negligence occurred. All that matters is whether a reasonable person, under those circumstances, would have known that the act of balancing six jars on the balcony created a substantial and unjustifiable risk of harm to others.

---

e. Distinguishing Criminal from Civil Negligence. [§100]

The concept of negligence appears in tort as well as in the criminal law. While negligence in tort and in the criminal law are similar, they are not identical. **Criminal** negligence generally requires a **higher level** of "unreasonableness" than **civil** negligence in tort. (That is, the threshold level for criminal negligence is higher.) *Blueflame Gas, Inc. v. Van Hoose*, 679 P.2d 579 (Colo. 1984).

f. Common Point of Confusion: Are the More Heinous Mental States Associated with the More Heinous Crimes? [§101]

The general answer to this question is **no** — the more serious crimes do not necessarily require the most heinous mental states. Similarly, just because negligence is the least heinous mental state does not always mean that it is the basis for the least culpable crimes. The crime of rape is an instructive example: It required only a negligent mental state at common law. Attempted rape, on the other hand, a lesser included offense of rape, requires a specific intent to commit the crime, meaning the act must occur either purposefully or knowingly. Thus, an attempted rape requires a more heinous mental state than the more severe crime, rape. Further, a rape committed negligently is considered to be a more serious offense than a petty theft committed purposefully, just as a negligent homicide is considered to be more heinous than an attempted battery.

g. Specific and General Intent. [§102]

The words "specific" and "general" intent arise often in describing the mens rea requirements of crimes. Specific intent comprises conduct performed either purposefully or knowingly. Many other terms are used synonymously with specific intent. (See Case Squibs Section, *Morissette v. United States*; *United States v. Flores*, 753 F.2d 1499, 1505 (9th Cir. 1985).) These terms include "willful," "willful and wanton," and "intentional." General intent, on the other hand, denotes any of the four mental states — negligence, recklessness, knowledge, or purposefulness — that can satisfy the mens rea requirement. *Ricketts v. State*, 291 Md. 701, 436 A.2d 906 (1981). General intent also has many synonyms, most notably conduct performed "unlawfully."

> **(1) Example of a Specific Intent Crime.** Larceny at common law required the "trespassory taking and carrying away of the personal property of another with the intent to deprive the other of that property permanently." The "intent to permanently deprive another of property permanently" requires intentional behavior, which can be either purposeful or knowing. Thus, larceny is a specific intent crime.

> **(2) Example of a General Intent Crime.** Battery is the unlawful touching of another person. "Unlawful" is a synonym for general intent, and is satisfied by negligent behavior as well as by reckless, knowing, or purposeful behavior.

(3) Comparing the Mens Rea of Completed Crimes and Attempt Crimes. [§105]

The type of mens rea required for a crime may not be the same required to commit an attempt of that same crime. All attempt crimes require specific intent at common law because they demand an intent (either purposeful or knowing conduct) to commit the underlying crime. In contrast, if the attempt is completed, it might require either general or specific intent. An attempted battery (i.e., an assault), for example, requires specific intent, and is only satisfied by purposeful or knowing behavior. A battery, as noted above, however, is a general intent crime and satisfied by negligent conduct.

h. Malice. [§106]

"Malice" is an important criminal law mental state. It serves as the mens rea requirement for the common law crimes of **murder** and **arson**. A dictionary definition of the word "malice" will reveal such terms as "ill will" or "spite." The legal definition is quite different. Simply put, malice is a **mental state requiring purpose, knowledge, or recklessness**. In other words, at common law malice can be satisfied if the person acted intentionally (meaning either purposefully or knowingly), or recklessly.

> **(1) Example of Malice.** Sarah Silgum knows she should not try to flick her half-smoked cigarette into a waste canister ten feet away because of the potential danger, but she does so anyway. After successfully flicking cigarettes for several months, she finally misses the canister. The drapes catch fire and the house burns down. Sarah acted maliciously. Even though there was no ill will or spite on her behalf, she was reckless when she consciously disregarded the substantial and unjustifiable risk of fire by flicking the lighted cigarettes into a canister ten feet away.

i. "Transferred Intent." [§108]

In tort law, if the actor harms a person different than the intended victim, the **intent** to harm may be "transferred" from the intended victim to the actual one to hold the defendant liable. This **fiction** is sometimes used in criminal law as well. Yet, it is technically erroneous and unnecessary. An **alternative and preferable approach exists**, which involves determining whether an intent to kill a human being existed, and to hold the defendant liable even though the person killed was not the human being the defendant desired to kill. The alternative formulation rests on the premise that an intent to kill a human being is all that is necessary to satisfy the mens rea, not an intent to kill the actual person harmed.

> **(1) EXAMPLE.** Al intends to kill Bo and shoots at him. Al misses Bo, but kills Cy, an innocent bystander. Is Al liable for intent to kill murder? The answer is yes. Some courts would reason that Al's intent to kill Bo transfers to Cy. Instead, the preferable way to view this issue is that Al intended to kill a human being when he acted. The fact that Al killed a different human being than the one he wanted to kill is irrelevant; all that is necessary is an intent to kill a human being. Since the actus reus occurred concurrently with his intent to kill, and he caused the required result, a dead body, Al has met the requirements of intent to kill murder. *Mayweather v. State*, 29 Ariz. 460, 242 P. 864 (1926).

j. Strict Liability. [§110]

A certain group of lesser crimes known as "**public welfare**" **offenses** are strict liability crimes. No mens rea whatsoever is required to commit these offenses, which include the "sale of adulterated food," or the "sale of liquor to minors." These crimes are generally considered "**malum prohibitum**," which means they are wrong because they are prohibited. Most other crimes, including all crimes requiring a mens rea, are "**malum in se**," meaning they are bad in and of themselves. *State v. Horton*, 139 N.C. 588, 51 S.E. 945 (1905).

(1) Crimes with No Stated Mens Rea. [§111]

Where no mens rea is expressly stated in the statutory definition of the crime, a mens rea will be **implied** in the law because of the integral part played by mens rea in determining criminal culpability. At common law, the mens rea, when implied, is negligence. (See Case Squibs Section, *Morisette v. U.S.*)

> **(2) EXAMPLE.** According to law, "all unauthorized uses of a motor vehicle are prohibited." No mental state is required on the face of the law, so negligence will be implied at common law as the required minimum. Thus, a person can be held to have violated the law only if that person negligently, recklessly, knowingly, or purposefully engaged in the unauthorized use of a motor vehicle.

k. The Model Penal Code. [§113]

The MPC also divides mental states into categories of purpose, knowledge, recklessness, and negligence. The Code requires a mental state for all of the material elements of an offense. In addition, the MPC recognizes that some crimes require specific circumstances that are accorded their own mental states.

The MPC also generally implies a mental state requirement for crimes without a stated mental state. Unlike the common law, which implies negligence, the MPC **implies** at a minimum a **recklessness** mens rea.

l. Crimes With More Than One Mens Rea. [§114]

Some crimes have more than one mental state within their definition. When this occurs, each mental state applies only to a component part of the crime, such as the circumstances required for the crime to occur.

> **(1) EXAMPLE.** If rape is defined as "knowingly having sexual intercourse with a woman while negligently failing to obtain consent," the knowledge requirement would apply to having sexual intercourse with a woman, and the negligence standard would apply to whether consent existed.

PROBLEM 1. "Afterburn." Following a long day at work, Bugsy burns down one of the office buildings he owns in order to reap the insurance proceeds. Unbeknownst to Bugsy, a secretary who was diligently working overtime in the building is overcome by smoke and dies. Did Bugsy commit either arson or homicide?

> **Answer:** Arson at common law is "the malicious burning of the dwelling house of another." Bugsy meets the malice requirement, because it includes acting purposefully, knowingly, or recklessly. Here, Bugsy did the burning purposefully with the motive of collecting the insurance. However, at common law, Bugsy would not be guilty of arson because he burned down his office building, and not a dwelling house in which another person resided. Thus, the requirements of the law have not been met. (Modern statutes have expanded the definition of arson to include the burning of any building, so Bugsy may be held liable under this more expansive approach.)

A more difficult question is whether Bugsy committed criminal homicide when the secretary was killed. Murder, the most egregious form of homicide, requires malice. Bugsy did not intend to kill the secretary, and his intent to burn the building will not "transfer" to the homicide. He may still be guilty of murder, however, if he was grossly reckless in exposing employees or occupants of the building to the unjustifiable and substantial risk of a burning building. If he was consciously aware of the risk of serious bodily harm to others at the time he set the fire, and a reasonable person would find the risk of harm to be substantial and unjustifiable, Bugsy acted recklessly. To be considered murder, however, the recklessness must reach a level considered to be **gross**; otherwise, a reckless killing will be deemed manslaughter. Bugsy might be convicted of "gross recklessness" (i.e., depraved heart) murder if his recklessness was gross and the secretary's death is considered reasonably foreseeable. If Bugsy acted merely negligently with respect to the secretary, he may be guilty of criminal negligence manslaughter.

PROBLEM 2. "Me 'n' Bobby Magoo." Mr. Magoo, driving in the city for the first time, makes a wrong turn down a one-way street. He rationalizes his error by thinking, "I'm only going one way," but eventually he causes a 57 car collision. Did Bobby Magoo act with a culpable mental state?

> **Answer:** Mr. Magoo acted either recklessly or negligently. If he intentionally did the bad act of turning down the street in the prohibited direction, he consciously disregarded a risk of harm (i.e., driving in the wrong direction on a one-way street). If the risk of driving the wrong way down a one-way street is, to a reasonable person, substantial and unjustifiable, he acted recklessly.

It may be useful to understand that "intentionally doing the bad act" is the same thing as "consciously disregarding a substantial and unjustifiable risk of harm." "Conscious disregard" is equivalent to "intentional" and "bad act" is equivalent to "a substantial and unjustifiable risk of harm." If Magoo was not consciously aware of the risk of harm — no matter how unreasonable his conduct turns out to be — he has not acted recklessly. (Magoo must be subjectively aware of the risk of harm to be reckless.)

If Magoo actually did not know, but **should have known**, that there was a substantial and unjustifiable risk in driving the wrong way down a one-way street, he has acted negligently. (This standard is objective, based on a reasonable person under the circumstances.) If, on the other hand, Magoo should not have known about the risk, he would not be negligent or held criminally responsible for his conduct. *Commonwealth v. Welansky*, 316 Mass. 383, 55 N.E.2d 902 (1944).

PROBLEM 3. "More Misguided Parents." In the continuing saga of the "misguided parents," the parents try to cure their sick child by "starving" her fever. The child is starved and dies. Can these well-intentioned but misguided parents be held liable for any crimes?

Answer: To be held liable for criminal homicide, there must be an act, a result, and a mental state ("**ARM**"). Here, the actus reus exists. Even though the parents took no action against their child, and did nothing, they had a legal duty to affirmatively act to assist their child under "**SCRAP**," due to the special parent-child relationship. Thus, they failed to meet their legal duty by their inaction. The necessary result for homicide is also present. The parents' omission to feed their child actually and proximately resulted in the child's death.

Whether the parents had the requisite culpable mental state is the most difficult issue. The parents here were empty-headed, and did not appear to be consciously aware of the risk of their behavior. Therefore, the parents probably did not act recklessly, and at most acted negligently. The test for negligence is whether a reasonable person under the parents' circumstances should have known of the substantial and unjustifiable risk of doing nothing to aid their child. In other words, should the parents have known better that their actions were dangerous? The answer likely appears to be yes, since parents not schooled in medicine are minimally expected to seek a professional opinion about their child's illness, and certainly to know better than to believe that starving a child is a healthy course of treatment.

PROBLEM 4. "Inflated GPA." Assume that it is a crime to "file a false statement with the state university registrar." Bubba McFarland, an applicant to the state university, erroneously states in his application that he has a 3.6 average, when in fact it is a 3.5. Bubba honestly believed that his average was a 3.6 at the time he filed his statement. Did Bubba violate the statute?

Answer: Bubba committed the actus reus of filing a false statement with the state university registrar when he submitted an incorrect GPA. The statute does not expressly require a mental state. If no mens rea is required, the offense might be a strict liability crime and met solely by the doing of the act. At common law, however, a crime without any stated mens rea is not interpreted to omit the mens rea, unless there is a clear intent to do so, and a negligence requirement (satisfied by either negligence, recklessness, knowledge, or purposefulness) is implied.

Sum & Substance QUICK REVIEW of Criminal Law

Thus, the issue is whether Bubba had a culpable mental state when he filed a false statement with the registrar. Since Bubba appeared not to have been consciously aware that the statement he filed was false at the time, Bubba was at most negligent. The "empty-head" rule of negligence governs. The operative question becomes whether a reasonable person in Bubba's position **should have known** that the statement he filed was false. Phrased differently, would a reasonable person have known that there was a substantial and unjustifiable risk of a false statement being filed? Bubba will be found not guilty if his mistaken belief was reasonable, i.e., not negligent. Additional facts are necessary to fully resolve this issue.

If this problem was based on the MPC, Bubba's guilt would depend on whether he recklessly filed the false statement, since that is the minimum implied mental state under the Code. To resolve this question under the Code also would require additional facts, particularly about Bubba's mental state at the time he filed his G.P.A.

PROBLEM 5. "Greek Tragedy." Mononucleosis knows his wife Aristophanes is scared of snakes. To collect on an insurance policy on his wife's life, Mononucleosis brings home several mean-looking snakes in a bag, and releases them in the house. Mononucleosis is aware that his wife was in the company of her sister, Semiotic, whom he knew also was deathly afraid of snakes. When his wife and sister-in-law arrive home, they observe the snakes, suffer severe attacks of fright, and die. What crimes, if any, has Mononucleosis committed?

Answer: Mononucleosis is guilty of two separate intent-to-kill murders. Murder requires "**ARM**:" an act, a result, and a mental state. Mononucleosis satisfied these elements with respect to both Aristophanes and Semiotic. He committed the act of bringing the snakes home and releasing them in the house. His act of setting the snakes loose actually and proximately caused the deaths of the two sisters, meeting the result requirement. Mononucleosis also formed the necessary mens rea. He released the snakes with the objective of killing his wife, and thus acted purposefully with respect to her. With respect to his wife's sister, he was consciously aware that if the snakes were released, it was practically certain that she too would suffer a heart attack and die from fright, constituting "knowing" conduct on his part. Since knowing conduct is considered intentional, he can be found liable for two intent-to-kill murders.

OUTLINE

E. CONCURRENCE REQUIREMENT. [§116]

While it does not arise as an issue very often, the requisite **mens rea** and **actus reus** of a crime must occur **simultaneously**, i.e., concurrently. This means that the mens rea of an actor is measured at the exact time of the actus reus. There must not be any delay between the occurrence of the act and the mental state.

> **a. EXAMPLE.** Joe hated his neighbor, and one day drove home intending to kill him. On the way home, a person darted out between two parked cars. Joe, while desperately trying to avoid the person, accidentally hit and killed him, even though he was driving quite carefully. If the person Joe hit and killed turned out to be Joe's neighbor, it would not be criminal homicide because at the time of impact, Joe was not trying to kill the person, but instead was attempting, with care, to avoid harming him. Thus, Joe did not have a culpable mental state at the time of the act.

> **1. EXAMPLE.** Abe is very angry at fellow construction worker Bari, and wants to punch her in the nose. After yelling at Bari, he decides not to punch her in the nose and picks up a shovel to return to work. As he spins to leave with the shovel, he carelessly turns and strikes Bari on the head, knocking her unconscious. Abe's mental state at the time he hit Bari is the only pertinent one. While at one time Abe wanted to intentionally strike Bari, when Abe hit Bari with the shovel, he did so "carelessly," indicating he acted with either negligence or recklessness.

F. CAUSATION. [§118]

Some crimes, such as criminal homicide, require the occurrence of a particular **result.** For a defendant to be found guilty of such a crime, she must cause the necessary result. A homicide will not have occurred, for example, if there was no death of a human being caused by another person.

There are two different types of causation — **causation in fact,** (also called "but for" causation), and **proximate causation** (also called "legal" causation). Proximate causation has received greater attention from the courts, but causation in fact is still important.

> **a. EXAMPLE.** A shoots at B, intending to kill her. A's shot misses B, but kills Sparky the dog. This would not be homicide, which requires the death of a person. However, if B had died of a heart attack after the shot, whether the death actually and directly resulted from the missed shot will determine whether a criminal homicide has been committed.

1. CAUSATION IN FACT. [§119]

Essentially, if there is a causal link between the actor's conduct and the resulting harm, causation in fact exists. A single event may have **numerous causes** in fact. For example, a car accident depends on the drivers being at a particular time and place, on their cars being manufactured and sold, on other drivers, and on many other causes (even the drivers being born). To satisfy this requirement, the perpetrator must only be **one** of the causes — not **the sole cause** — of the harmful result.

In practice, cause in fact is easier to ascertain if the words "**but for**" are used to analyze whether such causation exists. Thus, an action is a cause in fact of a result if, "but for" that initial action, the result would not have occurred at the time it did. *Fine v. State*, 193 Tenn. 422, 430, 246 S.W.2d 70, 73 (1952).

a. Simultaneous Causes (the "Substantial Factor" Test). [§120]

A special cause in fact problem sometimes arises. If two or more persons simultaneously cause harm so that neither person alone is a "but for" cause of the injury, a special problem exists. If the cause in fact test is strictly applied, neither person meets the "but for" test, because the harm would have occurred if either of the persons had acted alone. Consequently, both would go free. Such a result would be unfair.

Instead of letting both perpetrators go free, the law creates a fiction to allow both actors to be prosecuted for their actions. Rather than asking whether each actor is a "but for" cause, a different test applies. When there are **two simultaneous causes**, the courts ask whether each cause was a **substantial factor** in the outcome. This fiction, while not very convincing, achieves the justifiable result of holding all culpable actors responsible for their conduct. *Wilson v. State*, 24 S.W. 409 (Tex. Cr. 1893).

(1) **EXAMPLE.** Alice and Bob go hunting. They both shoot Carl at the exact same time, mistakenly thinking Carl is a deer. Each bullet would have killed Carl if it was the only one fired. Thus, it cannot be said that "but for" Alice's bullet, Carl would not have died at that particular time. Nor can it be said that "but for" Bob's bullet, Carl would not have died at that particular time. Pursuant to the substantial factor test, however, both Alice and Bob would be considered causes in fact of Carl's death because each person's conduct constituted a substantial factor in Carl's death.

b. Hastening an Inevitable Result. [§122]

Sometimes, the conduct of one actor hastens an inevitable result, such as death. The important question to ask in a situation involving multiple causes is whether, but for the act, the bad result would have occurred **at the precise time it did**.

(1) **EXAMPLE.** If Ari stabs Cleo in the abdomen, so that Cleo would have bled to death in one hour, but Beth comes along and shoots Cleo in the chest, hastening his death to within fifteen minutes, who is a cause in fact of Cleo's death? The answer is both Ari and Beth. Here, the victim would not have died at the time he did but for the severe wounds inflicted by both Ari and Beth.

(2) **EXAMPLE.** Smith hates his Neighbor, and lies in wait to ambush him. Smith shoots at Neighbor, but only grazes him. At the same time, a driver named Jones has fallen asleep at the wheel, and his out of control car careens onto Neighbor's lawn, killing Neighbor instantly. Smith is not a cause in fact of Neighbor's death, because it cannot be said that, but for Smith shooting at neighbor, he would not have been killed. Therefore, Smith cannot be prosecuted for the

crime of homicide. Jones, on the other hand, is a cause in fact of Neighbor's death, because "but for" Jones falling asleep at the wheel driving up on Neighbor's lawn and striking him, Neighbor would not have died at the time he did. (If it can be shown that "but for" the bullet shot by Smith, Neighbor would not have jumped into the path of Jones's out of control car, Smith might be an actual, or "but for," cause as well.)

It is important to remember that the existence of cause in fact does not necessarily mean that either proximate cause or criminal liability also exists. The other elements of the crime must still be proven.

(3) EXAMPLE. Barbie and Ken have a fight. Ken storms off in anger, and jumps into his car. As he is driving home, he is killed by a drunk driver. Barbie is a cause in fact of Ken's death, because "but for" their argument at that time, Ken would not have been driving in the car and on the road at the time he was killed. Barbie will not be held criminally liable for Ken's death, however, because she does not meet the other elements of the crime, namely proximate causation and the mens rea. (She did not intend for Ken to be killed, nor did she commit the act that proximately led to his death.)

Generally, the cause in fact determination is **not** a significant component of a criminal law examination. There are so many causes in fact of a particular event that this doctrine does not effectively limit criminal liability.

2. PROXIMATE CAUSATION ("LEGAL CAUSATION"). [§126]

Of the two causation issues, proximate cause is the more significant and more intricate one for purposes of both classroom discussion and examinations. Much like its function in torts, the doctrine of proximate causation serves to **limit** the number of persons subject to **liability**. The doctrine of proximate causation essentially decides which of the actors who are a cause in fact of harm should be held criminally responsible for that harm.

The magic words for determining if proximate causation exists are whether the bad results were "**reasonably foreseeable**" from the defendant's conduct. Phrased differently, the applicable question is whether any intervening causes occurred after the defendant's conduct to "break the chain" of moral culpability.

Whether consequences are "reasonably foreseeable" depends on different factors and diverse terminology, including: (1) the **remoteness** of the actor's conduct to the harm caused; (2) the **independence** of the **intervening causes** that occurred after the defendant's act; and (3) whether the actor **intended** the consequences.

a. Example of Remoteness in Causation. Johnny Goodtime and his wife Joanna were driving in their car when she asked him to wait at a particular store so she could run an errand. While he is waiting, a meteor falls on his car, killing him. While his wife is a cause in fact of his death, because "but for" her asking him to stop at the store at that particular time, he would not have been hit by the meteor, she is not a proximate cause of his death. Her conduct was too remote and of too little consequence to causally hold her responsible for his death by the meteor (i.e., Johnny's death by the meteor was not a reasonably foreseeable result of Joanna's conduct).

b. Subsequent Negligent Medical Care and Independent Intervening Factors. [§127]

Causation problems often arise when an injured person receives negligent medical care and treatment. If medical care is negligent, whether it breaks the "chain" of proximate causation depends on whether the negligence is deemed gross or simple. **Gross negligence breaks the proximate cause chain; simple negligence does not**.

c. EXAMPLE. Bill negligently injured Barbara in an auto accident. In the ambulance on the way to the hospital, Dr. Gangrene negligently operates on Barbara, killing her. Bill is certainly a cause in fact of Barbara's death, because "but for" his conduct, Barbara would not have been in the ambulance at that time being operated on by Dr. Gangrene. Dr. Gangrene also is a cause in fact of Barbara's death, because "but for" Dr. Gangrene operating on Barbara, she would not have died when she did. The doctrine of proximate causation is necessary to determine whether Bill and/or Dr. Gangrene can be held responsible for Barbara's death. The common law rule is that subsequent gross negligence in medical care is considered to be an independent intervening factor, and it breaks the chain of responsibility. Subsequent simple negligence in medical care, on the other hand, is a dependent — i.e., reasonably foreseeable — intervening factor and does not break the chain of criminal responsibility.

Thus, in the previous problem, if Dr. Gangrene was **grossly negligent** in performing the operation on Barbara, his conduct would be considered an independent intervening factor, and Bill would not be a proximate cause of Barbara's death. On the other hand, if Dr. Gangrene's conduct constituted **simple negligence**, his conduct would be considered a dependent intervening cause, meaning it was a reasonably foreseeable event, and Bill may be held liable for Barbara's death.

d. Intended Consequences. [§129]

A finding of proximate causation is more likely to occur with an actor who **intends** harmful consequences, such as the death of another.

(1) EXAMPLE. Carl wanted to kill his wife, Katrina. He gave the housekeeper a bottle of poison and falsely told her it was medication for his ailing wife. The housekeeper negligently left the bottle on the counter, forgetting to give it to the wife. The couple's child, however, mistakenly picked it up, drank from it, and died. In this case, Carl was a cause in fact of the death of his child, because "but for" his conduct in giving the housekeeper the bottle, the child would not have obtained the poison and swallowed it at the precise time she did. Carl also is a proximate cause of his child's death, because the courts often hold that **intended consequences can never be too remote**. Otherwise, a culpable actor would be excused from liability. Even though several intervening causes occurred, and an unintended person died, the law often will extend the scope of proximate causation until it finds an actor who intended the wrongful consequences. The first actor in this situation who intended the harmful result of killing another human being is Carl, and he is likely a proximate cause of the child's death.

3. THE YEAR AND A DAY RULE — A LIMIT ON PROSECUTIONS FOR HOMICIDE. [§131]

At common law, a person could not be held responsible for causing a criminal homicide if the **death occurred more than one year and a day after the injury** was inflicted. The reason for this rule is that it was conclusively presumed that if the victim did not die within a year and a day, the initial harm was believed not to have caused the death. Since the harm was **too remote**, it would be unfair to hold the defendant responsible.

> **a. EXAMPLE.** Amy shoots Bud, intending to kill him. Bud is seriously injured and hospitalized, but does not die. Five years later, as a result of complications from the gunshot wounds inflicted by Amy, Bud dies. Under common law, Amy cannot be held liable for a criminal homicide, because Bud's death occurred more than a year and a day after the initial injury.

Under many **modern statutes**, however, the year and a day rule has been **abrogated** and Amy could be charged with criminal homicide. The existence of proximate causation, however, is still required. *Commonwealth v. Ladd*, 402 Pa. 164, 166 A.2d 501 (1960).

4. THE MODEL PENAL CODE. [§133]

The MPC attempts to clear up the morass of confusing rules and terminology surrounding the doctrines of causation, particularly that of proximate causation. For crimes requiring a mens rea, the Code asks whether the harmful result was "too remote or accidental in its occurrence to have a bearing on the actor's liability or on the gravity of the offense." [MPC §2.03(2)(b).] Thus, the Code dispenses with a considerable amount of ineffective legal jargon, including "independent superseding causes," "dependent intervening causes," and "reasonable foreseeability." The Code also provides that with respect to strict liability offenses, no causation exists "unless the actual result is a probable consequence of the actor's conduct." [MPC §2.03(4).] This is a more restrictive standard than the common law, and focuses on the probability of the result, not simply whether the result is too remote or accidental.

PROBLEM 1. "Ace of Clubs." Ace, intending to kill Brett, swings wildly at Brett with a club. Ace seriously injures Brett, who goes crazy from the pain and then jumps out of the eighth floor window, committing suicide. Did Ace cause Brett's suicide?

> **Answer:** Causation in fact exists here, because "but for" Ace clubbing Brett, Brett would not have been in such pain, and would not have committed suicide at the precise time he did. Proximate cause exists as well, because it is reasonably foreseeable that a person who is seriously wounded with a club, like Brett, may commit suicide as a result of the pain. Thus, Brett's decision to commit suicide would be considered a dependent intervening factor, because it flowed from Ace's initial conduct, and not an independent intervening factor separate from A's actions that would "break the chain" of proximate causation.

PROBLEM 2. "Buckshot Badshot." Arthur shoots at Biff with the intention of killing him. Arthur, however, graduated from the "school of bad marksmen," and misses Biff completely. Despite the miss, Biff was very frightened as a result of being the target of a shooting, had a heart attack and died. Can Arthur be held responsible?

> **Answer:** Arthur was the cause in fact of Biff's death, because "but for" Arthur shooting at Biff, Biff likely would not have had a heart attack **at the precise time he did**, and would not have died. In addition, Arthur is a proximate cause of Biff's death, because it is reasonably foreseeable that a person at whom a shot is fired would be very frightened, to the extent that the victim might even "die of fright." Hence, while the manner of death here was unanticipated, it was still proximately caused. In addition, courts are more likely to hold Arthur responsible because he intended the bad result, in this case, the death of Biff.

PROBLEM 3. "12th Avenue Freeze Out." One very cold winter night, Donald and his wife Arlene had a verbal altercation. Arlene stormed out of their 12th Avenue house, and Donald locked her out. Instead of going next door to her aunt's home, Arlene decided to sleep immediately outside of the locked front door. She froze to death during the night. Is Donald the cause of death?

> **Answer:** Donald is a cause in fact of his wife's death, because "but for" their fight and his locking her out, she would not have been outside the house in the cold at that time, freezing to death. Donald will not likely be considered a proximate cause of Arlene's death, however. Her decision to sleep outside instead of going to her aunt's house, which she easily could have done, broke the causation chain, and constituted an independent intervening cause. Arlene will be held responsible for her own independent decision to sleep outside, and not Donald.

PROBLEM 4. "58 Seconds." A's mortal enemy B is dying of a terminal disease. A, wishing to be the individual who ends B's life, sneaks into the hospital and kills B approximately 58 seconds before B would have expired from his illness. Is A liable for B's death?

Answer: A is the actual cause of B's death, because "but for" A acting to kill B, B would not have died precisely when he did. A is also the proximate cause of B's death, since it is reasonably foreseeable that A's actions would lead to the death of another. Thus, even though A shortened B's life only by 58 seconds, what matters is that A did in fact shorten B's life. A is consequently both the actual and proximate cause of B's death. Thus, if the mental state requirement is met, B may be prosecuted for criminal homicide.

A. BACKGROUND.
[§134]

Most criminal law courses cover the **major common law crimes**. These crimes include **homicide**, **larceny**, **arson**, **assault**, **battery**, and **burglary**. Many criminal law courses also include other common law crimes, such as **rape** and **robbery**. The large majority of criminal law examinations include questions about whether these crimes have been committed by participants in extended fact patterns. Thus, it is important to understand what the elements of the common law crimes are, and how they apply in different fact situations.

In this part of the Quick Review, sections B-D will discuss the common law inchoate crimes, crimes against the person, crimes against property, and their elements. The common law will be contrasted with the MPC. In the final section, E, certain statutory crimes and their elements will be discussed.

B. INCHOATE
CRIMES. [§135]

Unlike tort law, the criminal law uses the strategy of **early intervention** to prevent a subsequent harm from occurring. This **preventative** strategy entails criminalizing incomplete as well as failed efforts to commit a crime. The **incomplete and failed crime**s are called "inchoate" crimes, and include **solicitation, conspiracy,** and **attempt**. The common law does not look at these incomplete or failed acts as "no harm, no foul." Rather, failed or incomplete efforts are still considered to be dangerous conduct warranting prohibition before harm to others or to property can occur. (Note that the crime of **possession** sometimes is viewed as an inchoate crime as well. Criminalizing possession serves as early intervention for the harm resulting from the use of the contraband possessed.)

1. SOLICITATION. [§136]

This crime, originally called "incitement" in its antecedent form in England, occurs when the following three elements are met: a person (1) **knowingly** (2) **invites, entices, advises, orders, or encourages another person to** (3) **commit either (a) a felony or (b) a misdemeanor which involves a breach of the peace or the obstruction of justice**. The **actus reus** is the inviting, enticing, advising, ordering or encouraging of another to commit a felony or a misdemeanor involving obstruction of justice or breach of the peace. The mens rea is knowingly, which means a specific intent for the person solicited to commit the object offense.

Solicitation statutes have over time supplemented or replaced the common law version. Historically, the statutes were directed at specific offenses, such as solicitation to commit prostitution. Despite the widespread use of solicitation laws, many jurisdictions still do not have a general solicitation statute.

The solicitation offense illustrates that **words alone** can create criminal liability. On criminal law examinations, encouragement of another to commit a crime often indicates that a solicitation offense may have been committed.

> **a. EXAMPLE.** Freddy "Dead Beat" Kruger is charged with a laundry list of crimes. He offers the judge a bribe to dismiss the numerous charges against him. The judge refuses. Freddy has added to his laundry list of crimes with the crime of solicitation to obstruct justice. Even though the bad result (the obstruction of justice) has not occurred, and even though the individual he encouraged to break the law (the judge) refused to do so, the crime was completed when Freddy, with the requisite mental state (the intent that the judge obstruct justice), engaged in the act of encouraging the judge to obstruct justice.

Merely asking another to commit a crime is not necessarily solicitation. There are several rules that define and limit when a solicitation has occurred.

b. The Problem of a Failure to Communicate. [§138]

If the actor solicits another individual, but that individual is either **deaf** or simply **does not hear** or otherwise receive the communication, at common law **no solicitation** has occurred. (The actor perhaps could be prosecuted for an attempted solicitation, a crime recognized in some jurisdictions.)

c. The "Primary Actor" Requirement. [§139]

A solicitation occurs at common law only when the person solicited is asked to be the **primary actor** in committing the crime. (That is, the solicitee is asked to be the principal actor; to "do it for the solicitor.") If the person solicited is asked merely to assist the solicitor, a common-law solicitation has not occurred.

> **(1) EXAMPLE.** Geneviere asks her sister to stand lookout while Geneviere kills her mortal enemy, Othello. Has Geneviere committed common law solicitation? No. For solicitation to commit murder to occur, Geneviere must ask her sister to be the primary actor in the murder. Geneviere would have to say, "Sister of mine, please do the murder for me."

d. The "Innocent Instrumentality" Rule. [§141]

Individuals who are solicited to commit a crime must be told or made aware of the fact that they are being asked to engage in criminal conduct, and not merely to perform an act that appears to be lawful. If the solicited person is **duped** or **tricked** into committing a crime, that person becomes an "innocent instrumentality," and no solicitation has occurred. (Note, however, that when one person uses another through trickery, and manipulates an innocent instrumentality to achieve criminal ends, the "user" may be held liable for either an attempt or a completed crime, depending on whether the intended harm occurs.)

> **(1) EXAMPLE.** Jones decides to kill Mr. Big by poisoning him. He asks his trusting but very naive friend Gomer to bring Mr. Big a "package full of brownies." Unbeknownst to Gomer, the package contains poisoned brownies. No solicitation has occurred, because Gomer was not made aware that he was going to commit a crime by delivering poisoned brownies to Mr. Big.

e. Solicitation and Accomplice Liability. [§143]

If a crime is solicited and the solicitee successfully completes the object offense, the solicitation merges into the completed offense and the solicitor may be held liable for the completed crime. In effect, the **solicitor** is an aider and abettor of the completed crime — i.e., **an accomplice**. (See §311.5.) If the object crime does not occur, then the solicitor still can be held liable for solicitation.

f. The Mens Rea. [§144]

Like most crimes, solicitation requires not only an act, but a concurrent mental state as well. The mental state required for solicitation is the **intentional** commission of the actus reus. Thus, an individual who entices, encourages, aids, abets, commands, etc. another to commit a crime is not guilty of solicitation unless the individual acts with the intent that the other person commit the crime. In other words, **solicitation**, like the other inchoate offenses, is a **specific intent offense** requiring either purposeful or knowing conduct by the perpetrator. *People v. Heston*, 1 Cal. App. 4th 471, 2 Cal. Rptr. 2d 26 (1991).

> **(1) EXAMPLE.** Arturo, an ardent Cubs fan, is disappointed with the umpire's calls during a close game. Arturo disgustedly states to his friend, Rambo, who is sitting next to him, "Rambo! That umpire is terrible. Go kill the umpire!" If Rambo subsequently goes ahead and kills the umpire as Arturo suggested, Arturo is still not liable for solicitation if he did not actually intend for Rambo to commit the crime. In all likelihood, Arturo was merely releasing his frustration, and did not have the minimum mens rea.

g. The Model Penal Code. [§146]

Under the MPC §5.02, a person is guilty of solicitation if that person (1) **intentionally** (2) **encourages, commands, or requests another to commit a crime**, even if the encouragement is not communicated to the solicitee.

> **(1) EXAMPLE.** Teddy Mangrove solicits Charles Oak to steal Juniper's baseball card collection. As Oak trots off to commit the larceny, the solicitor, Mangrove, has a change of heart, and warns Juniper, preventing the theft. Because the criminal purpose was voluntarily renounced, and the crime was prevented from occurring, Mangrove would not be guilty of solicitation.

PROBLEM 1. "Change of Heart." Jane Doe, a prostitute, spotted a potential customer walking nearby and she offered him sex for money. When he pulled out a police badge, Jane changed her mind, saying "I forgot, I was just leaving town." Has Jane committed a crime?

Answer: Jane is guilty of solicitation to commit prostitution. She committed the actus reus when she offered the undercover officer sex for money. Based on the circumstances, it appears that the offer was made concurrently with the requisite mens rea, an intent to carry out the criminal act solicited. The crime was completed the minute the words were uttered, because the words themselves constitute the actus reus. (The fact that Jane changed her mind after seeing the police badge does not negate her criminal responsibility, since abandonment is generally not a defense to solicitation at the common law (although it is recognized as a defense under the MPC). Jane would not be able to successfully assert the defense of abandonment under the Model Penal Code, however, since the renunciation of her criminal purpose was not voluntary, but rather coerced by the prospect of apprehension by the police.)

PROBLEM 2. "Martini, Shaken, Not Stirred." Bond, a private investigator, asked his friend M to create a special trunk in his car with a false bottom, to be used for "work-related equipment and the like." M obliges. In reality, Bond wanted a false trunk to smuggle illegal aliens into the country. Is Bond guilty of solicitation?

Answer: Bond is not guilty of criminal solicitation for three reasons. (1) While Bond requested assistance from M, he did not request that M be the **primary actor** in committing a crime. Thus, the primary actor rule, which can be remembered as the "**do it for me**" requirement, was not met. (2) In addition, M was an **innocent instrumentality**, because he was duped into believing that Bond was using the trunk for legal purposes. Thus, the requirement that the solicitee be made aware that he was being asked to commit a crime was not met. (3) Finally, at common law, only the solicitation of specific offenses constituted a crime. Smuggling illegal aliens was not such an offense.

2. ATTEMPT. [§148]

An attempt crime is defined as (1) an **incomplete** or **unsuccessful effort** to commit an **offense** (2) with the **intent** to commit that offense. The actus reus, (1) above, is more specifically defined as the incomplete or unsuccessful **overt act** toward the commission of an object offense. The mens rea, (2) above, requires the specific intent to commit the object offense.

"Failed attempts" is a less controversial category of crime than "incomplete attempts." A failed attempt is readily seen as dangerous, and may have resulted in serious harm but for the accused's incompetence or fortuitous circumstances. **Incomplete** attempts, however, are more ambiguous in their apparent dangerousness. Whether the accused is in a position to harm others, or even truly intends to do so, is much less clear. Thus, this category of offenses raises the question of when intervention is too soon. The answer to this question determines how much of an act is required for a crime to occur.

a. How Minimal an Act is Enough? [§149]

A threshold issue in the law of attempts is how much conduct toward the completion of the offense is required to satisfy the act requirement. Although many different terms are used to describe the minimum act, the short answer is that an overt act towards the crime's completion is necessary. An **overt act** with a **close proximity** to the successful completion of the object offense is necessary. (In other words, just like in the game of horseshoes, in the law of attempts "**close counts**.") *People v. Rizzo*, 246 N.Y. 334, 158 N.E. 888 (1927).

b. The Overt Act Requirement. [§150]

The actus reus for attempts is not just any act in furtherance of the object crime. There must be an **overt act**, one that **goes beyond mere preparation**. *People v. Gallardo*, 41 Cal. 2d 57, 257 P.2d 29 (1953). The precise labels given to overt acts vary from jurisdiction to jurisdiction. These descriptions include "**dangerous proximity**," "**last proximate act**," "**res ipsa loquitur**" (meaning, "the thing speaks for itself") "**substantial step**" or "**indispensable element**." These terms can be distinguished by whether they ask: (1) how much conduct **remains** for the crime to be completed, or (2) looking backwards, how much conduct towards the commission of the crime already **has occurred**.

Despite their differences, these definitions are functionally similar. The definitions ensure that the act is more than "mere preparation," and is instead "close enough" to completion to provide an **unequivocal**, **symbolic**, or **manifest** indication that the individual was intending to commit a crime, and was sufficiently close to the goal to make such conduct dangerous to society. Acts that are "**ambiguous**" or "**equivocal**," on the other hand, are considered mere preparation and insufficient to form the basis of an attempt charge.

OUTLINE

(1) Examples of conduct which meet the **overt act** (i.e., "close enough") requirment are:

(a) Two "cat burglars" show up at a house they intend to burglarize carrying the burglary tools of the trade. (See Case Squibs Section, *People v. Bowen & Rouse*).

(b) Defendant pulls out a loaded gun and takes aim at the victim. As he is about to shoot, he is arrested.

(c) Defendant, after demanding money from the victim in a robbery attempt, trips and falls and never receives any valuables.

(2) **Examples** of **mere preparation** (which are not "close enough") are:

(a) Defendant purchases a gun, ammunition and other accessories of a robbery and sets out for the intended scene of the crime, but is arrested before she can reach it.

(b) A defendant who has previously been convicted of sexual enticement of a minor invites a thirteen-year old boy into his automobile. The defendant is then arrested. *People v. Pippin*, 316 Mich. 191, 25 N.W.2d 164 (1946).

(c) A defendant who intends to rob a payroll clerk becomes lost on the way to find the clerk and is arrested instead. *People v. Youngs*, 122 Mich. 292, 81 N.W. 114 (1899).

c. Attempt Crimes and the Innocent Instrumentality Issue. [§151]

Attempts may be perpetrated by a solitary individual, as compared to solicitation and conspiracy, which require a second individual in some capacity. An attempt crime also may result from group activity (see Conspiracy and Accomplice Liability, §157 and §311.5).

A special situation in which an attempt involves more than one person involves the use of an "**innocent instrumentality**" (see §136, on Solicitation). This situation occurs when the defendant dupes or tricks another person to assist him in the commission of a crime, without revealing the criminal nature of the endeavor. If the assistance of the innocent instrumentality constitutes an overt act — i.e., the innocent person's conduct is "close enough" to the completion of the object offense — an attempt crime has occurred. Thus, a defendant who uses an "innocent instrumentality" to do the "dirty work" can still be charged with an attempt crime without having lifted a finger in the commission of the overt act. *United States v. Rovetuso*, 768 F.2d 809 (7th Cir. 1985).

---

(1) **EXAMPLE.** Bonnie and Clyde ask their neighbor, Innocent Irma, to assist them in closing out a bank account. They give Irma an envelope with a note in it and tell Irma to give this note to a teller. In return, she will get a bag full of money. Unbeknownst to Irma, the note is in fact a robbery note that threatens to blow up the bank if the demand for money is not met. Irma hands over the note, but the crime is thwarted. Bonnie and Clyde may be liable for attempted robbery because they used Irma to commit the overt act

---

for the crime of attempted robbery. Irma's conduct went beyond mere preparation and surpassed the minimum act requirement. Further, Bonnie and Clyde appeared to have intended that Irma commit the crime, satisfying the mens rea requirement as well. (Irma will not be guilty of a crime because she lacked a culpable mental state.)

d. The Mens Rea Requirement. [§153]

Attempts, like solicitation and conspiracy, are **specific intent** crimes, requiring that the defendant intend to commit the object offense. (As noted above, intent equals either a "purposeful" or "knowing" mental state.)

> **(1) EXAMPLE.** Sluggo, a construction worker, carelessly drops a can of paint off of a roof top, narrowly missing pedestrians walking many stories below. Is Sluggo guilty of attempted murder? At common law, the answer is no. Sluggo did not have the intent to commit murder at the time he dropped the paint; he was careless, which connotes negligence or, at most, recklessness. He, therefore, did not have the requisite mens rea for the specific intent crime of attempted murder, no matter how close Sluggo came to killing the pedestrians below.

e. The "Attempt Family of Crimes." [§155]

Two apparently complete crimes really belong to the attempt "family" of offenses — **assault** and **burglary**. **Assault**, when defined as an **attempted battery**, its common law definition, constitutes an attempt to commit a greater criminal offense. **Burglary** is an inchoate attempt offense as well. At common law, it was defined as the breaking and entering of the dwelling house of another at night time **with the intent to commit a felony therein**. The actual commission of a "felony therein" completes the object crime, but is not required to commit the offense of burglary. Thus, burglary occurs even though the criminal objective is not reached.

f. The Model Penal Code. [§156]

The MPC defines an **attempt** crime as (1) conduct constituting a "**substantial step**" towards the commission of an offense, with (2) the **purpose** of committing that offense. [MPC §5.01.] The Code offers several examples of a "substantial step:" lying in wait for the victim; an unlawful entry into a structure in which a crime will be committed; possessing implements of the crime at or near the selected scene; and soliciting an innocent person to participate in committing the crime (i.e., the "innocent instrumentality"). An attempt under the Code also includes an effort to enlist another person's assistance as an accomplice in committing a crime, abrogating the common law requirement that the person be solicited as the primary actor. According to the Code, mere preparation is not enough. Furthermore, the Code recognizes the defense of abandonment [MPC §5.01(4)], provided that there is a complete and voluntary renunciation of the criminal purpose and a thwarting of the crime.

OUTLINE

g. Punishment. [§156.5]

Although a person can be <u>prosecuted</u> for both the completed offense and the lesser included attempt to commit the same offense, it is not permissible to <u>convict</u> a person of both the completed offense and the attempt. The attempt merges into the completed offense. The Model Penal Code [MPC §5.05(1)] punishes attempts at the same grade and degree as the offense attempted, except in the cases of capital felonies.

REVIEW PROBLEMS — ATTEMPTS

PROBLEM 1. "Snakes II." Junior, forgetting that his grandmother hates snakes, brings home his pet python to show it to her. She lapses into a coma from the fright, coming very close to death, but eventually recovers. Is Junior guilty of attempted murder?

Answer: Junior has not committed attempted murder because he lacked the necessary mens rea. While his act in bringing home the snakes likely meets the "overt act" requirement because it was 'close enough' to killing his grandmother, his mental state was insufficiently culpable. An attempt is a specific intent crime requiring the actor to intend that the crime be committed. Junior's forgetfulness does not satisfy the "intent-to-kill" requirement for attempted murder. If Junior had brought the snakes home with the intent of frightening his grandmother to death, then the crime of attempted murder would have occurred.

PROBLEM 2. "Double Vision." Joe, a convicted arsonist, is seen entering into his enemy's home through an open door, lighting a match, and holding it in front of him near extremely flammable drapes. Has he committed a crime?

Answer: It depends on whether Joe committed an overt act. No matter how an overt act is defined, Joe's conduct still must go beyond mere preparation to satisfy the actus reas requirement. Joe's conduct serves as a manifest corroboration of his criminal intent, and is symbolic of his criminal purpose. In the facts given, the action is sufficiently vague and ambiguous to fail the "close enough" requirement. Joe may have been lighting a match to see better, or lighting a cigarette. While Joe's prior conviction for arson makes his match lighting suspicious, it does not make the act unambiguous or unequivocal. Furthermore, there is insufficient information to determine whether his entry into the house was unlawful — he entered through an open door — and unless additional information is available, his entry will not satisfy the overt act requirement. In essence, more facts are necessary to find Joe guilty of attempted arson.

PROBLEM 3. "No, No Van Gogh." George decides to steal the art work from an acquaintance's home, including a priceless Van Gogh, while the acquaintance is on vacation. One night, George breaks a basement window to enter the house. To his astonishment, the home is completely empty. It appears that the family is completely remodeling the interior of the home and has removed all of the furnishings. George, in great despair, consequently changes his mind about the theft, and leaves as quietly as he came. Has George committed a crime?

Answer: George committed the felony of burglary once he broke and entered his acquaintance's home at night with the intent to commit a felony — larceny of the art work — therein. The more difficult question is whether he committed an attempted larceny of the art work. George had the requisite intent to commit larceny because his subjective purpose in breaking into the home was to steal another's property. The remaining question is whether he committed an overt act. Breaking into the house, particularly with burglary tools in his possession, would likely be "close enough" to the object offense of larceny to satisfy the "substantial step" requirement of the MPC or alternative formulations of the overt act standard. (See Case Squibs Section, *People v. Bowen & Rouse.*) Thus, it would appear that George committed attempted larceny.

George still may assert the defense of legal impossibility (see Section on Defenses). He would argue that had the act been completed, he still would not have committed the crime of larceny since there were no paintings to steal. The prosecution would respond by claiming that only a factual impossibility occurred; the theft was prevented solely as a result of the unforeseen fact that the paintings had been removed. A court likely would consider this to be factual impossibility since it is functionally similar to the pickpocket cases, where defendants attempted to pick empty pockets, and were still found to have been properly convicted. *State v. Utley*, 82 N.C. 556 (1880). If George claims abandonment, he again would likely lose, since at common law the defense of abandonment was not generally recognized. Furthermore, George's "change of heart" was not completely voluntary because it occurred only upon discovering the absence of the art work, and he did not completely and voluntarily renounce his criminal purpose as required.

3. CONSPIRACY. [§157]

A conspiracy is: (1) **an agreement between two or more people to commit a crime** with (2) the **intent** to (a) **agree to commit the offense** and (b) **to commit the offense**. The actus reus is the agreement, and the mens rea is comprised of the twin intents to agree and to commit the crime.

In essence, a conspiracy is a **criminal business venture**. Since two or more persons must participate, it is best viewed as a **joint venture**.

Conspiracy has been called "**the prosecutor's darling**" for good reason. The crime provides the government with several advantages. One significant benefit to the police is the opportunity for **early intervention**, well prior to the realization of the object offense. The rationale for intervening when only an agreement has been reached is that **individuals acting in concert are especially dangerous**, much more dangerous and likely to follow through on their intentions than individuals acting alone. A second significant governmental advantage is that **conspirators can be held liable for certain acts of their co-conspirators**, allowing a wide range of charges to be brought even though a conspirator's actual participation in the crime was minimal. Prosecutors also have certain procedural and evidentiary advantages at trial, with the **admissibility of a co-conspirator's statements against other conspirators** being the most noteworthy. If a conspirator makes a statement during and in furtherance of the conspiracy, most evidence codes will permit the state to offer those statements at trial against other conspirators under an agency theory.

---

a. Example of Conspiracy. Bob and Carol agree with Ted and Alice to rob the local bank. They are all lazy, however, and no one does anything about the agreement. Have they committed a crime? Yes, the four have committed conspiracy. The agreement alone suffices to meet the actus reus requirement. At common law, no additional act in furtherance of the crime is required. If all four people intended to agree and to commit the crime, the mental state is also present. Consequently, all four can be charged with and convicted of conspiracy to commit bank robbery.

---

b. The Actus Reus. [§159]

At **common law**, an express or implied **agreement** satisfies the **actus reus requirement**. Many **modern jurisdictions** have expanded the actus reus by requiring the commission of **an act in furtherance of the conspiracy**, sometimes referred to as an "**overt act**," in addition to the agreement. *People v. Burleson*, 50 Ill. App. 3d 629, 365 N.E.2d 1162 (1977). The overt act requirement in conspiracy is completely distinct from the "overt act" requirement in attempt law. **In conspiracy law, if an overt act is required**, **any act** in furtherance of the conspiracy by a co-conspirator **will suffice**. It need not exceed a certain standard or be "close enough" to the object crime, as is required for a criminal attempt. *Braverman v. United States*, 317 U.S. 49, 63 S.Ct. 99 (1942).

---

(1) EXAMPLE. Eanie, Meanie, and Miney Moe agree to burglarize a home. Eanie goes out and buys a mask. Does this satisfy the overt act requirement for conspiracy if one is imposed by statute? The answer is yes, since any act committed in furtherance of the object of the conspiracy suffices.

---

c. The Mens Rea. [§160.5]

At common law, an individual must have two intents to satisfy the mental state required for conspiracy. The individual must have intended to conspire and intended to commit the object crime of the agreement. Thus, if the alleged conspirator, intended to commit or assist in committing the object crime but did not intend to agree with the other(s), the mental state required would not be met. Likewise, if the individual only intended to agree to commit the crimes, and not to participate or otherwise commit the object crimes, the mere intent to agree would not suffice.

d. The Number of Conspiracies. [§161]

The number of conspiracies that exist depends on the number of agreements made, not the number of crimes the parties agree to commit. Conspirators can enter into a single agreement to commit a multitude of crimes, or several different agreements, each of which may have a single crime as its objective. (There is a striking similarity to contract law principles in determining the number of conspiracies.)

> **(1) EXAMPLE.** One autumn evening, Bonnie and Clyde agree to rob five banks and four supermarkets. Before they get a chance to commit any of the crimes, they are arrested. What crimes, if any, have they committed? In this case, they have committed one conspiracy to commit multiple crimes. As noted above, the key to the number of conspiracy charges is the number of agreements, not the quantity of crimes to be committed.

e. The Problem of the Lawful Supplier. [§162]

Generally, it is fairly clear as to whether a person should or should not be considered a conspirator. The question of inclusion in a conspiracy becomes murkier, however, when a person lawfully sells goods or services to conspirators that the seller knows will be used to further the conspiracy. When is a lawful supplier of goods and services to a conspiracy a part of that conspiracy? Unless the supplier knows the sale of goods or services is furthering an egregious felony (where knowledge alone may be enough), **mere knowledge** of the unlawful use of lawfully provided goods or services **will not satisfy the mens rea** requirement for conspiracy. *People v. Lauria*, 251 Cal. App. 2d 471, 59 Cal. Rptr. 628 (1967).

Certain circumstances exist, however, where a merchant's intent to participate in the conspiracy may be inferred. The primary touchstone of whether an intent to participate in a conspiracy exists is if the merchant has a "**stake in the outcome**" of the conspiracy, meaning the merchant is profiting from the unlawful joint venture, even though her sales are legal. The situations in which **conspiratorial intent will be inferred** include:

(1) When a merchant charges an **excessive price** because of the unlawful use to which the goods or services are put;

(2) When **no legitimate use** exists for the goods or services provided (even though the goods or services themselves are lawful); or

(3) When the merchant does an **excessively large volume** of business with the unlawful user.

If any of these situations occur, and the merchant is intentionally reaping rewards from the unlawful nature of the conspiracy, the requisite mens rea likely will be inferred from the circumstances.

> **(a) EXAMPLE.** A drug wholesaler sells large quantities of legal drugs to an individual whom the wholesaler knows is using those drugs unlawfully. If the wholesaler is reaping an excessive profit, or does an extra large volume of business with the buyer, the intent to participate in the conspiracy can be inferred on the part of the supplier. *Direct Sales Co. v. United States*, 319 U.S. 703 (1943).

> **(b) EXAMPLE.** Betty of Betty's Hardware store supplies Arnie with specially made wrenches that have but one use — as a burglary tool. While the wrench itself is not unlawful, Betty's intent to participate in Arnie's conspiracy to burgle houses may be implied, and Betty may be held liable for conspiracy.

f. Bilateral Versus Unilateral Conspiracies. [§165]

Does a conspiracy still occur when only **one** of the parties to the conspiracy **actually intends** to agree and to commit the crime? This question arises when a participating party (or parties) is **faking** participation or is **incapable** of forming the requisite intent, such as a police undercover officer participating in a "sting operation," or an insane person, respectively.

If the jurisdiction adopts a **bilateral approach**, this means that **two or more individuals** must not only **agree** to commit a crime, **but** also **actually intend** at the time of the agreement to carry that agreement out. In essence, in a bilateral jurisdiction, it takes "two to tango." An individual who conspires with an insane person or an undercover police officer — neither of whom intend to carry out the agreement — thus cannot be held liable for conspiracy.

Some jurisdictions have adopted a **unilateral approach**. In a unilateral jurisdiction, if **one conspirator** with the requisite two intents (the intent to agree and the intent to carry out the object crime), agrees with another person to commit the crime, the sole conspirator **can be held liable** even if the other person did not intend to agree or to carry out the agreement. In a unilateral jurisdiction, it takes only one to tango.

> **(1) EXAMPLE.** Roseanne hates her mother and suggests to her younger cousin Elana that they kill her. Elana is very frightened and says "sure," but only because she fears upsetting Roseanne even further. Elana then informs the police and they arrest Roseanne. Roseanne is guilty of conspiracy in a unilateral jurisdiction, but not in a bilateral one. That is because Elana did not intend to agree and to carry out the crime at the time she said "sure," and thus lacked the mens rea necessary for a bilateral agreement.

g. The Multiple Conviction Requirement. [§167]

In a **bilateral** jurisdiction at common law, if all conspirators but one are acquitted, a conviction of the remaining co-conspirator cannot stand. If it "takes two to tango," there must be **at least two** conspirators convicted. *Gebardi v. United States*, 287 U.S. 112 (1932). This requirement is not generally followed today.

h. The Unknown Conspirator. [§168]

Those who are involved in a conspiracy need not know each other personally, but can simply know **of** each other. *United States v. Bruno*, 105 F.2d 921 (2d Cir. 1939).

> **(1) EXAMPLE.** Thurston agrees to sell to Gilligan contraband. Gilligan in turn promises to distribute the contraband to three unnamed "retailers" in another state. Who is involved in this conspiracy? Thurston, Gilligan and the three "retailers" are all part of the same conspiracy if the three retailers agreed to participate. It is of no consequence that the three retailers have never met Gilligan, or that Gilligan does not know them by name.

i. Types of Conspiracies. [§170]

Just like lawful businesses, conspiracies have many different organizational structures. Two major types stand out: (1) **"wheel"** and (2) **"chain"** conspiracies.

(1) The "Wheel" Conspiracy. [§171]

The **wheel conspiracy** has a **controlling** person, or persons, located at the figurative **center** of the wheel, and other less central members of the conspiracy connected to the center figuratively by "**spokes**." The controlling center deals with each of the "spokes," who need not deal with each other at all.

(2) The Chain Conspiracy. [§172]

The **chain conspiracy**, on the other hand, looks like a **straight line**, and involves conspirators connected to each other in a linear fashion. There is no controlling center, and participants might only have contact with members of the chain who precede and follow them. (Both the chain and wheel conspiracies are illustrated in *United States v. Bruno*, 105 F.2d 921 (2d Cir. 1939).)

> **(a) Example of a Wheel Conspiracy.** The defendant, acting as a broker, obtained fraudulent loans from the government for 31 people. The defendant acted as the central command post and the 31 conspirators as the spokes. Consequently, all 32 people participated in one conspiracy. *Kotteakos v. United States*, 328 U.S. 750 (1946). *United States v. Sutherland*, 656 F.2d 1181 (5th Cir. 1981).

> **(b) Example of a Chain Conspiracy.** Marvin, Amy, George and Sage had the following plan: Marvin would import drugs and sell them to Amy, who would distribute them to George, who would give them to Sage to sell. This is a chain conspiracy because the participants acted **sequentially**, or consecutively, in a joint venture to sell or distribute narcotics. *United States v. Bruno*, 105 F.2d 921 (2d Cir. 1939).

j. Liability for the Acts of Others — The "Pinkerton" Rule. [§175]

Conspiracy is different than most crimes in that, at common law, a conspirator could be held **vicariously liable** for some of the acts committed by co-conspirators. The common law rule, often called the **Pinkerton** rule, after the precedent-setting case, *Pinkerton v. United States*, 328 U.S. 640 (1946), states that a conspirator is responsible for all acts (and criminal offenses) by co-conspirators committed **during and in furtherance of the conspiracy**. An offense "in furtherance of" a conspiracy has been defined as any offense that is a **natural and probable consequence** of the conspiracy. A natural and probable consequence of the conspiracy is one that is "**reasonably foreseeable**."

> **(1) EXAMPLE.** The 25-member group, "Freedom Now," decides to blow up the public library to protest the poor selection of magazines offered there. Joe participates in the agreement, but subsequently does nothing to further it. Several of the other conspirators act to advance the conspiracy. Some members rob two banks to obtain money to finance the operation, another conspirator steals dynamite from the local gun store, two homes are burglarized by still other conspirators to obtain needed plans of the library, and a different conspirator, seeing his mortal enemy on the street, shoots him dead. For what crimes, if any, can Joe be held liable?
>
> Pursuant to the **Pinkerton rule**, Joe can be held liable for all of the crimes, with the exception of the homicide. The non- homicidal acts of the co-conspirators occurred during and in furtherance of the conspiracy objective of blowing up the public library. It is reasonably foreseeable, moreover, that in planning to blow up the library, the conspirators may very well steal dynamite, plans, and money. The homicide, however, is too remote and distant from the conspiracy objective to hold Joe and the other non-participating conspirators liable; it did not in any way further the criminal endeavor. Even so, this example illustrates the potency of vicarious conspirator liability.

k. Wharton's Rule (The "Plus One" Requirement). [§177]

Some crimes, such as **adultery**, **dueling**, **bigamy** and **incest**, require at least two persons for the commission of the offense. Under Wharton's Rule, a conspiracy to commit these offenses will be recognized only if: (1) at least **one person more than the minimum number** of individuals required to commit the offense participates in the conspiracy (meaning there must be at least three persons in the conspiracy if the offense requires two persons); or (2) **two persons** who are **not required to participate** in the crime enter into a conspiracy to commit the crime. This rule is discussed and explained in *Iannelli v. United States*, 420 U.S. 770 (1975); [contra, MPC §5.04 (comment to this section rejects the Wharton Rule)].

> **(1) EXAMPLE.** Hamilton, Burr, and their seconds, Jefferson and Adams, all agree that Hamilton and Burr will duel at high noon in a fortnight. Can the foursome be convicted of conspiracy to duel? Even under Wharton's Rule, the four can be convicted of conspiracy to duel. More than the two persons who intend to duel entered into the agreement. Even if the two seconds, or one of the seconds and a participant, had agreed to the duel, each person still could be convicted of conspiracy to duel. Only if Hamilton and Burr, the two intended participants, had by themselves agreed to duel, would they have been exempt under Wharton's Rule from a prosecution for conspiracy.

l. Legislative-Exemption Rule. [§178.5]

This defense is a cousin of Wharton's Rule, described above. Some crimes require the victimization of another person, regardless of whether that person consents. The legislative exemption rule exempts from conspiracies those crimes that require a victim, even if the victim consents. This situation will most likely occur in a prosecution under the Mann Act, 18 U.S.C. §2421 (1982). That Act essentially prohibits the transportation of any women across state lines for the purpose of prostitution.

m. The Punishment for Conspiracy. [§179.5]

The punishment for conspiracies varies widely from state to state depending upon the particular statute that applies. At common law, however, conspiracy generally was considered a misdemeanor, punishable by a maximum incarceration of one year in prison.

n. The Model Penal Code. [§179]

The MPC modifies the common law of conspiracy in various respects, and continues it in others. The MPC adopts:

(1) a **unilateral approach** to conspiracy. [MPC §5.03(1)(a) and (b); §5.04(1)(b)];

(2) the "**no identity**" rule is similar to the common law, in which a co-conspirator need not know the identities of all of the individuals who participate in the conspiracy. [MPC §5.03(2)];

(3) a "**multiple objectives of one conspiracy**" approach, is consistent with the common law, in which a single conspiracy can have multiple criminal objectives. [MPC §5.03(3)];

(4) the **common law approach to impossibility** (i.e., it is **no defense** to conspiracy) [MPC §5.03(1)];

(5) an **affirmative defense of abandonment**, unlike the common law, but only so long as the conspirator **completely** and **voluntarily** renounces his criminal purpose and **thwarts** the commission of the object offense or offenses. [MPC §5.03(6)];

(6) a scheme permitting a conspiracy offense to be tried in any jurisdiction in which the conspiracy was created, or where an overt act in furtherance of the conspiracy was committed. [MPC §5.03(4)(b)(1)];

(7) a position **contrary to Wharton's Rule**, such that there need not be one more person in the conspiracy than the number of persons required to commit the underlying crime. [MPC §1.07(1); §5.03(1); §5.04(1)];

(8) an actus reus which requires (1) an **agreement** between the parties, **plus**, when the charge is either a **felony in the third degree or a misdemeanor**, (2) an **overt act** by at least one of the conspirators in **furtherance** of the conspiracy. (**No act in furtherance** of the conspiracy is required if the charge is a **felony in the first or second degree**.) [MPC §5.03(5)]; and

(9) a standard **contrary** to the common law **Pinkerton Rule**. Under the MPC, conspirators are not held liable for the reasonably foreseeable acts of other co-conspirators (although extended liability for the acts of others may occur through accomplice liability). [MPC §2.06].

OUTLINE

PROBLEM 1. "Clemente!" Abel and Baker hatch a plan to steal a Roberto Clemente baseball card from Charlie. Unbeknownst to Abel and Baker, at the time of their plan, Charlie had sold the card to an overseas trader in the Netherlands. The plan is later forgotten after Abel wins the lottery. Have Abel and Baker committed a crime?

> **Answer:** To commit a conspiracy at common law, Abel and Baker must satisfy the **actus reus** of an agreement to commit a crime. They did that when Abel and Baker agreed to steal the baseball card. The two defendants also satisfied the necessary **mens rea**, which requires "two intents," the intent to agree and the intent to commit the object offense. Abel and Baker both intended to agree and to steal the card. Thus, they had the requisite mental state.
>
> The fact that Charlie did not have possession of the card at the time of the agreement does not negate the conspiracy, since "impossibility" is generally not a defense. Furthermore, the fact that the plan was later abandoned also would be irrelevant at common law, since once the act and the two intents occur simultaneously, the crime is complete.
>
> Under the **MPC**, Abel and Baker would not have committed the actus reus because there was no overt act committed in furtherance of the agreement. Even if Abel or Baker had committed such an overt act, the defendants would be able to assert the defense of abandonment under the Code if they had completely and voluntarily renounced their criminal purpose and, if applicable, thwarted the objective(s) of the conspiracy.

PROBLEM 2. "The Terminator." Arnold Terminator and Rambo D. Blood agree to jointly commit armed robberies of three convenience stores over a period of three days to escape bankruptcy. Arnold forgets to show up, and Rambo proceeds to commit two of the robberies alone, shooting and killing a store clerk who tried to stop him during the first robbery. For what crimes may Arnold be held liable?

> **Answer:** For Arnold to be convicted of conspiracy at common law, Arnold must have had the requisite act and mental state. Arnold agreed to commit the three robberies, thus satisfying the common law act requirement. At the time of the agreement, it appears he intended to agree and to commit the object offenses to satisfy his debts. Therefore, he also fulfilled the requisite mental state. Although there were three separate crimes, there was **only one agreement**, and therefore, only one conspiracy.
>
> Arnold also will be held liable at common law for the object offenses and, pursuant to the **Pinkerton rule**, for all acts during and in furtherance of the conspiracy committed by a co-conspirator. Even though Arnold did not participate in the two robberies committed by Rambo, he can be held liable for both robberies, as well as for the murder of the clerk. The robberies were object offenses, and the death of the clerk was likely reasonably foreseeable — i.e., a natural and probable consequence of the commission

of the robbery — because it can be reasonably anticipated that a robbery may be resisted by force. If such resistance occurs, and especially if weapons are involved, someone could easily get seriously hurt. Thus, simply because Arnold did not in any way further the conspiracy after the agreement does **not** mean he will be able to escape the "long-arm" of conspiracy liability.

Arnold also may be held liable for conspiracy under the **MPC**. He committed the act of agreeing, and since armed robbery is not a third degree felony or misdemeanor, no overt act is required. Even if it was such a felony, an overt act was committed by Rambo, who performed two of the robberies. No abandonment occurred as a result of Arnold "forgetting to show up," because he did not thwart the commission of the target offenses; moreover, forgetting is not a "complete and voluntary" abandonment.

o. Merger. [§180]

The "**merger doctrine**" states that a criminal defendant cannot be convicted of **both a crime and any of its lesser included offenses**. Since a lesser included offense is **part of** the larger crime, allowing convictions to stand for the whole crime as well as its component parts would violate double jeopardy and due process of law fairness principles. The merger doctrine often applies when a defendant is convicted of both an inchoate crime (such as attempt or solicitation) and the completed crime arising from the same actions or transaction.

> **(1) EXAMPLE.** A person who is charged with robbery and an attempt to commit the same robbery, all stemming from the exact same conduct, cannot be convicted of both, since the attempt is a lesser included offense of the completed robbery. The attempt "merges" with the completed crime.

> **(2) EXAMPLE.** If a murder is solicited, and then successfully completed, the solicitation to commit murder merges with the object offense, murder. The solicitor can be convicted of the completed murder as an accomplice. In a sense, the completed crime devours the incomplete crime. *State v. Hardison*, 99 N.J. 379, 492 A.2d 1009 (1985).

(3) Exception to the Merger Doctrine. [§183]

A glaring exception to the merger doctrine exists. Under the **later common law** (contrary to an earlier rule), **conspiracy convictions did not merge** with the completed offense. *Callanan v. United States*, 364 U.S. 587 (1961). Instead, convictions for conspiracy and the object offense of the conspiracy can both occur.

> **(a) EXAMPLE.** Travis, Garth, and Conway agree to steal banjos from the Old Banjo Store. The three steal the banjos, but are then apprehended and prosecuted for three crimes: conspiracy to commit larceny, attempted larceny, and larceny. The defendants cannot be convicted of three crimes. Instead, the conspirators can only be convicted of the conspiracy and either the larceny or attempted larceny. The attempted larceny is part of the larceny, and thus will merge into it upon a conviction of both crimes. The conspiracy, while arguably a lesser included part of the object crime of larceny, does not merge into it under the later common law approach.

p. Merger under the Model Penal Code. [§185]

Under MPC §1.07(1)(b), **conspiracy generally merges** with the completed object offense. An **exception** to this rule exists, however, if the conspirators intend to commit **other offenses** in addition to the object offense. [MPC §5.03(3).]

> **(1) EXAMPLE.** Sam and Susie agree to murder Farhquar. They attempt to murder Farhquar, but fail. Sam and Susie will be held liable for the crime of attempted murder, but not for conspiracy to commit murder as well. The conspiracy charge will merge into the attempt under the MPC, since it is a lesser part of the attempt. If Sam

and Susie had decided not only to murder Farhquar, but intended to commit five additional murders as well, they could be held liable for both conspiracy and the object offense of attempted murder. In this situation, the exception to the merger rule for conspiracy applies, since the conspirators intended to commit additional offenses.

4. POSSESSION. [§187]

Possession requires (1) **the act of exercising dominion and control over the thing possessed**, having had the **opportunity to dispossess** it, along with (2) **the mental state of knowingly doing the act**. A "knowing" mental state means knowingly exercising dominion and control over a thing. *United States v. Martorano*, 709 F.2d 863 (3rd Cir. 1983).

The crime of possession is an anomaly, since it is both a completed crime and an inchoate one as well. It is a "**place holder**" crime for the **use** of contraband, and it is a complete crime since the act of possession is distinct from the ultimate harmful conduct it is intended to prevent (a person who possesses an item can be viewed as at rest or in repose). In still another sense, the crime of possession can be viewed as requiring no act at all, but rather a status, since possession entails no action, but simply the exercising of dominion and control. *Baender v. Barnett*, 255 U.S. 224 (1921). Regardless of the perspective, the crime of possession holds persons responsible for controlling or having authority over harmful or dangerous property.

a. Actual and Constructive Possession. [§188]

Possession is considered **actual** if the thing possessed is on the person of the possessor or within arm's reach. Possession is considered **constructive** if it is outside of the individual's actual possession but still within her dominion and control. *State v. Florine*, 226 N.W.2d 609 (Minn. 1975).

b. Joint Versus Exclusive Possession. [§189]

Possession of a thing may be joint, **between two or more people**, or **exclusive, by one person only**. *United States v. Morando-Alvarez*, 520 F.2d 882 (9th Cir. 1975).

(1) EXAMPLE. Alice, a college student, asks her good friend, Betty, to drive Alice's car back to school for her. Alice also asks Betty to bring back a "fragile" package. The package was tightly wrapped in newspaper, and was placed by Alice gingerly in the unlocked glove compartment of the car. The package contained cocaine, and Betty is subsequently charged with the unlawful possession of narcotics. Is Betty guilty of possession?

The **act** requirement is met, since (1) Betty exercised dominion and control over the package by controlling the car and the unlocked glove compartment. There is actual possession if the glove compartment in the car is within arm's reach. If not, it is constructive possession. Whether (2) the requisite **mental state** exists is questionable, however. There is no indication that Betty had knowledge of what she was controlling in the package — she was not "consciously aware" that the package was "practically certain" to contain cocaine, which is required for a "knowing" mental state. If Betty did not know what the contents of the package were, and she was used as an innocent instrumentality, she would not be guilty of criminal possession. *State v. Flaherty*, 400 A.2d 363 (Me. 1979).

> **(2) EXAMPLE.** Gordon finds a bag of marijuana on the street, observes that the bag contains marijuana, and mindlessly puts it in his jacket, forgetting about it. He is later charged with the possession of marijuana. Since Gordon (1) committed the **act** of exercising dominion and control over the thing; and (2) had **knowledge** of what the bag contained, the only issue remaining is whether Gordon (3) had a reasonable opportunity to **dispossess** himself of the bag. If Gordon ended up taking the bag and its contents home — and not to the police station, for example — where he forgot about it, he likely could be held liable.

C. CRIMES AGAINST THE PERSON

1. HOMICIDE. [§192]

A homicide occurs when a **person causes the death of another** person or persons. It is the most serious and harmful consequence of a person's conduct. Yet a homicide is not always criminal. "**Non-criminal homicide**" includes accidents in which the actors were not culpable, such as some automobile accidents, and excused or justifiable killings.

Criminal homicide involves a **culpable** perpetrator who engages in morally blameworthy conduct: intentional killings, drunk driving killings, killings provoked by passion, and reckless killings are but a few examples of criminal homicide.

> **NOTE: The Common Law — Murder Distinguished from Manslaughter.** Within criminal homicide at common law, there are **two** major categories — **murder** and **manslaughter**. The major dividing line between the two categories is the mental state of malice: **murder requires malice**, and **manslaughter does not**. The crime of murder is subdivided further based on different forms of malice. Manslaughter is similarly sub-divided based on types of non-malicious conduct. (See §232.)

In the **early common law**, all homicides were **capital offenses** — meaning guilty perpetrators were put to death — and no gradations of culpability were necessary. Only later did jurisdictions distinguish homicides and its punishment based on culpability.

In modern times, statutes often distinguish criminal homicides by the heinousness of the perpetrator's mental state. In these jurisdictions, homicides are divided into categories labeled **degrees**, such as first degree murder, second degree murder, and third degree murder. It is important not to confuse the common law **homicide distinctions** (see §203) with the statutorily-created **homicide degrees** (see §208). First degree homicide, for example, not only includes intent-to-kill crimes, but in many jurisdictions it also includes felony murder as well.

a. Elements of Murder. [§193]

Murder is defined as the (1) **unlawful** (**unexcused or unjustified**) (2) **killing of** (3) **another human being** (4) **with malice aforethought**.

The two elements most likely to be in dispute on an examination or in a courtroom are malice — the necessary mental state — and causation — whether the accused actually and proximately caused the death of another.

(1) "Unlawful." [§194]

Some killings of other human beings, such as those committed in self-defense, are lawful, and therefore are not criminal homicide.

(a) EXAMPLE. Jones is sentenced to death. The executioner is not committing unlawful homicide when the state, via the death penalty, has made the executioner's act lawful.

(b) EXAMPLE. Susie kills her ex-husband in self-defense. She has not committed the crime of murder because self-defense is a justification defense, and her conduct is lawful.

(c) EXAMPLE. A tire on Horace's car accidentally punctures while he is riding on the highway. The puncture was not Horace's or any other person's fault. However, it caused a multiple car collision and the death of another person. Horace will not be guilty of criminal homicide because his conduct, while causing the death of another human being, was not culpable.

---

(2) "Killing." [§198]

The victim must be killed.

(a) EXAMPLE. Elouise lapses into an irreversible coma after Jenny tries to kill her with poisoned chocolate. Jenny can be charged with attempted murder, but not murder, because Elouise did not die.

---

(3) "Of Another Human Being". [§200]

Another human being must be killed. (Similarly, an attempted murder requires an attempt on the life of another, not attempted suicide.)

(a) EXAMPLE. A, with an intensity and fury rarely seen, intentionally runs over a stray dog, killing it. A has not committed murder because murder only applies to the killing of another human being, not an animal.

---

(4) "With Malice Aforethought". [§202]

Malice is the required mental state for murder. For most crimes, **malice** is defined as the **intentional** (purposeful or knowing) **or reckless commission** of an act. For the purposes of common law murder, malice equals either **intentional or grossly reckless conduct**. Merely reckless killings are considered manslaughter.

The term "**aforethought**" originally indicated that some sort of premeditation or deliberation was a prerequisite to a murder conviction. Over the years, however, the word "aforethought" became irrelevant to the determination of criminal culpability. It is now largely a historical appendage that is not interpreted literally.

> **(a) EXAMPLE.** "A" negligently drops a lighted cigarette while smoking in bed. Consequently, his house burns down, killing his in-laws. A's conduct, while causing the death of other human beings, is not malicious. Malicious behavior is either purposeful, knowing, or reckless, and A's actions are merely negligent. Therefore, A could be prosecuted at most for manslaughter, but not for murder.

b. The Four Types of Common Law Murder. [§203]

Historically, murder was described by a wide variety of legal terminology, which often confused instead of simplified the subject. Four types of murder predominated, each distinguished by a different mental state: (a) **intent to kill**; (b) **intent to commit serious bodily harm** against another; (c) **"depraved heart"** (i.e., gross recklessness) **murder**; and (d) **felony murder**.

> **(1) Example of Intent to Kill Murder.** Susan sees her ex-husband walking across the street. She purposefully committed the act of running him over with her car, intending to kill him. The ex-husband dies as a **result** of being run over. The elements of **"ARM"** — Act, Result and Mental state — are all satisfied, and Susan can be prosecuted for intent to kill murder.

> **(2) Example of Intent to Commit Serious Bodily Harm Murder.** The coach, Lou, tells Klinger, the defensive captain, to "take out the quarterback." Klinger pulls out his AK 47 assault rifle and aims for the quarterback's legs. Klinger is a bad shot, and hits the quarterback in the chest and head, killing him. Since Klinger did not desire the death of the quarterback, but intended serious bodily harm instead, the result is intent to commit serious bodily harm murder. (The fact that Klinger's shot killed the quarterback is not the proper measure of what Klinger subjectively intended.) *Bantum v. State*, 46 Del. 487, 85 A.2d 741 (1952).

> **(3) Example of "Depraved Heart" Murder.** After receiving a new rifle as a present, Johnny decides to try it out by shooting out the windows of passing commuter trains during rush hour. He is aware that there are people who are traveling in the trains who could get harmed. Although he does not intend to harm anyone — he only desires to try out his new rifle — Johnny kills two people while shooting out the windows. Johnny's gross indifference to human life is likely to be so reckless that it is considered gross recklessness, satisfying the "depraved heart" standard.

> **(4) Example of Felony Murder.** While committing an armed robbery, Boris Nogoodman stumbles and the gun he is holding discharges, accidentally killing the victim of the armed robbery. Even though the killing was purely accidental, Boris may be held liable for felony murder because the killing occurred during the commission of a dangerous felony, an armed robbery.

c. Culpability and Common Law Murder. [§207.5]

In most jurisdictions, the most **heinous** type of murder is intent to kill murder, followed by the intent to commit serious bodily harm murder and certain types of felony murder. "Depraved heart" murder is based on gross recklessness, which is defined as a gross indifference towards human life. Depraved heart murder is less heinous than the two types of intentional murder, because the act is not done with an intent to harm another. It is still sufficiently culpable, however, to be considered murder. The culpability of someone who commits felony murder varies, and often depends on the seriousness or dangerousness of the underlying felony or attempted felony committed. The more serious the felony, the more culpable the perpetrator. *Commonwealth v. Buzard*, 365 Pa. 511, 76 A.2d 394 (1950).

d. Statutory Degrees of Murder. [§208]

Many jurisdictions **divide** up the crime of murder not just by mental states, but by special categories labeled "**degrees**." *People v. Anderson*, 70 Cal. 2d 15, 73 Cal. Rptr. 550, 447 P.2d 942 (1968). The degree of the offense determines its seriousness and the potential severity of punishment.

Many jurisdictions have at least **three degrees** of murder. **First degree** murder is punished the most severely, sometimes even by death. Second and third degree murder include crimes with lower levels of culpability, such as depraved heart murder and some felony murder.

Murder in the first degree is often defined as a killing that is "**willful**, **premeditated**, and **deliberate**." Taken literally, "willful" means intentional, "premeditated" means to think about beforehand, and "deliberate" means to measure and evaluate the choices. These words indicate that for a killing to be considered a first degree murder, it must be considered or planned beforehand, or carefully weighed. Many courts blur the meaning of these three words, however, and simply **collapse** their meaning into the categories of purposeful or knowing behavior. Thus, the "dictionary" meanings as stated above have lost their significance. In the large majority of jurisdictions that have a first degree murder statute, there need not be any measurable amount of time prior to the killing in which the intent to act was formed.

e. Felony Murder at Common Law. [§209]

Originally, felony murder was defined as a *murder* **committed during the course of a felony or an attempted felony**. When defined in this manner, the crime required a showing of **malice** like any other common law *murder*. Since a *murder* committed during the commission of a felony or attempted felony was considered to be even more heinous than murders committed under other circumstances, the punishment was accordingly increased.

Over time, however, the definition of felony murder changed dramatically. No longer did a felony murder require both a felony (or attempted felony) and a murder. Instead, felony murder required simply a killing during the commission of a felony or attempted felony. Rather than require a showing that the killing was malicious (and therefore murder), the malice was presumed from the commission or attempted commission of the felony. *People v. Root*, 524 F.2d 195, 197 (9th Cir. 1975).

Consequently, by the time of the **later common law**, a **felony murder** was defined as: (1) a **killing** (2) **during the commission of a felony or attempted felony**. The killing, when defined in this way, can be accidental, negligent, reckless, knowing, or purposeful. Prosecutors favor this felony murder rule because they do not have to prove any mental state associated with the killing. The mental state is implied. All that has to be proven is that the killing occurred during, and resulted from, the commission of the felony or attempted felony.

Note that an **attempted felony is sufficient** to serve as the basis for felony murder. If A attempts to rob B, but never receives any money, and A kills B accidentally in the process, a felony murder charge may still be successful. *Amlotte v. State*, 456 So. 2d 448 (Fla. 1984).

---

(1) Example of Felony Murder. Joanna, a veteran burglar, is in the process of burglarizing Lawrence's house. As she enters the house, she accidentally falls on Lawrence, killing him. Joanna is guilty of felony murder because a killing occurred during the commission of the burglary, which is a felony.

---

(2) The "D.I.D.I." Limitations of Felony Murder. [§211]

Not all felonies and not all killings meet the felony murder requirements. Several significant limitations exist, characterized in this outline as "**D.I.D.I.**" — Direct (the **death** must be "**directly**" **caused** by the commission of the felony or attempted felony); Inherently **D**angerous (the **felony** or **attempted felony** must be "**inherently dangerous**"); and Independent (the **felony** must be **independent** of **murder**, meaning it must not be a lesser included offense). These limitations will be discussed below.

(a) Direct. [§212]

("**D.**"I.D.I.) The death must be directly caused by the felony or attempted felony. This is simply another way of saying that the death must be a **natural and probable**, (i.e., reasonably foreseeable) **consequence** of the felony; both **actual** and **proximate causation** must exist for the death to be attributable to the felon or felons. *State v. Glover*, 330 Mo. 709, 50 S.W.2d 1049 (1932).

(i) EXAMPLE. A robs B. During the robbery, an out of control car unrelated to the robbery suddenly appears and kills B instantly. A is not liable for felony murder because the death is not a direct result of the felony; in other words, the death is not reasonably attributable to the commission of the felony.

(b) Inherently Dangerous Felonies. [§214]

(D."**I.D.**"I.) At common law (and in many penal codes), not all felonies or attempted felonies can serve as a basis for a felony murder charge. Only those felonies or attempted felonies that are considered "inherently dangerous" qualify. Inherent dangerousness depends on how **dangerous** the felony is to **human life**.

> **(i) Examples of "Non-Inherently Dangerous" Felonies.** Felonies that are not "inherently dangerous" include: practicing medicine without a license; the unlawful possession of a firearm; and grand larceny.

> **(ii) Examples of "Inherently Dangerous" Felonies.** Rape, robbery, arson, and burglary are all considered to be inherently dangerous felonies.

(iii) "Inherently Dangerousness" Tests. [§217]

Two different approaches have been used to define "inherent dangerousness": (1) **in the "abstract,"** where the dangerousness of the felony is determined **objectively**, based on the **reasonable probability** of **serious harm** being caused by that **general type of crime**; and (2) **"as applied,"** where the **dangerousness** of the felony depends not only on its dangerousness in the abstract, but also on the **particular circumstances** of the case. This second definition is more expansive in scope and can include a wider variety of felonies. A shorthand description of the "as applied" test is "**abstract plus**" (i.e., plus the circumstances).

> **(iv) Examples of the Two Approaches.** Johnny Dangerously gets into an argument about business with an old nemesis. Johnny is carrying a loaded gun in his pocket without a safety catch, and it accidentally goes off, killing his nemesis. Johnny, an ex-felon, is charged with the felony of "the unlawful possession of a firearm after a felony conviction." If viewed **abstractly**, the possession of a firearm is not in and of itself inherently dangerous to others. Objectively, it is only when the gun is used that it becomes dangerous, not when it is merely possessed. If looked at "**as applied**," which includes consideration of the circumstances of the case, it may be concluded that concealing a loaded firearm without a safety catch in one's pocket during a heated argument, which may involve a sudden jerk or movement, might indeed be quite dangerous to human life. Thus, the "as applied," "abstract plus," method may yield a very different result than the "abstract" approach.

(c) Independent Felony. [§219]

(D.I.D."**I.**") The inherently dangerous felony must also be **independent** of murder. This means that the **felony cannot be a lesser included offense** of murder. If this limitation did not exist, all forms of manslaughter, battery, and other lesser included offenses to murder that resulted in the death of the victim automatically would be elevated to murder; the death would occur during the commission of an inherently dangerous (i.e., a violent) felony.

OUTLINE

(i) EXAMPLE. Harry negligently shoots and kills Sue. Without the limitation of independence, Harry would be guilty of felony murder. He directly killed another person during the commission of an inherently dangerous felony, manslaughter (i.e., the unlawful negligent killing of another human being). If the independence limitation applies, however, Harry can only be convicted of negligent manslaughter, since the felony of manslaughter is not independent of murder.

(ii) EXAMPLE. Sluggo, on a rampage, intentionally breaks all four limbs of a former friend, who thereupon dies. Sluggo has not committed felony murder, because he has committed the crime of aggravated battery, a lesser included offense of murder. The felony of aggravated battery violates the rule of independence. Sluggo would not go free, however, because he still could be charged with intent to commit serious bodily harm murder, although the prosecutor would have to prove malice to convict him.

(iii) EXAMPLE. A intentionally shoots at B, trying to kill her, but misses, and B dies of fright. A can be charged with murder, but not on a felony murder theory. Attempted murder is a lesser included offense of murder, and consequently is not an independent felony, as required for felony murder.

(iv) EXAMPLE. A intentionally scratches B, a hemophiliac, who subsequently dies from the scratch. A cannot be charged with felony murder. The scratch is a battery, and battery is a lesser included offense, and not independent of, murder.

(v) EXAMPLE. A robs B. During the robbery, B trips and is killed on impact. A can be charged with felony murder, since robbery is not a lesser included offense of murder. The larceny component of robbery is separate from (i.e., independent of) murder. (Calling larceny "independent" is just another way of saying that larceny will not be proven if the elements of murder are proved by the prosecution. If larceny was a lesser included offense, like battery, it would be proven upon a showing of murder.)

Note that the independent felony rule only prevents a felony murder charge based on certain non-dangerous felonies; the rule does not preclude a direct charge of intent-to-kill, intent-to-commit-serious-bodily harm or depraved heart murder for any killing. (Prosecutors often prefer a felony murder charge, however, because they do not have to prove malice.)

(3) Felony Murder Liability When a Non-Felon Kills. [§225]

A non-felon is a person who **is not an accomplice** participating in the crime. Non-felons include **bystanders** or **police officers**. Special rules apply if a non-felon kills during the commission or attempted commission of a felony. If a felon (i.e., perpetrator of the crime) kills, conspirator or accomplice liability will be used to hold the co-felons liable for the death. *Jackson v. State*, 286 Md. 430, 408 A.2d 711 (1979). If a non-felon does the killing, several different approaches exist to determine if a felon can be held liable for the acts of the non-felon. (A jurisdiction may adopt any one of these approaches, or a combination of them.) These approaches are discussed below.

(a) The Agency Theory (Majority Rule). [§226]

Under this majority theory, co-felons will be held responsible under a felony murder theory **only if one of the felons does the killing**. This approach is based on the premise that the felons are **agents of each other** and should be held responsible only for each other's conduct. *State v. Canola*, 73 N.J. 206, 374 A.2d 20 (1977).

> **(i) EXAMPLE.** The Fred Schmerd gang enters a liquor store for the purpose of robbing it. The store clerk shoots and kills Joey Schmerd, a member of the gang. Since the killing was not done by one of the accomplices who committed the crime, but by one of the robbery victims, no "agency" relationship exists, and the members of the Schmerd gang will not be held liable for murder.

(b) The Proximate Cause Theory. [§228]

Under this approach, the defendant felons are **liable for any deaths proximately caused** by the felons' conduct. The rationale for this wide open approach is that since the felons set the events in motion, they should be held responsible for **reasonably foreseeable deaths**, regardless of whether the killing was committed by a felon or a non-felon (this rule can be characterized as "you asked for it, you got it ...," felony murder). *State v. Baker*, 607 S.W.2d 153 (1980).

> **(i) EXAMPLE.** The Fred Schmerd gang robs a liquor store in a "proximate cause" jurisdiction, and this time Jimmy Schmerd, a member of the gang, is shot and killed by the store clerk. The surviving members of the Schmerd gang can be held responsible for felony murder since it is reasonably foreseeable that someone may get shot during the course of a robbery of a liquor store. The surviving Schmerd gang members also can be held responsible if a police officer or some other innocent bystander had done the killing. *Commonwealth v. Moyer*, 357 Pa. 181, 53 A.2d 736 (1947).

(c) The Limited Proximate Cause Theory. [§230]

Under this compromise view, co-felons (the perpetrators of the crime) are liable for **all reasonably foreseeable deaths** of **non-felons only**. If a non-felon kills a felon, the result is considered justifiable (i.e., acceptable under the circumstances), and the surviving felons will not be held responsible. If a non-felon kills another non-felon, such as a bystander accidentally shooting another bystander, the non-felon is excused. The felons, however, will be held liable for creating the events leading to an innocent person's death. *People v. Morris*, 1 Ill. App. 3d 566, 274 N.E.2d 898 (1978).

(i) EXAMPLE. A gunfight erupts during the Fred Schmerd gang's robbery of the convenience store, and the store clerk kills a customer as well as Fred Schmerd. Pursuant to the limited proximate cause approach, the surviving members of the Schmerd gang can be charged with felony murder of the customer, but not for the death of Fred Schmerd. Schmerd's death is considered justifiable and not subject to a felony murder prosecution. However, the surviving gang members can be held responsible for the customer's death because they triggered the events that led to an innocent person's death.

REVIEW PROBLEMS — MURDER

PROBLEM 1. "Cheerleader." Jane loses a cheerleading contest to her fierce rival, Edwina. She decides to get even by killing Edwina. Later that same day, Jane turns and shoots a person she thinks is Edwina, although it turns out to be Edwina's older brother, Carl. What crime did Jane commit, if any?

> **Answer:** Jane committed **intent-to-kill murder**. She met the requirements of "**ARM**:" she did the **act** of shooting that led to the death of Carl, thus meeting the actus reus requirement; the shooting that **resulted** in Carl's death was both the **actual** and **proximate cause** of his death, since "**but for**" the shooting, Carl would not have died when he did, and it was reasonably foreseeable that the shooting would lead to Carl's death. Jane meets the intent to kill requirement because she **intended** to kill a human being; the mere fact that she intended to kill a different human being than the one who died is not significant; all that is required is a concurrent act and intent to kill another human being.

PROBLEM 2. "Butt Really." A hits B with the butt of a loaded gun, intending to break his jaw and "put a real hurt on him." The gun accidentally discharges, and the bullet ricochets around the room before killing B. For what crime is A liable, if any?

> **Answer:** A may be convicted of intent to commit serious bodily harm murder. The elements of "ARM" are met: A's **act** of hitting B with the gun butt led to the death of another person. A's actions **resulted** in B's death. Specifically, A was both the **actual** and **proximate** cause of B's death. "But for" A hitting B with the gun, the bullet would not have discharged and killed B. It also was reasonably foreseeable that a loaded gun intentionally used in that manner could discharge and kill another individual, even if the particular manner of B's death was not anticipated. A's intent to "put a hurt on B," and break B's jaw with a gun butt, indicates an intent to commit serious bodily harm.

> A could not be prosecuted under a felony murder theory. The felony of aggravated battery, occurring when A struck B, would be a lesser included offense of murder. Therefore, it would fail the **"D.I.D.I." rule**, which requires that the underlying felony be independent of murder.

PROBLEM 3. "Foiled Again." Eeny, Meeny, and Miney Moe decide to rob Jim Tiger by tiptoeing up behind him and jumping him. During the commission of the robbery, the police arrive on the scene and shoot Eeny Moe dead. The robbery is foiled. For what crimes can Meeny and Miney Moe be held responsible?

> **Answer:** Meeny and Miney Moe can be charged either with attempted **robbery or robbery**, depending on whether the crime was completed. They also may be charged with **felony murder**, since there was a (1) **killing** (2) **during the commission or attempted commission of a robbery**, a felony. Furthermore, the **"D.I.D.I."** limitations are met: the death was directly (actually and proximately) caused by the robbery; robbery qualifies as an inherently dangerous offense; and robbery is independent of murder, since it is not a lesser included offense of murder, due to its larceny component.

A non-felon, namely a police officer, did the killing. Thus, the only question remaining is whether the co-felons can be held liable for the death. The answer depends on whether the agency, wide open proximate cause, or limited proximate cause theory applies. Under the **agency theory**, the co-felons cannot be held liable when a non-felon kills. So Meeny and Miney Moe would not be subject to a felony murder prosecution. Under the **wide open proximate cause approach**, the co-felons can be held liable for the death of Eeny Moe because they set the events in motion and are liable for all reasonably foreseeable deaths resulting from the commission of the qualifying felony, including the death of a co-felon. Under the **limited proximate cause theory**, however, the felons may be held liable only when a non-felon kills another non-felon, and not a felon, as in this case. Thus, Meeny and Miney would not be held liable for felony murder if the limited proximate cause theory governed.

f. Manslaughter. [§232]

Manslaughter is the **unlawful (unjustified and unexcused) killing of another human being without malice aforethought**. The lack of malice is manslaughter's distinguishing feature in the world of criminal homicide. There are **four types** of manslaughter: (1) **heat of passion** (or **provocation**) **manslaughter**; (2) **imperfect justification manslaughter**; (3) **negligence/recklessness manslaughter**; and (4) **bad misdemeanor (sometimes called "Bad Act") manslaughter**. These divisions have been rearranged by many legislatures, which have created special separate statutory offenses such as negligent homicide and driving under the influence manslaughter.

At common law, heat of passion and imperfect justification manslaughter are considered to be types of "**voluntary manslaughter**;" recklessness and bad act manslaughter are treated as types of "**involuntary manslaughter**." The words "voluntary" and "involuntary" are terms of art, and do **not** refer to whether the act committed is voluntary or involuntary. Thus, involuntary manslaughter does not mean that there was no free will involved in the commission of the act. If anything, "voluntary" and "involuntary" can be viewed as synonyms for "**intentionally**" and "**unintentionally**," respectively. Both heat of passion and imperfect justification manslaughter involve intentional (but partly excused) killings. Recklessness and bad act manslaughter, on the other hand, involve unintentional killings.

(1) Heat of Passion Manslaughter. [§233]

Heat of passion (or provocation) manslaughter is the **unlawful but provoked intentional killing of another human being**. It is a partial defense to a murder charge, and indicates that a defendant's actions are an understandable example of human weakness, even if not completely excusable. The elements of heat of passion manslaughter are: (1) **an unlawful** (2) **intentional** (3) **killing that** (4) **results from provocation**, i.e., **an (a) actual and (b) objectively reasonable sudden heat of passion**; (5) which is considered **legally adequate**; and (6) which occurred **before** the defendant had a reasonable opportunity to "**cool off**" (this last element is known as the "cooling off" doctrine). These elements are discussed below.

(a) "**Unlawful**" requires that the killing be without a justification or excuse which would render the conduct lawful.

(b) "**Intentional**" indicates that the killing is committed purposefully or knowingly.

(c) "**Killing**" mandates that the death of a human being occur.

(d) "**Actual**" provocation means that the defendant was not faking a disturbance while acting, but became in fact upset or provoked. "**Objectively reasonable**" provocation requires that a reasonable, ordinary person be provoked under the circumstances as well; no partial excuse is granted to an ultra-sensitive person who is easily angered or provoked, to a much greater extent than the average person. (This element greatly limits the scope of the excuse.)

(e) **"Legally Adequate" Provocation** has been interpreted by courts to **limit** the permissible types of provoking incidents. To illustrate, **mere words are not enough to legally provoke** (although words plus an assault generally are sufficient), nor is a breach of a contract legally adequate provocation. Observing adultery by the spouse of the defendant, however, constitutes legally adequate provocation, as is an aggravated assault or battery, or when a significant crime is committed against an immediate relative of the defendant.

(f) The "**Cooling Off Doctrine**" limits the **time** in which a defendant may justifiably respond to a provoking incident. If a **reasonable person would have cooled off** from the provoking event by the time the defendant responded to the provocation, then the defendant is not deserving of a partial excuse, and cannot claim heat of passion. Rather, the defendant's tardy response increases his or her level of blameworthiness to the extent that a murder charge is once again warranted.

(i) Example of Heat of Passion Manslaughter. Freddie was called a "sissy" in front of his family and friends by a co-worker, to which he took great offense. He was then pushed and shoved almost simultaneously by the same co-worker. Freddie thereupon picked up a steel rod and, with his temper unleashed, angrily bashed the co-worker over the head, killing him. Freddie can assert the partial excuse of heat of passion if he is charged with murder. Freddie (1) **unlawfully** (i.e., without any legal justification such as self defense, or excuse such as insanity), (2) **intentionally**, that is, purposefully, (3) **killed** the co-worker by striking him over the head. He also was (4)(a) **actually provoked**, because he took great offense to the victim's comments, responding "angrily" and "with his temper unleashed." He also was (4)(b) **reasonably provoked**, because a reasonable person could be expected to be humiliated under the circumstances and respond strongly. Since he was shoved as well as called names, his conduct was (5) **legally adequate** (while mere insults are insufficient, words plus a battery qualify). Further, (6) Freddie did not have time to **cool off**. (See Case Squibs Section, *Freddo v. State*.)

(ii) Example of the "Cooling Off" Doctrine. Husband Biff returned home earlier than expected from a sales trip and found his wife Betty in bed with her lover, Bart. Biff, extremely angry, stormed out of the house. Four months later, he returned to the house still angry brandishing a shotgun. He proceeded to shoot his wife dead, yelling at her "That'll teach you for messing around on me!" This would be murder, not heat of passion manslaughter. Biff certainly acted under actual heat of passion — even four months later — and the events that provoked him were both legally adequate and reasonable under the circumstances, but Biff had **adequate time to cool off** about the event. That is, a **reasonable person** would have cooled off four months after the incident. The heat of passion was no longer sudden, as required, and a reasonable person after four months would not have acted the way Biff did. *State v. Gounagias*, 88 Wash. 304, 153 P. 9 (1915).

Sum & Substance QUICK REVIEW of Criminal Law

(iii) Example of the "Reasonableness" Requirement. Kenny's longstanding girlfriend broke up with him, telling him she never wanted to see him again. Kenny was distraught. He showed up at her door and pleaded with her to go out with him again. When she refused, he stabbed her to death. Kenny is guilty of murder. This is not heat of passion manslaughter because, while the provocation may be considered actual, sudden, and even legally adequate, the response was not reasonable to an objective person under the circumstances. It is not reasonable for a spurned lover in this situation to be so distraught as to kill the other person (it may happen, but that does not make it a reasonable response).

Note that some jurisdictions have adopted, by statute, a broader heat of passion partial defense for defendants who act as a result of an actual and reasonable provocation defined as an "extreme **emotional disturbance**". This generally refers to a mental disturbance that falls short of insanity. *People v. Casassa*, 49 N.Y.2d 668, 427 N.Y.S.2d 769, 404 N.E.2d 1310 (1980).

(2) Imperfect Justification Manslaughter. [§237]

Imperfect justification manslaughter is an unlawful intentional killing under particular circumstances. The defendant must honestly but unreasonably believe that the use of lethal force is necessary. *People v. Bobo*, 271 Cal. Rptr. 277 (1990). The elements of imperfect justification are: (1) an **unlawful** (2) **intentional** (3) **killing** resulting from an (4) **actual belief** that the use of **lethal force was necessary** under the circumstances, but which is (5) **unreasonable** (it is based on an unreasonable mistake about the factual circumstances). While the defendant believes her actions were justified, the **erroneous** nature of her belief makes the justification **imperfect**. Because the defendant's mistaken belief is unreasonable, the defendant is still culpable — unreasonable conduct is the rough equivalent of negligence. The defendant is considered less culpable than a murderer, however, because there was at least an honest belief that lethal force was necessary to prevent a greater harm from occurring. (By comparison, if the defendant's mistake in the need to use lethal force is both honest and reasonable, the defendant generally is not considered culpable at all, and she will be completely exonerated.) *State v. Mendoza*, 80 Wis. 2d 122, 258 N.W.2d 260 (1977).

(a) EXAMPLE. Early one morning, the defendant sees a man in a trench coat and dark glasses walk up his front steps and reach into his pocket. The defendant, after watching several Stephen King movies, unreasonably believes the man is reaching for a gun with which to kill him. The defendant shoots the man first, killing him. It turns out that the victim was a United Parcel Service employee delivering a package. A reasonable person under the circumstances would have recognized that it was a United Parcel Service employee doing his duty. Thus, the defendant was honestly but unreasonably mistaken about the need to use deadly force in self-defense, and is guilty of imperfect justification manslaughter.

(b) EXAMPLE. Donnie Defendant erroneously believed that self-defense using lethal force is permissible to repel a perceived imminent attack. Donnie's belief was an honest one, based on a misreading of the applicable penal code. If Donnie kills a perceived assailant, he likely will be found guilty of murder because an honest but unreasonable mistaken justification about the **applicable law** is not a defense; only a mistake about an **applicable fact** will suffice (i.e., ignorance of the law is no defense).

(c) EXAMPLE. Defendant is wrongly arrested for attempted robbery. The defendant resists, correctly believing the arrest is improper. The resistance includes deadly force, and the arresting officer, Link, is killed. Defendant can be held liable for imperfect justification manslaughter.

(3) Recklessness or Negligence Manslaughter. [§241]

Recklessness or negligence manslaughter requires (1) **the unlawful** (2) **reckless or negligent** (3) **killing of another human being**. Recklessness/negligence manslaughter is separated from depraved heart/gross recklessness murder by a matter of degree. The recklessness in recklessness manslaughter does **not** rise to the level of gross recklessness evidencing "a depraved or malignant heart," but rather constitutes recklessness of a lower order. In other words, recklessness manslaughter does not require that the defendant be consciously aware of an extremely high or inordinate risk of serious bodily harm or death to others. *Palmer v. State*, 223 Md. 341, 164 A.2d 467 (1960).

(a) EXAMPLE. Nevin, a relatively new juggler, decides to try juggling lighted sticks. As he is practicing, Nevin recklessly allows one of the sticks to fly away from him. It hits a passerby, setting the passerby's clothes on fire and subsequently killing him. Nevin could be found guilty of recklessness manslaughter. His conduct was not so grossly reckless as to evince a grave indifference towards human life, but was sufficiently reckless, since he was a "relatively new juggler," to possibly hold him liable for manslaughter.

(4) Misdemeanor ("Bad Act") Manslaughter. [§243]

While the name misdemeanor manslaughter is often used, what is actually required is the **death of a human being during the commission or attempted commission of a specified unlawful act**. In many respects, this category is the functional equivalent of felony murder. Most of the unlawful acts supporting this type of crime are, in fact, misdemeanors. Some jurisdictions, however, construe this type of crime more narrowly, and permit only qualifying misdemeanors that are **malum in se**, bad in and of themselves, and not **malum prohibitum**, bad because they are prohibited by law. Other jurisdictions treat this category more expansively, and permit a manslaughter charge for any deaths occurring during the commission of any unlawful act, even ordinance violations that are not misdemeanors. *People v. Stuart*, 47 Cal. 2d 167, 302 P.2d 5 (1956).

(5) The Model Penal Code on Criminal Homicide. [§244]

The MPC both modifies and perpetuates the common law of criminal homicide. **Under the MPC**:

(a) Criminal homicide is divided into **three categories**: **murder**; **manslaughter**; and **negligent homicide**. [MPC §§210.2, 210.3, 210.4.]

(b) The **mental state terminology** for intent to kill, intent to commit serious bodily harm, and "depraved heart" murder has been slightly **modified** in favor of requiring the defendant to purposely or knowingly kill the victim, or to kill the victim recklessly "under circumstances manifesting extreme indifference to the value of human life." [MPC §210.2(1).]

(c) The category of intent to commit serious bodily harm is not expressly included in the MPC. Instead, the intent to seriously harm another is treated as gross recklessness, becoming murder if it manifests "extreme indifference to the value of human life." [MPC §210.2(1).] Thus, the intent to commit serious bodily harm homicides would appear to be subsumed into the gross recklessness category.

(d) **Felony murder is preserved**, but in a less potent form. A killing occurring during the commission or attempted commission of, (including the flight from), certain enumerated felonies presumptively constitutes extreme recklessness, but evidence can be offered by the defendant to rebut this presumption. If the presumption is rebutted, the prosecutor must prove malice. [MPC §210.2(1)(b).]

(e) Instead of heat of passion manslaughter, the Code adopts broader terminology, providing a partial defense to persons whose actions result from an "**extreme mental or emotional disturbance**." [MPC §210.3(b).] This kind of disturbance appears to embrace, but is not limited to, mental illness short of insanity. To determine whether an extreme mental or emotional disturbance existed, (1) the explanation or excuse must be reasonable, and (2) "determined from the viewpoint of a person in the actor's situation under the circumstances as he believes them to be." Thus, an objective test is used, but in the context of subjective circumstances. (See Case Squibs Section, *People v. Casassa*.)

PROBLEM 1. "Abbott!!" Abbott and Costello attempt to commit a petty larceny together. They get in each other's way and start arguing. Abbott starts pushing and spitting at Costello, who thinks to himself that it is a good time to finally do away with his dear friend Abbott. After being pushed for a sixth time, Costello pulls out a gun and shoots Abbott dead. Is this murder or manslaughter?

> **Answer:** Costello meets the "**ARM**" elements of act, result and mental state required for murder. Costello committed the **act** of shooting Abbott that was both the **actual** "but for" and **proximate** — i.e., reasonably foreseeable — **cause** of Abbott's **resulting** death. Costello **purposefully** killed Abbott, thus satisfying the **mens rea** requirement of intent to kill murder.
>
> The next question is whether Costello can successfully assert the partial excuse of **provocation** and reduce the offense for this intentional killing from murder to manslaughter. Since Abbott pushed and spit at Costello, each a battery, Costello's response was **legally adequate**. In addition, an **objectively reasonable** person may indeed have responded to the battery of spitting and pushing as Costello did under the circumstances. Further, Costello did not have a reasonable opportunity to **cool off**, but instead acted in the heat of the moment. Despite meeting all of these requirements, Costello still will be found guilty of murder. To be eligible for provocation manslaughter, there must also be **actual heat of passion**, and the facts indicate that Costello thought rationally "that it is a good time to do away with his dear friend Abbott." Thus, because he apparently did the killing calmly, without a sudden heat of passion, he has not satisfied all of the elements of provocation manslaughter.

PROBLEM 2. "The Law Firm." Roxanne, recently hired as a secretary at the law firm of Smith and Smith, is called by senior partner Arnie into his office. Roxanne had been sexually attacked by a co-worker as she was leaving work in her previous job, and she mistakenly believed that when Arnie sipped his cup of coffee, he was about to do the same. Fearing for her life, she picked up a lamp and bashed Arnie over the head with it, killing him. What crime, if any, has Roxanne committed?

> **Answer:** Roxanne likely has committed imperfect justification manslaughter. Roxanne met the "**ARM**" requirements of intent-to-kill murder. By bashing Arnie over the head, she did the **act** of killing that **actually and proximately resulted** in Arnie's death. She also had a **purposeful mental state**, desiring to hit and kill Arnie at the time of her act.
>
> However, Roxanne would likely claim she acted in self-defense because she believed lethal force was necessary. While her belief in the need to defend herself was honest, it also was mistaken and unreasonable under the circumstances. An objectively reasonable person would not construe sipping a cup of coffee as preparation for an attack on another, especially when the alleged preparatory conduct was quite dissimilar to the context in which the defendant had been previously assaulted. Thus, Roxanne is still culpable in her behavior. Yet, because her belief in the need to use self-defense was honest, she will likely be partially excused, and found guilty of **imperfect justification manslaughter**, not murder.

Spotting and Analyzing Criminal Homicide for the Exam

SPOT : Dead Body

ANALYZE : The Three Big Issues:

#1: | Mental State |

    a. Intentional or gross reckless killing? = Murder unless heat of passion or imperfect justification.

    b. Reckless or negligent? = Manslaughter

#2: | Defenses |

    Justification or excuse?
    [Self defense, duress, necessity, entrapment, insanity, etc.]

#3: | Special Problems |

    a. Heat of Passion (= Manslaughter)?

    b. Killing during felony (= felony murder)?

    c. Killing during bad act non-felony (= bad act Manslaughter)?

2. ASSAULT AND BATTERY. [§245]

The crimes of assault and battery have distinct meanings at common law, although the lines between them often have been blurred by judges, lawyers, and commentators.

Yet the two crimes share common characteristics. Both are crimes of violence, encompassing a wide variety of intimidation and conflict. In their simple forms, both are misdemeanors, meaning that the maximum incarceration that could result from a violation of each is one year in jail. Aggravated assaults and aggravated batteries, on the other hand, are often felonies, punishable by more than one year in prison.

a. Assault. [§246]

There are **two types** of assault: (1) an **attempted battery**, or (2) the **intentional creation of the imminent apprehension of a battery** (i.e., the **intentional scaring of another person**). In either case, an assault does not involve the actual touching of another person — either there was a failed effort to touch another, or simply an effort to scare another. For intentional scaring to constitute an assault, the defendant must have an apparent present ability to commit the battery. *Proffitt v. Ricci*, 463 A.2d 514 (R.I. 1983).

Both definitions of assault require **specific intent** (purposeful or knowing behavior); consequently, assault is a specific intent crime.

---

(1) EXAMPLE. Boris and Natasha observe their archenemy Bullwinkle walking down the street. Boris decides to end their feud once and for all, and he takes out a huge rock and throws it at Bullwinkle. It misses, without Bullwinkle ever realizing that it has been thrown. Has Boris committed a crime? The answer is yes, he has committed an assault in the form of an **attempted battery** (i.e., an attempted unlawful touching of another person). The fact that Bullwinkle did not realize what had happened is irrelevant to the commission of an attempted battery assault. (Boris's conduct was dangerous, and worthy of moral condemnation and even punishment.)

---

(2) EXAMPLE. Arnold "the terminator" Zisselle walked up to the neighborhood bully and said in a menacing tone of voice, "I'm going to take my fist and place it on your nose, and I don't mean gently." With that statement, Arnold drew back his fist in a fighting stance, as if to get ready to punch, and the bully ran. Has Arnold committed an assault? The answer is yes. Arnold has committed an **intent to scare** assault. Arnold intended to frighten the bully into believing that a battery was imminent. Arnold also had the apparent present ability to inflict harm on the bully. (If Arnold had spoken these same words in a telephone conversation with the bully, or while in police custody in handcuffs, no assault would have occurred because there would not have been any apparent present ability to harm the bully. In addition, if the victim did not notice the intended fright, or did not actually get scared, no intent to scare assault would have occurred.)

---

b. Battery. [§249]

Battery is the (1) **unlawful** (2) **touching of another person**. An unlawful touching means that the touching is either **harmful** or **offensive**. Thus, battery is more specifically defined as the (1)(a) **harmful** or (b) **offensive** (2) **touching of another person**. The mental state required for battery is not expressly defined. When a crime requires that the act be committed "**unlawfully**," it generally is construed to mean any of the four culpable mental states: purpose, knowledge, recklessness, or negligence ("PKRN"). Battery, consequently, is a **general intent** crime requiring **negligence** at a minimum. *State v. Rullis*, 79 N.J. Super. 221, 191 A.2d 197 (1963).

> **(1) EXAMPLE.** Gwendolyn, while carrying a ladder to a construction site, thinks she hears her name being called and swings around suddenly in the opposite direction. When she does this, she knocks over Leslie, who is walking behind her. Gwendolyn is guilty of **battery**. In swinging around, Gwendolyn harmfully touched Leslie, committing the actus reus. Her conduct was negligent, and therefore unlawful, because she did not use reasonable care to check if anyone was behind her before she swung around. That she did not in fact see Leslie or intend to hit her is irrelevant, since the harmful or offensive touching need only be negligent, not intentional.

c. The Model Penal Code. [§251]

The MPC **groups** both **assault and battery together** under the label "**assault**." [MPC §211.1.] A simple (or basic) assault occurs when an individual either (1) **attempts to cause**, or (2) **purposely, knowingly, or recklessly causes**, the **bodily injury of another**, or (3) **negligently causes** the **bodily injury of another with a deadly weapon**, or (4) **attempts** through **physical menace** to put another person in **fear of imminent serious bodily injury**. Thus, the MPC changes and regroups the common law definitions.

> **(1) EXAMPLE.** Quinn, a karate expert, is demonstrating her prowess in the martial arts in the corner of a crowded area. Unbeknownst to Quinn, Jesus and Elvira turn the corner and are accidentally struck by Quinn and slightly injured. Quinn has committed an assault under the Model Penal Code if: (1) she was negligent in unreasonably demonstrating her skills; (2) the bruises suffered by Jesus and Elvira are considered a "bodily injury"; and (3) Quinn's hands are considered deadly weapons. (Some jurisdictions may find that a karate expert's hands are in fact deadly weapons.) Therefore, Quinn would be held liable because her (1) negligence (practicing in a crowded area) caused the (2) bodily injury of another (the injuries to Jesus and Elvira) (3) with a deadly weapon (her hands). If her hands are not considered deadly weapons, no assault will be deemed to have been committed as a result of Quinn's negligence.

OUTLINE

3. ROBBERY. [§253]

Robbery is defined at common law as the (1) **trespassory** (2) **taking** and **carrying away** (3) of the **personal property of another** (4) with the **intent to deprive the other of the property permanently** (5) from the **other's person or presence** (6) **by force or fear**. *Lear v. State*, 39 Ariz. 313, 6 P.2d 426 (1931). Simplified, a robbery can be viewed as a **larceny** (see §0.2) from another's person or presence **accompanied by an assault**. *State v. Davis*, 242 N.C. 476, 87 S.E.2d 906 (1955) (overruled on other grounds, *State v. Hurst*, 359 S.E.2d 776 (1987)). In still different terms, a robbery constitutes larceny by force or fear from the person or presence of another.

> **a. EXAMPLE.** Shana stopped walking to tie her sneaker. As she did so, Sluggo pulled Shana's pocketbook out from under her arm, yelled "If you try to stop me, I'll hurt you," and ran away. Sluggo has committed **robbery** of the pocketbook, because he (1) trespassorily (without permission) (2) took and carried away (3) the pocketbook of another, Shana, (4) with the intent to permanently deprive Shana of the pocketbook (5) from Shana's presence, (6) saying "I'll hurt you!", creating fear in the victim of imminent harm, and pulling it from her arm by force. Note that a robbery is not complete until the perpetrator comes to a point of repose in escaping apprehension. In addition, a robbery is considered more egregious if it is committed with a weapon; an armed robbery has a greater potential for danger.

4. RAPE. [§255]

Rape is defined at common law as (1) the **carnal knowledge** (2) **by a man** (3) **of a woman** (4) **by force or fear and against her will**.

This crime has undergone considerable change over the centuries. Originally, the crime at common law was a quasi-property crime intended to protect the proprietary interests of husbands and fathers in their wives and daughters. Until fairly recently, moreover, rape only occurred if the victim was not the defendant's wife; in essence, there could be no rape of the defendant wife. There also existed several other requirements that tilted the scales against complainants — corroboration of the allegations was required, and some showing of the alleged victim's resistance was necessary. In most jurisdictions, these requirements have been repealed, and special statutes protecting victims, particularly from defense allegations about the alleged victim's prior sexual conduct, have been enacted. These statutory protections are often known as "**rape shield**" laws. (Also see §308, Statutory Rape.)

The social dimension of the crime of rape is significant. The crime raises questions about gender, socio-economic status, race, and American culture. For example, some view rape as a crime of power, not sex, and view the crime in the context of gender relations. Others look at the disparate ways society treats a rape by strangers as compared to those by acquaintances, and heterosexual versus homosexual rape. These deep-rooted issues raise questions about the efficacy and propensity of the criminal justice system and its underlying values.

a. Carnal Knowledge. [§256]

Rape requires penetration, that is, sexual intercourse. For different types of sexual abuse, other crimes exist.

b. By a Man. [§257]

A woman, however, can be charged with aiding and abetting a male rapist.

c. Of a Woman. [§258]

Contrary to the long-standing rule, the current trend in the law permits prosecution when the woman raped is the defendant's wife. *State v. Smith*, 85 N.J. 193, 426 A.2d 38 (1981).

d. "By Force or Fear and Against Her Will." [§259]

This requirement has uniformly been interpreted to mean **without consent**. Consent is often the primary issue in acquaintance rape cases, as compared to cases in which the assailant and victim did not know each other. The issue of consent, particularly in the way that non-verbal cues are interpreted by the defendant, is often controversial.

e. Intent. [§260]

Rape is a **general intent crime**, satisfied by a minimum of **negligence**. Recklessness, knowledge, or a purposeful mental state also will suffice. Even though the word negligence will not be found in the definition, it is implied as the minimum culpable mental state. That rape only requires negligence does not mean it is a less heinous offense than specific intent crimes such as attempted robbery or even attempted rape. As noted above in the introduction to mens rea (see §V(d)), the heinousness of the mental state does not determine the seriousness of the crime.

> **f. EXAMPLE.** Michael has sexual intercourse with Betty after she has passed out from alcohol consumption. Michael has committed rape because Michael, (1) a man, had (2) carnal knowledge (sexual intercourse) with Betty, (3) a woman, (4) by force or fear, because there is no evidence of consent on Betty's part. This example illustrates that consent means affirmative agreement. Without such an expression by the victim, either tacit or express, a rape has occurred.

5. FALSE IMPRISONMENT. [§262]

A person commits false imprisonment if she: (1) **unlawfully confines the victim**, (2) **against her will**, so that, (3) **the victim does not have the freedom to leave**.

a. "Unlawful confinement." [§263]

This crime requires the unlawful confinement of a person. Sometimes confinement is lawful, such as the detention of prisoners sentenced to incarceration, or the lawful pre-arrest detention by the police. If confinement is lawful, false imprisonment has not occurred.

b. "Against her will." [§264]

The constraint must be without the victim's consent.

c. "Without the freedom to leave." [§265]

The victim must have a reasonable belief that the constraint is against her will. The victim must be restrained by **force** or the **threat** of force so that, to a reasonable person, she can not leave by her own volition.

> **d. EXAMPLE.** Bar Bat is forcibly prevented from entering the Hard Rock Cafe. Bar Bat has not been falsely imprisoned because he has not been confined. However, if Bar Bat enters and then wishes to leave the Hard Rock Cafe, but is prevented from exiting by force or threat of force, it is likely that Bar Bat is now falsely imprisoned. Note, however, that consent to confinement is a valid defense to the charge of false imprisonment.

6. KIDNAPPING. [§267]

This crime requires:

(1) the **confinement of a person**, (2) **against her will**, (3) who is **transported or secretly confined**. (Note that in some jurisdictions, secret confinement alone is required and transportation is irrelevant.)

a. "Confinement." [§268]

The victim must be restrained in a bounded area.

b. "Of a person". [§268.5]

No age limitation exists, but kidnapping of a child is often considered a more heinous offense than the kidnapping of an adult.

c. "Against her will." [§269]

This requirement means the confinement must occur without the victim's consent.

d. "Transported and/or secretly confined." [§270]

The transportation or secret confinement requirement distinguishes kidnapping from the crime of false imprisonment. Kidnapping statutes fall into **two categories**: those which **require either transportation or secret confinement**, and those statutes which **only require secret confinement** (no transportation, i.e., "asportation," is necessary).

Where asportation (transportation) is an element of the crime and asportation has occurred, it is not sufficient if the movement is incidental to the commission of a separate crime or of minimal duration. *People v. Daniels*, 459 P.2d 225 (Cal. 1969) (movement of the victim incidental to a robbery is not the type of movement which will satisfy a kidnapping charge); to compare, see MPC §212.1 (kidnapping requires movement from a residence or business, or of a substantial distance, or confinement in an isolated place for a substantial period of time).

With either type of kidnapping statute, it appears that **secret confinement** is the essence of the crime. In those jurisdictions requiring either transportation or secrecy, secrecy is **presumed** if transportation of the victim is shown. If there is no movement of the victim, a kidnapping charge will be sustained only if it is shown that the victim was, in fact, secretly confined.

e. Aggravated kidnapping is the most serious type of kidnapping offense. Examples of aggravated kidnapping include, kidnapping for ransom, kidnapping for purposes of committing other crimes, kidnapping for offensive purposes (intent to harm or sexually abuse), and child stealing.

7. MAYHEM. [§271]

Mayhem requires: (a) an **intentional act**, (b) to **disfigure, dismember, or disable**, (c) another **human being**.

a. "Intentional." [§272]

Mayhem requires that the defendant's act be intentional — purposeful or knowing. Reckless or negligent acts cannot support a mayhem charge.

b. "Disfigure, dismember, or disable." [§273]

The defendant must intend to disfigure, dismember, or disable, and must be successful. That is, the defendant must, in fact, permanently disfigure or disable the victim. However, the intent to disfigure or disable a particular body part need not result in the disfigurement or disabling of that body part; mayhem still occurs when the defendant disfigures, disables, or dismembers a body part different than the body part originally intended to be harmed.

> **(1) EXAMPLE.** Defendant mangles Vinny the Victim's right hand, although defendant had intended to mangle the left. Defendant can still be held liable for mayhem, since the defendant acted intentionally to disfigure or maim, with the result that the victim was maimed. The fact that a different part of the body was maimed than that intended to be harmed by defendant does not prevent liability.

c. "Another human being." [§275]

Only injuries to humans suffice. The common law crime of mayhem has been abolished in most jurisdictions. However, modern statutes retain this crime in the form of a similar crime, **aggravated battery**, which involves great bodily harm inflicted upon the victim.

D. CRIMES AGAINST PROPERTY

1. ARSON. [§276]

At common law, arson is defined as the (a) **malicious** (b) **burning** of the (c) **dwelling house of another**. The burning need not be complete; scorching will suffice. Further, the "dwelling house of another" has been interpreted to mean the residence of another, regardless of ownership. *State v. Vickers*, 306 N.C. 90, 291 S.E.2d 599 (1982).

A criminal law examination is likely to test any of the elements of arson, but the mental state requirement is particularly susceptible to inquiry.

> **a. EXAMPLE.** Defendant Jones, while visiting his friend Smith at the house Smith was renting, carelessly dropped a cigarette on the floor, burning the house down. Is Jones guilty of arson? It depends. He did (b) burn down the (c) dwelling house resided in by another, namely Smith's rental property. Whether Jones acted with malice, however, is questionable. Jones will only be guilty of arson if his "carelessness" means recklessness, the minimum level of culpability required for (a) malice. If Jones was merely negligent, he would not have acted maliciously, and therefore could not be held responsible for the common law crime of arson.

b. Model Penal Code. [§278]

Under the MPC, arson occurs when a person (1) starts a fire or an explosion (2) with the purpose of destroying a building or occupied structure of another or to (3) destroy or damage his own or another's property to collect insurance. [MPC §220.1(1)(a)(b)]. The Code has created a separate lesser offense called "recklessly burning or exploding." [MPC §220.1(2)(a)(b)]. This provision applies to persons who (1) purposely start a fire or an explosion and (2) recklessly place (a) a person in danger (of death or bodily harm), or (b) a building or occupied structure of another in danger of damage or destruction.

---

(1) EXAMPLE. On the 4th of July, Matthew lit a bonfire in his back yard. When Matthew went inside his house to find some marshmallows to roast, one of the neighbor's children wandered too close to the fire, and his hair was singed. The bonfire then hit a gas line and blew up the neighbor's porch. What crimes, if any, has Matthew committed? Under the Model Penal Code, Matthew has not committed **arson**, since he did not purposefully start a fire or explosion with the purpose of either (1) destroying a building or structure or (2) damaging property to recover insurance. He may be guilty, however, of "reckless burning," because he (1) purposely started a fire on his own property, and (2) recklessly (a) placed a neighborhood child in danger of bodily injury and (b) placed an occupied structure of another, namely his neighbor's house, in danger of damage or destruction. Thus, he may be held liable on two counts of "reckless burning."

---

2. LARCENY. [§280]

At common law, larceny is defined as the (a) **trespassory** (b) **taking and carrying away** (c) of the **personal property of another** (4) with the **intent to deprive the other person of that property permanently**. *Commonwealth v. Johnson*, 379 Mass. 177, 396 N.E.2d 974 (1979).

a. Trespassory. [§281]

This means that the property must have been taken **without** the owner's (or rightful possessor's) **permission**. If the owner gives tacit or express permission, no larceny has occurred.

---

(1) EXAMPLE. Amy asks Billy Joe if she could take a ride on Billy Joe's horse. Billy Joe says "Sure." Amy takes a ride on the horse, rides off into the sunset, and never returns. Amy has not committed larceny at common law because the taking was not trespassory. When Amy was given permission to ride the horse, she was granted custody of it. When custody over property is given by an owner, any subsequent taking is generally not considered to be trespassory.

An exception exists, however, which is called "**larceny by trick**." This form of larceny, as the name implies, involves the use of **trickery** (i.e., fraud) to obtain **custody** over another person's property. This special type of larceny is discussed below at §288.

b. Taking and Carrying Away. [§282]

This is commonly known as the "asportation" requirement. To satisfy this element, the property must be **physically moved** by the perpetrator (Note: large or heavy items need not actually be "carried" away, just moved). *State v. Rozeboom*, 124 N.W. 783 (1910). An issue that often arises is how far the property must be moved "away." The answer to this question is, the property need only be moved infinitesimally; not even off of the owner's property; just enough so that the entire property is moved. *People v. Olivio*, 52 N.Y.2d 309, 438 N.Y. 242, 420 N.E.2d 40 (1981); *People v. Alamo*, 358 N.Y.S. 375 (1974) (sufficient movement to establish dominion and control). Thus, a person who takes and carries away the property of another must first acquire possession. Possession may be actual or constructive. Actual possession means the property is on the person or within arm's reach. Constructive possession means the person exercises dominion and control over a thing that is not within arm's reach. For example, for someone who has your car keys on their person and constructively possess your car even though it is located hundreds of yards away. Some courts also distinguish between possession and custody. Custody is another way of saying that there is a more temporary or limited use of the property compared to possession. The legal fiction of cutody occurs in several specific contexts, including an employee who is holding property for an employer or a bailee who is in control of property which is placed in containers. Under common law, a taking of the property has not occurred if the perpetrator obtains mere custody of it and not full possession.

---

(1) EXAMPLE. Jennifer, at a fancy fund raising party held in the home of a wealthy donor, sneaks into the master bedroom, lifts out some diamond earrings, and starts to walk out of the room with them. Hearing a noise, she drops the diamonds six feet away from where she picked them up. Jennifer has met the "trespassory taking and carrying away" requirement, even though she had possession for less than one minute and moved the diamonds only six feet from their initial resting place. If she also had the intent to steal the diamonds (and deprive the owner of them permanently), at the time she took and carried them away, she can be held liable for larceny.

---

c. The Personal Property of Another. [§284]

Larceny can occur only if the **tangible personal property of another**, namely goods and chattels, are taken. This requirement seems intuitively obvious. After all, it is difficult to take and carry away real property (even with a dump truck), or to steal from yourself. Yet this element is not so easily resolved when the property is subject to joint ownership and one of the joint owners is the perpetrator.

> **(1) EXAMPLE.** Roy and Kate were married but not getting along. Roy became very angry at Kate one day, and took their prized antique clock out of the house, yelling "I'm leaving!" Has Roy committed larceny? Jurisdictions are currently split on this issue, although at common law it was generally the view that one **co-owner could not commit larceny against another co-owner**. Thus, at the common law, Roy would not be guilty of larceny of the clock.

d. Intent to Deprive the Other of That Property Permanently. [§286]

The mens rea element requires an **intent to steal the property**, not just to borrow it. The perpetrator's intent is determined at the time of the taking, and not at any later time. Thus, a person who originally intends to deprive another of property permanently can later change her mind and decide to return the property, and yet still have committed larceny. *Barfield v. U.S.*, 229 F.2d 936 (5th Cir. 1956).

> **(1) EXAMPLE.** Lenny admired Amy's bicycle so he decided to steal it from where it was stored. After riding around on it for a day or two, he became bored with it, and returned it. Has he committed larceny? The answer is yes, because all of the elements, including the intent to steal, were met at the time he took the bike. (If Lenny had taken the bicycle originally only intending to borrow it, or believing that it was rightfully his, no intent to steal would be present.)

e. Larceny by Trick. [§288]

In larceny by trick, the perpetrator **obtains possession of the property by fraudulent means** (i.e., by "tricking" the owner or lawful possessor). Securing possession by fraud is considered to be a trespassory taking. (Note that if the **title** to the property, as opposed to its mere possession, is obtained by fraudulent means, the crime is not larceny by trick, but instead the statutory crime of false pretenses, discussed below in §299. *People v. Miller*, 169 N.Y. 339, 62 N.E. 418 (1902).

> **(1) Example of "Larceny by Trick".** Stan and Fran drive their Jaguar convertible up to Capriccio's restaurant to enjoy a fancy meal out. Mel, pretending to be the parking valet, takes the keys to the car, telling Stan and Fran "Don't worry, I'll take good care of it." When everyone is out of sight, however, Mel drives it away, intending to keep it. Mel has committed a larceny called "larceny by trick," because he obtained possession of the car through fraudulent means, intending to steal it.

3. BURGLARY. [§290]

At common law, burglary is defined as (a) the **breaking and entering** (b) of the **dwelling house of another** (c) at **nighttime** (d) with the **intent to commit a felony therein**.

Although it is generally treated as a completed crime, burglary is **inchoate**, i.e., incomplete, because it does not require the actual commission of a felony once inside the dwelling house, just the intent to do so. The mental state is measured at the time of the break-in. Thus, the perpetrator who changes her mind and decides not to commit a crime after breaking and entering the dwelling house of another at night-time with the intent to steal valuables within (generally a felony) or harm one of the occupants (also a felony), already has committed a burglary.

a. "Breaking and Entering." [§291]

There must be both a breaking and an entering of the dwelling house. Permission to enter, or entry through an already open door, does not satisfy the "breaking" requirement at common law. *State v. Dunbar*, 282 S.C. 169, 318 S.E.2d 16 (1984). If the perpetrator opens a door or a window which is not locked, however, a sufficient breaking has occurred. *State v. Boon*, 35 N.C. 244 (1852). The word "breaking" is not meant literally; nothing actually need be broken for a breaking and entering to occur. An "entering" is considered to occur when any part of the perpetrator's body enters the house, *Mattex v. State*, 179 Ind. 57, 101 N.E. 1009 (1913); the whole body need not enter the house for this component to be met (an arm or leg will do). See *People v. Davis*, 54 Ill. App. 3d 517, 369 N.E.2d 1376 (Ill. 1977).

b. "Dwelling House of Another." [§292]

A dwelling house is considered "of another" if someone other than the perpetrator lawfully occupies the premises. The ownership of the dwelling is not controlling on the issue of whether the structure is "of another." *State v. Ervin*, 96 N.M. 366, 630 P.2d 765 (1981).

c. "At Nighttime." [§293]

At common law, "nighttime" depended upon whether a person could be seen by natural light, not whether the sun had technically set. (Crimes committed in the dark are potentially more dangerous than those committed in the light.)

d. "Intent to Commit a Felony Therein." [§294]

If, at the time of the breaking and entering, the perpetrator was not intending to commit a crime inside, but thereafter changed her mind once inside, a burglary has not occurred. The intent to commit a felony must occur simultaneously with the breaking and entering of the other's dwelling house. In essence, what counts is the perpetrator's mental state at the precise moment of her breaking and entering. *People v. Hill*, 67 Cal. 2d 105, 60 Cal. Rptr. 234, 429 P.2d 586 (1967).

> **(1) EXAMPLE.** Joe and Amy break into their neighbor's house one night, intending on a lark to just "take a look around." Once inside, they find a drawer full of diamonds, and steal them. Joe and Amy have not committed burglary. While they (1) broke and entered their (2) neighbor's house, a dwelling house of another, (3) at night time, at the time they broke in there was no intent to commit a felony inside, just a desire to "look around." The fact that a felony theft subsequently occurred does not retroactively make the initial break-in a burglary.

4. MALICIOUS MISCHIEF. [§296]

A defendant is guilty of this crime if she: (a) intentionally, (b) destroys or damages, (c) the property of another (note that the property need not be physically decimated, but only damaged as to its utility or value). This crime is generally not a significant component of criminal law courses.

E. STATUTORY CRIMES

This section lists the elements of certain statutory crimes listed in this section are offenses which the legislature has declared criminal and were not traditionally classified as common law crimes.

1. EMBEZZLEMENT. [§297]

Embezzlement is generally defined as the (a) **fraudulent** (b) **conversion** of the (c) **personal property** of another by (d) an individual in **lawful possession** of that property. *State v. Frasher*, 265 S.E.2d 43 (1980). Embezzlement is distinguishable from larceny in that the **embezzler** already **is in lawful possession** of the property, which is then appropriated for her own use. In comparison, larceny requires that a perpetrator obtain custody of the property by stealth or deceit. Embezzlement is further distinguishable from larceny since it is statutory in origin, and not a common law offense.

> **a. EXAMPLE.** Frances is employed as a cashier at the local supermarket. Her job is to take the money she receives from supermarket sales and place it in the cash register. Her philosophy, however, is "one for the cash register, and one for me." Frances is committing embezzlement. The money is (1) in her lawful possession but (2) is still the personal property of another, the supermarket owner, which she is (3) fraudulently converting for her own use. She has not committed larceny, however, because the property was lawfully in her own possession, and was not taken by trespass.

2. FALSE PRETENSES. [§299]

False pretenses is a statutory-based crime. It requires a wrongdoer who, with (a) the **intent to defraud another** (b) **knowingly** makes a (c) **false** and (d) **material** (e) **representation of fact**, which results in the perpetrator (f) **obtaining title** to another's property.

a. Comparison with Embezzlement and Larceny by Trick. [§300]

The primary difference between the crimes of false pretenses, embezzlement, and larceny by trick is the way the property is **obtained**. In embezzlement, the defendant already has lawful possession of the property, whereas in larceny by trick, the defendant obtains possession — but not title — by fraud. In false pretenses, the defendant obtains title to the property — not just possession — by fraud.

> **(1) Example of False Pretenses.** Simone agrees to sell her horse to Pasqual for Pasqual's stock certificates, which Pasqual claims are valued at $20,000. Pasqual knows before the exchange that the stock is absolutely worthless. Thus, at the time of the trade, Pasqual has committed the crime of false pretenses, because with the (1) intent to defraud Simone, he has (2) knowingly made a (3) false and (4) material (5) representation of fact about the value of the stock, thereby (6) fraudulently obtaining title to another's property, namely Simone's horse.

3. FORGERY. [§301.5]

This crime requires: (a) **making or altering,** (b) **a writing with apparent legal significance** (e.g. check, contract), (c) **so that it is false,** (d) **with the intent to defraud.** The crime of "uttering" a forged document is when a person offers the forged document to another with the intent to defraud.

4. RECEIVING STOLEN PROPERTY. [§302]

To commit the crime of receiving stolen property, the defendant must: (a) **knowingly,** (b) **receive stolen property,** (c) with the **intent to permanently deprive** the true owner of the property.

a. "Knowingly." [§303]

A defendant must actually know that the property received is stolen. This means that the defendant must be consciously aware that it is practically certain the property in question was stolen. "Knowledge" can be inferred from the totality of the circumstances.

b. "Receiving stolen property." [§304]

A perpetrator receives stolen property if it is in her **actual** or **constructive possession** or **control**.

c. "Intent to permanently deprive the true owner of the property." [§305]

The intent to permanently deprive means that the accused intends, either purposefully or knowingly, to **permanently dispose** of the stolen property. Disposal can occur, for example, by either destroying, selling, or distributing the property. The intent to permanently deprive is a **specific intent**.

Receiving goods which a defendant believes are stolen, but which in fact are not, does not constitute the crime of attempting to receive stolen property. There is no attempted receipt of stolen property because courts view the circumstances as a **legal impossibility**, which is a complete defense to the attempt charge. (See Case Squibs Section, *People v. Jaffe*, 78 N.E. 169 (N.Y. 1906); contra, *People v. Comodeca*, 338 P.2d 903 (Cal. 1959) (a defendant can be guilty of receiving stolen property so long as he believes the property he is receiving was stolen).)

Similarly, receiving goods which at one time were stolen but are no longer stolen (e.g., stolen property which has been returned to the owner or recovered by the police, who then set up a "fence" operation) does not constitute the crime of receiving stolen property.

> **(1) EXAMPLE.** The police recover a stolen coat and set up a sting operation. Some time later, an undercover police officer sells the defendant the "stolen" coat. The defendant is not guilty of either attempting to receive stolen property or receiving stolen property. There is no receipt of stolen property because the coat was no longer stolen when it was received (the coat had lost the character of being stolen). See Case Squibs Section, *People v. Jaffe*. Also, there was no **attempted** receipt of stolen property because it is legally impossible to attempt to receive stolen property where the property is, in fact, not stolen.

5. THEFT. [§307]

This crime requires the: (a) **unlawful**, (b) **appropriation**, (c) of the **property of another**, (d) by a person who **intends to deprive the true property owner** of the property **permanently** or **temporarily**.

Theft is often used as an umbrella offense which combines and includes a variety of related crimes of stealing such as larceny, embezzlement, receiving stolen goods, fraudulent conversion, extortion, and false pretenses. (MPC §223.)

6. STATUTORY RAPE. [§308]

This crime requires: (a) **sexual intercourse**, (b) with a **female under the age of consent** (generally under the age of 18).

There is no mens rea requirement pertaining to the age of consent, and it is tantamount to a strict liability offense. Accordingly, consent by the female is not a defense to this charge. However, a minority of courts allow an honest and reasonable mistake as to the age of the female as a valid defense to this crime. *State v. Guest*, 583 P.2d 836 (Alaska 1978).

7. INCEST. [§309]

This statutory offense occurs when the defendant has: (a) **sexual intercourse** with, **or** (b) **is married to**, (c) a **blood relative**. A minority of jurisdictions extend liability to situations in which the defendant marries certain non-blood relatives.

VII. VICARIOUS LIABILITY (OR "COMPLICITY")

A. VICARIOUS LIABILITY. [§310]

Vicarious liability means that a **defendant can be held liable for the acts of others**. This is the most powerful form of criminal responsibility. There are two major forms of vicarious liability: (1) **conspiracy liability** and (2) **accomplice liability**.

1. COMPARING CONSPIRACY AND ACCOMPLICE LIABILITY. [§310.5]

Conspiracy liability, discussed above in section §135, is similar to its vicarious liability cousin, accomplice liability, in that each generally involves a crime to be committed by two or more persons. Several differences exist, however. **Conspiracy liability** revolves around an **agreement** to commit a crime. It is based on the concept of a joint partnership or enterprise. The crime is complete without any steps being taken towards the commission of the object crime. **Accomplice liability**, on the other hand, is predicated on a person **actually assisting** another in committing a crime; the formation of an agreement to commit the crime is irrelevant to the existence of accomplice liability.

B. CONSPIRACY LIABILITY. [§311]

A conspirator will be held liable for the **acts of co-conspirators occurring during and in furtherance of the conspiracy**. A conspirator can be found liable even if she did nothing more than agree to participate in the conspiracy. (See §157.)

C. ACCOMPLICE LIABILITY. [§311.5]

Accomplice liability arises if a person (1) **knowingly** (2) **aids, abets, or assists** another in committing a crime. The principal actor need not know of or agree to the assistance, which can take a wide variety of forms. Further, the assistance can occur **before**, **during** or **after** the commission of the offense. Some accomplices can be held vicariously liable for the acts of other accomplices, most often for the object offense.

1. TYPES OF ACCOMPLICES. [§312]

The common law recognized different types of accomplices. These distinctions had a significant impact on the procedures and substance of accomplice prosecutions. The major distinctions were based on whether the accomplice helped **before**, **during** or **after** the commission of the **crime**, and whether the person had a primary or secondary role during the crime's commission. At common law, those persons who **actually carry out the crime** are called **principals**. Those who **assist before or after** the crime's commission are called **accessories** to the crime.

a. Types of Principals. [§313]

There are two types of principals.

(1) Principal in the First Degree. [§314]

The individuals who actively commit the crime are called the principals in the first degree. There may be more than one principal in the first degree. Note that those who are principals in the first degree are not necessarily in leadership positions in group criminal activity.

OUTLINE

Furthermore, a person still will be considered a principal in the first degree even if she uses an **innocent instrumentality**, a person who has been duped or tricked, to commit the actus reus of the crime.

(2) Principal in the Second Degree. [§315]

A person who **intentionally assists** in committing the crime, and is **present at the scene** in a **less than central position**, such as a lookout, a getaway driver, or the person who holds the bag in which the money is to be put during a robbery, is called a principal in the second degree. The dividing line between a principal in the first degree and a principal in the second degree is often based on the facts of the particular case. *United States v. Peichev*, 500 F.2d 917 (9th Cir. 1974).

b. Types of Accessories. [§316]

In addition to the two different kinds of principals, there are two distinct types of accessories to the crime. The accessories generally play a lesser role in the crime than either type of principal.

(1) Accessory Before the Fact. [§317]

An accessory before the fact is **not present at the scene** at all, but **intentionally assists** the principals **prior** to the crime's commission. *Moehring v. Commonwealth*, 223 Va. 564, 290 S.E.2d 891 (1982). This type of accessory assists in planning and preparing for the crime. She may purchase or repair equipment to be used in the crime, draw up diagrams or maps of the target, or strategize about possible courses of action.

(2) Accessory After the Fact. [§318]

An accessory after the fact is **not present at the scene**, but intentionally assists the felon in escaping or avoiding detection **after** the crime has been completed. *United States v. Thorton*, 178 F. Supp. 42 (E.D.N.Y. 1959). This type of accessory may provide a hide-out for the principals, or offer supplies or transportation to them by which they can better elude the police.

c. Significance of Distinctions at Common Law. [§319]

At common law, an accessory to a felony could not be convicted of a crime greater than the crime for which the principal was convicted. Further, unless a principal was convicted, an accessory could not lawfully be convicted either. No such distinctions applied, however, for **misdemeanors** or the felony of **treason**, where all participants were considered principals at common law.

2. THE SCOPE OF RESPONSIBILITY. [§320]

At common law, accessories before the fact, principals in the first degree and principals in the second degree could be held liable for the commission of the object crime. (Accessories after the fact were treated separately and were not liable for the object offense.)

> **a. EXAMPLE.** Jane acted as a lookout for Bob when he committed the crime of rape. Jane was an accomplice because she intentionally assisted Bob, and she can be held liable for rape as well. Specifically, Jane was a principal in the second degree because she was present at the scene in a secondary capacity.

b. "Long-Arm" (Vicarious) Accomplice Liability. [§322]

If the object crime is a homicide, in a minority of jurisdictions, the defendant also may be held responsible for the "**natural and probable consequences**" of the acts of other accomplices in committing the object homicide. This rule creates an extension of liability much like the **Pinkerton** Rule for conspirator liability (see section §175). Jurisdictions that apply the "natural and probable consequences" doctrine to accomplice liability, however, generally **restrict** its use to homicides committed in furtherance of an object crime.

3. ACCOMPLICE LIABILITY MENS REA. [§323]

Accomplice liability requires both an act and a mental state. (The act is the actual assistance of another in committing the crime, including encouragement or enticement.) The **mental state** is the **intent to commit, or to assist another in committing**, the object offense. *Alonzi v. People of Colorado*, 198 Colo. 160, 597 P.2d 560 (1979). Because accomplice liability requires an **intent** to commit or to assist in committing a crime, accomplice liability requires **specific intent**. See *People v. Beeman*, 35 Cal. 3d 547, 674 P.2d 1318 (1984).

4. THE LEGISLATIVE EXEMPTION RULE. [§324]

If an individual is in the **class of persons a criminal statute is designed to protect**, the person **cannot** be prosecuted as an accomplice.

> **a. EXAMPLE.** If a statute prohibited "corrupting the morals of a minor," or "transporting a minor across state lines for immoral purposes," the minor in such cases cannot be charged as an accomplice. Otherwise, that would defeat the purpose of the statute.

VIII. DEFENSES

A defense to a criminal charge can **partially or completely negate** liability. Yet defenses are not all alike. Certain defenses apply only to particular crimes (impossibility, for example, generally applies only to attempt charges). Depending on the statute or common law rule, sometimes prosecutors have to disprove defenses, and sometimes defendants must assert and offer some proof of defenses. Further, defenses can be subdivided based on how they operate — whether they **negate an element** of the crime, or whether they admit the crime but offer an **affirmative justification or** excuse.

The former group of defenses, such as intoxication, essentially denies the existence of an element by claiming that the prosecution's allegations are wrong. (This group can be remembered as "**you're wrong**" **defenses**.) The latter group of defenses is generally called "**affirmative defenses**." These affirmative defenses are perhaps more easily remembered as "yes, I did it, but ...," or simply "**yes, but**..." **defenses**. The various types of defenses will be discussed in greater detail below.

A. DEFENSES TO INCHOATE CRIMES. [§326]

1. DEFENSES TO SOLICITATION OFFENSES. [§326.5]

There is no clear consensus as to whether **abandonment** (also called a "change of heart") serves as a defense to solicitation (see §136 above) at common law. Several states, by statute, provide for such a defense when there is a **complete and voluntary renunciation** by the defendant of his **criminal purpose** (and, in some jurisdictions, the defendant must **thwart** the commission of the crime as well). The key to determining whether a renunciation is voluntary is whether it was influenced by the accused's perception of the opportunity for a successful completion of the crime, or whether it was truly motivated by a new-found belief that "crime does not pay." As a matter of logic and history, abandonment is not appropriate as a defense to solicitation since the crime is complete once the requisite act and mental state have occurred.

> **a. EXAMPLE.** Big Mama Red decides her husband must die. To this end, she asks a member of her country music band to kill her husband for her, saying, "Kill him for me, banjo player, after all, he got the gold mine, and I got the shaft." Minutes later, she patches things up with her husband, and quickly tells the band member to forget about what she has said. At common law, a solicitation still has occurred because Big Mama met both the act and mental state requirements before changing her mind.

2. DEFENSES TO ATTEMPT. [§327]

For a definition of attempt, see §148.

a. Impossibility. [§328]

"Impossibility" means that under the particular circumstances of the case, it is impossible for the defendant to complete the crime. The common law, and many statutes, have divided the defense of impossibility into two types — "factual" impossibility and "legal" impossibility. The law recognizes only legal impossibility as a valid defense to a criminal attempt charge.

(1) Legal Impossibility. [§329]

Legal impossibility has been defined as: (1) **conduct** which, (2) **had it been completed, would not constitute a criminal offense**. *Wilson v. State*, 85 Miss. 687, 38 So. 46 (1905). This definition simply asks whether the incomplete action, carried out to its logical conclusion, would have been a crime.

> **(a) EXAMPLE.** A person who receives goods **believing** they have been **stolen**, when in fact, they were not, is **not guilty** of attempting to receive stolen property. *People v. Jaffe*, 185 N.Y. 497, 78 N.E. 169 (1906). (The reasoning here is that no matter what the accused's mens rea, she cannot be found guilty if an essential element of the crime, the stolen nature of the goods, is missing.)

> **(b) EXAMPLE.** A hunter who shoots a **stuffed deer** after the hunting season has ended is **not guilty** of attempting to shoot a deer out of season (again there exists a culpable mens rea, but an element of the crime, that a real deer must be shot, is missing.)

> **(c) EXAMPLE.** A defendant who attempts to **bribe** a person the defendant incorrectly thinks is a juror, is **not guilty** of attempting to bribe a juror. (Had the defendant completed the act, there would not have been a crime, because the essential element of bribing a person who is a juror is missing.)

(2) Factual Impossibility. [§330]

Factual impossibility has been defined as: (1) **conduct** which is **impossible to complete** (2) due to some **unforeseen fact or physical condition**. *People v. Fiegelman*, 33 Cal. App. 2d 100, 91 P.2d 156 (1939). Factual impossibility is not a defense to an attempt charge. The **central difference** between factual and legal impossibility seems to be their focus: factual impossibility asks whether the failure to complete the crime is due to a fortuity (i.e., an unforeseen fact), and legal impossibility asks whether the attempt, had it been successful, would have constituted a completed criminal offense.

> **(a) EXAMPLE.** A person who attempts to **pick an empty pocket** is still **guilty** of attempted larceny. *People v. Fiegelman*, 33 Cal. App. 2d 100, 91 P.2d 156 (1939). (The unforeseen fact presenting the successful completion of the crime was the lack of money in the victim's pocket; but for the unforeseen circumstance, a lack of money, the crime of larceny would have occurred.)

(b) EXAMPLE. A person who attempts to kill another person by shooting a loaded gun at that person, but is unable to fire **because the gun accidentally jams**, is still **guilty** of attempted murder. *Mullen v. State*, 45 Ala. 43 (1871). (The unforeseen fact preventing the successful completion of the offense was the mechanical problem with the gun; but for the gun jamming, the crime of murder would have taken place.)

(c) EXAMPLE. A doctor who attempts to **perform an abortion on a woman who is not pregnant** is still **guilty** of attempting to perform an unlawful abortion. *People v. Cummings*, 141 Cal. App. 2d 193, 296 P.2d 610 (1956). (The unforeseen fact preventing the successful completion of the offense is the non-pregnant condition of the woman; but for the woman not being pregnant, the doctor would have committed the offense of performing an unlawful abortion.)

(3) EXAMPLE. Distinguishing Factual from Legal Impossibility. While courts often have managed to differentiate between legal and factual impossibility, the two appear to be generally **interchangeable**. This is because a single situation often involves both a failure attributable to an unforeseen fact (factual impossibility), and circumstances such that, had the act been completed, it still would not have been a crime (legal impossibility). In effect, legal impossibility often depends on unforeseen factual circumstances. When there is one type of impossibility, there is also usually the other.

(a) EXAMPLE. When a person receives goods that are not stolen but believes that they are, the situation can be construed as either factual or legal impossibility. It is **factual impossibility** because the reason the crime could not have been completed was the unforeseen factual circumstance of the goods not being stolen. Yet, the same situation also could be interpreted as **legal impossibility**. If the act of receiving the goods had been completed, it still would not be a crime because an essential element of the crime, the stolen nature of the goods, is missing. This analysis demonstrates that a particular scenario can be viewed either as factual or legal impossibility. (The one major **exception** to this interchangeability is **"true" legal impossibility**, discussed below.)

Despite the ambiguous and elusive nature of the line dividing factual and legal impossibility on an examination, be prepared to argue which type of impossibility a fact pattern represents. To do so, use precedent, if any exists, in bolstering your analysis.

(4) True Legal Impossibility. [§333]

The only clear-cut case of legal impossibility occurs when the defendant mistakenly believes the object "offense" is unlawful, but in actuality the object conduct is perfectly lawful. With true legal impossibility, there is **no fact** that prevents the accused's conduct from being a crime, merely the **accused's erroneous belief about what the criminal law prohibits**.

(a) Example of True Legal Impossibility. Sarah, having obtained two tickets to a Springsteen concert, attempts to scalp them for an amount far exceeding their face value. Sarah mistakenly believes this conduct is unlawful, so she sneaks around the arena whispering her price for the tickets. Sarah will not be guilty of attempted ticket scalping if scalping itself is not unlawful in that jurisdiction. The uncompleted attempt to do something lawful — e.g., ticket scalping — is itself lawful.

(5) Comparison: Inherent Legal Impossibility. [§335]

This type of impossibility is more likely to appear on a criminal law examination than in the appellate case reports. It involves persons who intend to achieve a criminal objective through woefully inadequate, **de minimus conduct**. Generally, the actor will **not** be held liable for an attempt if only de minimis conduct occurs. The conduct is not sufficiently dangerous.

(a) EXAMPLE. A voodoo doctor sticks pins in a doll for the purpose of killing a human being. Is this conduct attempted murder? No, because the act is so de minimis it would be unfair to hold the voodoo practitioner criminally liable for such a heinous crime, attempted murder. *Commonwealth v. Johnson*, 312 Pa. 140, 167 A. 344 (1933).

b. Abandonment. [§337]

Although the rules on abandonment differ from jurisdiction to jurisdiction, abandonment was generally **not available** as a defense to an attempt crime at **common law**. Once the elements of an attempt occurred, an offense was deemed to have been committed. If a jurisdiction recognized abandonment as a defense, however, the abandonment was permitted **only** if it was **complete and voluntary**. The abandoning defendant must also move, if appropriate to the circumstances, to **thwart** the object offense.

(1) EXAMPLE. Lou is in the process of breaking into the local hardware store at 2:00 a.m. in order to steal the contents of the cash register. Lou sees a police car nearby, and consequently runs away before he can break in. While Lou aborted his attempt to burglarize the store, it was precipitated by Lou's observation of a police officer nearby. Therefore, it is not voluntary, and would not serve as a valid abandonment defense. *Pyle v. State*, 476 N.E.2d 124 (Ind. 1985).

3. DEFENSES TO CONSPIRACY. [§338]

Because of the extended scope of conspiracy liability, defenses are particularly significant.

a. Impossibility. [§338.1]

Impossibility is generally **not** a defense to a conspiracy charge. The primary reason is that impossibility is rarely an issue in conspiracy prosecutions, where the act requirement is completed solely by an agreement to commit the offense. The question of impossibility, however, can sometimes arise. Specifically, a true legal impossibility situation, where the parties agree to commit an act they believe is unlawful, but is in fact lawful, likely will serve to exonerate the defendants from liability. *People v. Jaffe*, 185 N.Y. 497, 78 N.E. 169 (1906). Cf. *Commonwealth v. Donoghue*, 250 Ky. 343, 63 S.W.2d 3 (1933).

b. Abandonment and Withdrawal. [§338.2]

Abandonment of a conspiracy generally is not considered a defense to conspiracy at common law. Yet a **withdrawal** from a **continuing conspiracy** may be significant for several reasons: (1) withdrawal may **toll** the **statute of limitations** for the withdrawing member, *Hyde v. United States*, 225 U.S. 347 (1912); (2) withdrawal may **terminate the use of hearsay statements** against the withdrawing members by co-conspirators in furtherance of and during the conspiracy; and (3) withdrawal from a conspiracy may **terminate the conspirator's vicarious liability** for the subsequent offenses of co-conspirators in furtherance of the conspiracy. *Loser v. Superior Ct.*, 78 Cal. App. 2d 30, 177 P.2d 320 (1947).

In order to effectively withdraw, a conspirator must **communicate** the fact of withdrawal to all other members of the conspiracy, and the withdrawing member must take **affirmative steps to thwart** the successful completion of the object of the conspiracy. *Marino v. United States*, 91 F.2d 691 (9th Cir. 1937).

4. ABANDONMENT OF ACCOMPLICE STATUS. [§339]

An accomplice can abandon her criminal activity and avoid future liability if she **communicates** the fact of abandonment to the other accomplices, and then attempts to **thwart** the criminal purpose. This rule is similar to the rule concerning the abandonment of attempt.

B. DEFENSES NEGATING AN ELEMENT OF THE CRIME. [§340]

1. MISTAKES. [§340.5]

There are **three major types** of mistake that occur in the criminal law. It is important to understand the differences between them, and to keep them separate for analytical purposes on an examination. A brief overview follows.

a. Mistake in Fact. [§341]

This form of mistake arises when the defendant bases her conduct on an **erroneous factual belief** constituting a misperception of reality. A mistake in fact can have the effect of negating the mens rea in either specific or general intent crimes (but not in strict liability "public welfare" offenses, which have no mens rea). Mistakes in fact will be discussed in §344 below.

b. Mistake in Law. [§342]

This type of mistake occurs when a person is mistaken about the **applicable law** (the person usually believes that the intended conduct is not prohibited, when in actuality it is). *United States v. Currier*, 621 F.2d 7 (1st Cir. 1980). This type of mistake does **not** negate the mens rea or any other element of the crime, but serves as a separate affirmative, "yes, I did it, but ..." defense. It is generally unsuccessful (**"ignorance of the law is no defense"**) and will be discussed in §354 below.

c. Mistake in Justification. [§343]

This category of mistake occurs when the actor **mistakenly believes** that a **justification defense** is warranted. That is, the actor is mistaken about the facts in such a way that she erroneously believes she is entitled to use an affirmative defense, such as self-defense. Thus, this type of mistake does not negate an element of the crime, but rather exonerates the defendant from criminal responsibility if the mistake is not only **honest** but **reasonable** as well. Mistake in justification will be discussed further in §390 below.

d. Analysis of Mistake in Fact. [§344]

Whether a mistake in fact will negate the mens rea of a crime usually depends on whether the crime is a **specific** or **general intent offense**.

(1) Specific Intent Crimes: [§345]

The applicable rule is that the mens rea in a specific intent crime can be negated by an (1) **honest mistake**, no matter how unreasonable. *Richardson v. United States*, 403 F.2d 574 (D.C. Cir. 1968).

(2) General Intent Crimes: [§346]

The mens rea in a general intent crime can be negated only by a mistake that is **both** (1) **honest** and (2) **reasonable**. If a mistake is unreasonable, it is in all likelihood negligent as well. Thus, a person who makes an unreasonable mistake about the facts, no matter how honest the mistake is, should not completely escape a conviction because the conduct is still culpable.

(3) Why Use Different Mistake Tests for General and Specific Intent Crimes? [§347]

Specific intent crimes only prohibit **intentional** "bad" conduct. Thus, if a mistake is inadvertent, meaning honest, the conduct is unintentional and not a violation of specific intent. On the other hand, general intent crimes prohibit negligent, inadvertent conduct. Consequently, if a mistake is reasonable, essentially meaning non-negligent (as well as honest), the conduct is not a violation of general intent.

(4) Which Mens Rea? [§348]

Sometimes crimes have **different** mental states associated with its component parts (i.e., the "circumstances" of the actus reus). When this occurs, evaluate the mistake to determine which part of the crime might be negated by the mistake defense.

(5) Example of a Multiple Mens Rea Crime. Paul is charged with the "carnal knowledge of a woman knowingly without consent." The "without consent" element requires knowledge at a minimum, whereas negligence is required with reference to whether Paul had carnal knowledge of a woman. If the defendant is mistaken about whether the woman consented, since consent is a specific intent element of the crime, the mistake simply must be honest. If the defendant is mistaken about whether there was carnal knowledge with a woman, the mistake must be both honest and reasonable because it relates to a general intent element of the crime.

(6) Example of a Mistake in Fact. Jessie Magoo mistakenly takes a Rolls Royce from his office parking lot, erroneously believing it is his own Ford Escort. Has he committed larceny? The answer is no, because the mistake in fact negated the intent to steal element of larceny. Larceny is a specific intent crime, and Magoo's mistake must only be honest, even if it is highly unreasonable. Thus, even though Magoo should not have mistaken a Rolls Royce for a Ford Escort, he will be exonerated because his mistake was honest.

(7) Example of a Mistake in Fact. Defendant Leon mistakenly believes that a woman he met in a bar consented to having sexual intercourse with him. They spoke to each other in French, which was not their native language. Since rape is a general intent crime, unless the defendant's mistake was both honest and reasonable (to an objective person under the same circumstances), a mistake in fact will not serve as a defense.

(8) A Simplified Mistake in Fact Analysis. [§352]

A simplified mistake in fact analysis exists that eliminates the need to determine whether a crime is a specific or general intent offense. This analysis yields the same result as the "specific or general intent" analysis. The **substitute analysis** asks one question: "**Did the alleged perpetrator have the required mens rea**?" With specific intent crimes, the question simply becomes whether the conduct was knowing or purposeful, and with general intent crimes, whether the conduct was negligent, reckless, knowing or purposeful.

(a) EXAMPLE. Mick hurls stones at dusk in a pond frequently used by recreational swimmers, and accidentally strikes Keith, who is swimming in the far end. Mick mistakenly believed no one was in the pond at the time. While Mick claims mistake in fact, he still can be charged with battery. This problem can be analyzed in two ways. **Method # 1 (specific and general intent analysis):** Since battery is a **general intent** crime, the mistake must be **both honest** and **reasonable** for it to serve as a defense. Mick's mistake, while honest, was not reasonable (because it was dark and Mick should have known someone might be swimming), and he can be held liable. **Method # 2 (the one step alternative):** Since battery requires negligence, Mick will be held liable if, operating under his mistaken belief, he acted negligently (i.e., unreasonably). Mick likely acted unreasonably, given the preceding analysis. Specifically, he should have known better.

e. Analysis of Mistake in Law. [§354]

As noted above, it is widely accepted that **ignorance of the law is no excuse**. *Lambert v. California*, 355 U.S. 225 (1957). People are presumed to know the law, and are held responsible if they violate it. Simply because the line drawn between "lawful" and "unlawful" conduct sometimes is not altogether clear does not mean that people can escape criminal liability by claiming a lack of knowledge about the law.

Despite the general rule prohibiting mistakes of law from constituting a defense, several exceptions exist. (These exceptions appear to be analogous to the contracts principle of promissory estoppel.)

(1) Exceptions. [§355]

A mistake about the law may serve as a defense if:

(a) A defendant relies on a state Supreme Court **ruling** that is later overruled;

(b) A defendant relies on a **statute** that is later declared void; or

(c) A defendant relies on an **official but erroneous interpretation** of a law by an individual or agency holding the power to execute the law.

---

(2) Example of Mistake in Law. Defendant Michael, relies on an official interpretation of a state regulation by the State Attorney General, which concludes that limited stakes gambling is legal. Michael proceeds to hold a small stakes poker game at his home. The official interpretation by the Attorney General turns out to be erroneous, and the defendant is prosecuted for gambling. The defendant in this situation may successfully assert the defense of mistake in law. *State v. Patten*, 353 N.W.2d 30 (N.D. 1984).

---

(3) Example of Mistake in Law. Defendant Michael now asks his lawyer Deborah, whether the weekly card game in which he plays is unlawful. Deborah says "Go ahead, there's no problem with the law." The defendant is subsequently arrested, however, and charged with unlawfully participating in a card game. The advice from the defendant's private attorney about the law will not provide a defense because **only "official interpretations"** of the law suffice. The defendant relied on his lawyer's advice at his own risk. *People v. Snyder*, 32 Cal. 3d 590, 186 Cal. Rptr. 485, 652 P.2d 42 (1982).

---

(4) Example of Mistake in Law. Les, a performance artist who routinely removed his clothes during his presentation, wanted to know whether his intended conduct would be unlawful, so he asked the local prosecutor Brigitte. The local prosecutor assured Les that his conduct was lawful. If Les is later prosecuted on obscenity charges, he will not be able to rely on the prosecutor's advice as a defense. The prosecutor is not considered to be a public official who provides an "official interpretation" of the law.

---

2. INTOXICATION. [§359]

This is a widely tested area in criminal law courses. Intoxication can be separated into two categories: (1) **voluntary**, and (2) **involuntary**. Different rules apply to each subject.

a. Voluntary Intoxication. [§360]

The common law rule is that voluntary intoxication may serve as a **defense** to a **specific intent crime**, but **not** to a **general intent crime**. *People v. Longworthy*, 331 N.W.2d 171 (Mich. 1982). In specific intent crimes, the intoxication may **negate** the **purposefulness** or **knowledge** required to commit the crime. *State v. Cameron*, 514 A.2d 1302 (N.J. 1986). Simply because the defendant is intoxicated, however, does not mean that she automatically will be excused from charges alleging that she committed a specific intent crime; there must be evidence that the intoxication eliminated her specific intent.

Voluntary intoxication is not a defense to a strict liability crime. Voluntary intoxication only negates the mens rea, and in strict liability offenses, there is no mens rea to negate.

---

(1) Example of Voluntary Intoxication. Defendant is charged with rape. The defendant contends that he was so intoxicated, he did not realize the victim did not consent to sexual intercourse. Even if the defendant's claim about his intoxication is correct, his voluntary intoxication will not serve as a defense to rape because rape is a **general intent** crime. The voluntary intoxication itself constitutes an unreasonable — i.e., negligent — act by the defendant, thus satisfying the minimum level of culpability required for the offense.

---

(2) Example of Voluntary Intoxication. Defendant Lenny is charged with larceny after stealing Leslie's 1992 Rolls Royce. Lenny claims that he was so high on drugs, he was unaware the car was not his 1978 Chrysler LeBaron. Even if the defendant's voluntary intoxication led him to such an unreasonable belief, if the intoxication negated the **specific intent** required for larceny, which it appears to have done, the defendant will not be held responsible. Lenny still can be convicted of a lesser included general intent crime, however, such as "the unlawful unauthorized use of a motor vehicle."

---

(3) Example of Voluntary Intoxication. Donny Defendant becomes intoxicated at a bar and attempts to rape Sheila Patron. He claims voluntary intoxication as a defense. **Attempted rape**, unlike the completed crime of rape, is a specific intent crime requiring that the actor intend the commission of the offense. Thus, voluntary intoxication can serve as a defense to the attempted rape charge. *People v. Guillett*, 69 N.W.2d 140 (Mich. 1955). (The applicability of the intoxication defense to an attempt crime such as attempted rape, and not its general intent completed crime, such as rape, can be confusing. To avoid this trap, look at the **mens rea** required for the crime, not the severity of the crime.)

---

(4) Voluntary Intoxication and Insanity. [§364]

Sometimes, an individual can become so intoxicated that his actions are the equivalent of "temporary insanity." *People v. Penman*, 271 Ill. 82, 110 N.E. 894 (1915). At other times, the ingestion of certain drugs, such as phencyclidine ("PCP"), can have a permanent damaging effect on the brain, causing organic brain syndrome, a severe mental disease. The organic brain syndrome that results may fall within the legal definition of mental disease or defect required to support a verdict of not guilty by reason of insanity. (The fact that criminal behavior resulted from a mental disease or defect, however, is only part of the showing required for a successful insanity defense.)

b. Involuntary Intoxication. [§365]

If a person becomes intoxicated **involuntarily** through **no fault** of her own, the intoxication **may serve as a defense** to any crimes committed under the influence of the intoxicant. Involuntary intoxication can serve as a defense to **all** crimes, including general intent offenses. A person who becomes intoxicated involuntarily is not considered culpable and therefore should not be held responsible or morally condemned for any subsequent conduct attributed to the intoxication. *People v. Scott*, 146 Cal. App. 3d 823, 194 Cal. Rptr. 633 (Ct. App. 4th Dist. 1983).

(1) Example of Involuntary Intoxication. Jonathan goes to a party, and sees what looks like M&Ms candies. He has several, especially the orange ones, which are his favorites. Unbeknownst to Jonathan, these orange ones are hallucinogenic drugs. Consequently, Jonathan panics and batters several individuals. Jonathan can claim involuntary intoxication as a defense, even to the general intent crime of battery.

c. The Model Penal Code. [§367]

The **MPC** recognizes three forms of intoxication: (1) **voluntary**, (2) **pathological**, and (3) **involuntary**. [MPC §2.08.] **Voluntary intoxication** under the Code **is a defense** to a **specific intent** crime, just like the common law. **Pathological intoxication**, on the other hand, occurs in very limited situations in which a person, who is generally suffering from a previous brain injury, has a **severe reaction to the voluntary ingestion of small amounts of intoxicants** such as alcohol. The key to this category is that there is an unanticipated disproportionate reaction to a small quantity of intoxicants. **Involuntary intoxication**, by comparison, is **not** self-induced, and is caused by substances which the actor does not knowingly introduce into her body. Involuntary intoxication is a defense to all crimes.

> **(1) EXAMPLE.** Joanne, a 35-year-old surgeon who never drinks, is persuaded by friends at a party to try the liquor tequila. She has a severe physical reaction after one drink, and as a result, intentionally punches the host of the party in the nose. Joanne may be able to assert the defense of voluntary intoxication to the charge of assault, because it is a specific intent crime under the Code. She also may be able to claim involuntary pathological intoxication, given the severity of the reaction in comparison to the amount of alcohol ingested. Further medical tests likely will be necessary to determine whether Joanne's response fits the legal definition.

C. AFFIRMATIVE DEFENSES. [§369]

There are **two major categories** of affirmative defenses: (1) **justification** and (2) **excuse**. Both types of affirmative defenses essentially admit that the defendant committed the elements of the crime (saying **"Yes, I did it"**), **but** further claim that because of special circumstances, the **defendant is not morally blameworthy**.

1. JUSTIFICATION AND EXCUSE COMPARED. [§370]

The defenses of justification and excuse can be distinguished from each other primarily in terms of how much society is willing to accept the results of the defendant's conduct. With **justification**, society **prefers the result** that occurs (compared to the alternative). When a person acts from justification, as in self-defense, society agrees that the **benefits** from avoiding potential harm to an innocent person **outweigh** the **costs** of the actor's conduct. With an **excuse**, society **abhors the result** that occurs, but due to some defect in or coercion of the actor, such as duress or insanity, finds that the actor is **not morally blameworthy**. *State v. Leidholm*, 334 N.W.2d 811 (N.D. 1983).

The categories of justification and excuse are not mutually exclusive, and some defenses have elements of both. Some of the **features shared by both types of defenses are**:

a. Coercion. [§371]

One similarity that exists in situations where an affirmative defense is raised, is that the defendant can be seen as being coerced into acting, either **by another person** (e.g., involving self-defense, defense of habitation, duress, and entrapment); by **nature** (e.g., involving the necessity defense); or **by herself** (e.g., involving the insanity defense). Thus, many defenses can be viewed as situations where the defendant's conduct has been understandably coerced.

b. Efficient Harm Avoidance. [§372]

The person who acts based on a defense is often motivated to commit the criminal act to **avoid** a **greater harm**. This **cost-benefit analysis** is recognized in self-defense, the defense of others, and the necessity defense, among others.

> **c. EXAMPLE.** Leslie is attacked by Peter, who wields a machete knife. In defending herself, Leslie kills Peter. A person who kills in self-defense has saved the life of an innocent person (Leslie) and taken the life of a culpable aggressor (Peter). While a life is taken, the innocent's life is considered more worthwhile than the blameworthy aggressor's.

2. JUSTIFICATION. [§374]

A defense of justification permits the **acquittal** of a defendant who otherwise meets all of the elements of a crime. Justifications generally occur when a person defends him or herself, either from an attack by another person (such as in self-defense or defense of habitation), or a natural calamity (such as in the necessity defense).

a. Self-Defense. [§375]

This doctrine arises when a person uses physical force to repel what the person reasonably believes is the imminent infliction of bodily harm. Self-defense requires (1) an **actual** and (2) **reasonable belief** of **imminent bodily harm**; (3) a **proportional response**; *Beard v. United States*, 158 U.S. 550 (1895); and (4) a defendant who is **not** considered to be the **aggressor**. *United States v. Middletown*, 690 F.2d 820 (11th Cir. 1982). The use of **lethal force** in self defense requires that the defendant **reasonably fear** the **imminent infliction** of **serious bodily harm or death**. The use of lethal force in self defense will be discussed separately below.

(1) Actual and Reasonable Belief. [§376]

The defendant must actually and reasonably believe that bodily harm is imminent; with respect to reasonableness, the operative question is whether the average prudent person would believe, under the same circumstances, that bodily harm was imminent.

(2) Proportional Response. [§377]

The amount of force considered proportional depends on how much force is being resisted. The force used in defense must be **equivalent** to the harm avoided; this approach is consistent with the value of **avoiding a greater harm** than the one that is inflicted. An "eye for an eye" equivalency determination applies; a person may use as much force as is necessary to repel the attacker. As noted earlier, even lethal force is justified in self-defense in certain, limited circumstances.

> **(a) EXAMPLE.** Ignatio raises his fist as if to punch Horatio. To defend himself, Horatio pulls out a miniature anti-tank gun and kills Ignatio. Can Horatio claim self-defense? The answer is no. Horatio was reasonable in his belief that he was subject to an imminent threat of bodily harm. Moreover, Horatio was not the aggressor. However, the amount of force used was not proportional to that threatened. The use of the anti-tank gun was **excessive**, and thus a claim of self-defense would not succeed.

(3) Non-Aggressor. [§379]

The determination of whether the defendant is the aggressor, and thus precluded from asserting self-defense, occurs at both the commencement of an altercation and as it develops. Generally, the **aggressor** is the person who **initiates** or **escalates** a **conflict**. If a person initiates the use of force, acting as an aggressor, the rationale underlying the defense — to permit self-preservation and self-help within limits — would be violated. An aggressor is morally blameworthy and not deserving of an acquittal. *United States v. Peterson*, 483 F.2d 1222 (D.C. Cir. 1973).

A defendant who initiates an altercation can completely **withdraw** or **terminate participation** in the affray. The defendant ceases to be the "aggressor" if the victim then chooses to escalate the dispute or fight. Similarly, a person who does not initiate an altercation, but escalates it to where lethal force is being used, loses the status of "non-aggressor".

(a) Example of the "Non-Aggressor" Rule. Defendant and Vinnie the Victim start arguing and the defendant pushes Victim to the ground. Victim gets up, pushes back, and a fistfight commences. Shortly thereafter, the defendant pulls out a knife, and Victim follows suit. The victim attacks, and the defendant kills Victim. The defendant, by initiating the conflict and the use of lethal weapons, will likely be considered the aggressor, and will not be able to successfully claim self-defense.

(b) EXAMPLE. If defendant Lenny punches Vinnie the Victim and Vinnie takes out a bazooka, Lenny can use deadly force to defend himself and still claim self-defense. Vinnie escalated the fight by initiating the use of lethal force. The "no aggressor" rule consequently has not been violated.

(c) EXAMPLE. If Amy defendant withdraws from a skirmish after acting as the initial aggressor, but the victim persists in attacking, the defendant once again can use self-defense.

(4) Imminence. [§383]

Self-defense can only be raised when an attack is **either occurring or is imminent**. *State v. Stewart*, 763 P.2d 572 (Kan. 1988).

(a) EXAMPLE. Vinnie the Victim spies the defendant walking with Vinnie's girlfriend. Vinnie runs up to defendant and says "I will kill thee with a gun that I shall buy in the store next week, after registering it properly, and waiting for my permit!" The defendant, in fear of his life, immediately shoots Vinnie the Victim dead in a pre-emptive strike. A self-defense claim will fail because the threat of force by Vinnie was far from imminent.

(5) Use of Lethal Force in Self-Defense. [§385]

A person may lawfully use lethal force in self-defense if: she (1) **actually** and (2) **reasonably believes** that (3) **lethal force** is **necessary** to repel the **apparent imminent application** of **lethal force** by another, and (4) she is **not the aggressor**. (Lethal force would cause either death or bodily harm.)

In a **minority** of jurisdictions, a fifth requirement exists: (5) a **duty to retreat**. A person who is outside of her own residence must refrain from using lethal force if she **knowingly can retreat in complete safety**. A significant and widely tested exception to the duty to retreat, however, exists.

(6) The Castle Doctrine. [§386]

The exception to the duty to retreat requirement is known as the "castle doctrine," because if a person is **in her own residence**, it is as if it is her castle. **She need not retreat,** even if she could do so safely. *People v. Caballos*, 12 Cal. 3d 470, 116 Cal. Rptr. 233, 526 P.2d 241 (1974). (In some jurisdictions, however, if both the victim and the defendant are lawful occupants of the same home, the duty to retreat still applies.)

> **(a) EXAMPLE.** Defendant Sharlene and her gardener Sloots get into a heated argument in defendant's home over which baseball team is better, the Dodgers or the Mets. The gardener, Sloots, pulls out a butcher's knife and starts to charge at the defendant. The defendant easily could have escaped through the back door, but instead pulls out a gun and kills the gardener. The "duty to retreat" rule does not apply because the defendant is in her own home. The defendant's self-defense claim will likely succeed because she proportionately repelled the imminent application of deadly force, and she was not the aggressor.

(7) The Model Penal Code. [§388]

The MPC is quite detailed and specific in the area of self-defense. An individual may use **non-deadly force** in self-defense under the MPC if the defendant believes it is **immediately necessary** to use such force to defend against the use of unlawful force by another. [MPC §3.04.] This test is completely **subjective**; the belief by the defendant as to the need for force need not be reasonable. Furthermore, the defendant must only believe that the use of force is immediately necessary, not that an attack is imminent. Thus, the defendant does not have to wait until the last second before responding.

(8) Lethal Force Under the MPC. [§389]

Significantly, the MPC allows the use of **lethal force** in self-defense **only** if a person believes such force is **necessary** to protect against one of four things: (1) **death**; (2) **serious bodily harm**; (3) **kidnapping**; or (4) **rape**. [MPC §3.04(2)(6).] In keeping with the common law, the MPC does not permit the use of deadly force if the accused is the aggressor. The Code also adopts the **minority retreat rule** — if a person knowingly can retreat in complete safety, she must do so. Under the Code, the **"castle" exception also exists** — a defendant has no duty to retreat in her own home. Importantly, the Code extends this exception to the defendant's **place of work**. Thus, there is no duty to retreat if the defendant is in either the home or the workplace.

b. Mistake in Justification. [§390]

At times, a person is mistaken when believing that the use of force is necessary to repel another. As noted above in the section on mistake, a person still can succeed in a claim of self-defense, however, if the **mistaken belief** is both (1) **honest** and (2) **reasonable**. Whether a mistake about the facts is **honest** is entirely **subjective**, and depends on what was in the accused's mind at the time she acted. The **reasonableness** of a mistake, however, is judged by an **objective**

standard under the particular circumstances. If the belief is honest but unreasonable, the actor has reduced culpability, but is still morally blameworthy. If the honest but unreasonable self-defense resulted in a homicide, the actor will be guilty of imperfect justification manslaughter (see section on imperfect justification manslaughter).

---

(1) EXAMPLE. Defendant watches a brutally violent thriller on television just before he goes to sleep. In the morning when he awakens, he hears a noise at the front door. Believing it to be an intruder with evil intentions, he takes his shotgun and fires wildly at the front door, killing the person behind it. He is mistaken. It is only the newspaper boy delivering the paper. The defendant is guilty of imperfect justification manslaughter, because his belief that he was about to be violently attacked was honest, but not reasonable.

---

c. The Battered Woman's Syndrome. [§392]

The Battered Woman's Syndrome is a defense that is increasingly being asserted in state courts. In many respects, the defense is an extension of the self-defense doctrine, although it can be thought of either as an excuse or as a justification defense. While it has been used by males and children, the defense is primarily used by women who are being abused by their spouses.

The defense is applicable when a **defendant kills while experiencing** the Battered Woman's Syndrome. The battered woman's syndrome takes place in a series of phases recognized and documented by psychologists. The **first phase** involves minor battering incidents. The **second phase** involves an escalation of the battering incidents until they become acute. The **third phase** involves contrition and a conciliatory attitude by the batterer. This three-phase cycle then repeats itself.

When a battered person kills her batterer just as he is about to inflict serious bodily harm upon her person, the conduct falls within generally accepted principles of the doctrine of self-defense. If, however, the battered person is **not** faced with imminent danger in fact, but the battered person proceeds to kill the batterer due to a belief that no viable alternative exists, a controversial question arises — whether it was **reasonable** for the battered person to **believe that deadly force was necessary**. Some have argued that a killing not based on a factual necessity removes the Battered Woman's Syndrome from the generally accepted parameters of a traditional self-defense claim. For the view that a battered person may reasonably believe that no alternative exists, see *State v. Kelley*, Case Squibs section.

---

(1) EXAMPLE. Jane kills her husband Tim while he lies sleeping in their bed. During their marriage of six years, Tim had regularly abused alcohol and beaten Jane in the cyclical fashion of the Battered Woman's Syndrome. In some jurisdictions, Jane can assert the Battered Woman's Syndrome as a defense. These jurisdictions have concluded that the defense is sufficiently accepted in the scientific community to overcome challenges such as unreliability.

---

d. The Defense of Law Enforcement. [§394]

At common law, a police officer is entitled to use **non-deadly force** to effectuate an arrest for what the officer reasonably believes is the commission of, or the prevention of: (1) either a **felony**, or (2) a **misdemeanor** involving a **breach of the peace**. **Deadly force** is permitted in the **prevention of a felony**, but not to prevent a misdemeanor. Most jurisdictions, however, only permit law enforcement officers to use deadly force to prevent the commission of **dangerous felonies** such as murder, robbery, arson, burglary, and rape, or to prevent a fleeing felon from escaping arrest, if the officer reasonably believes that the felon is a danger to others. (*Tennessee v. Garner*, 471 U.S. 1 (1985)). A private citizen can assert any defense available to a police officer if called to aid the officer. If the private citizen is acting alone, he or she may be privileged to use non-deadly force to make an arrest only when it is reasonably believed to be necessary to effectuate an arrest for a felony that has been committed. If, in fact, a felony was not committed, the citizen may be strictly liable.

> **(1) EXAMPLE.** Officer Jones chases after Bungy Barnes, for allegedly shoplifting from the Thrifty Cake Shop. Jones pulls out his gun and yells "Stop or I'll shoot!" While permissible in the movies, Jones cannot use any form of force, deadly or non-deadly, to arrest a person for a misdemeanor not involving a breach of the peace.

(2) Resisting an Unlawful Arrest. [§396]

A defendant is permitted to **resist** an unlawful arrest with **reasonable non-deadly force**. If deadly force is used to resist an unlawful arrest, the defendant generally will be held liable for manslaughter, and not murder. (Note: This situation presents another form of imperfect justification manslaughter.)

e. Defense of Others. [§397]

At common law, whether the doctrine of the defense of others can be raised depends on the **relationship** between the defendant and the person being protected.

(1) The "Family/Employment Rule." [§398]

Some common law jurisdictions followed the **early English rule** which permitted a defendant to **protect only** those with whom he had **a specially recognized relationship**, such as a member of the **defendant's family**, or an **employer and employee**. Thus, a person could not defend a friend, roommate, or total stranger from harm. This distinction has been dropped by modern statutes.

(2) The "Alter Ego" Rule. [§399]

Some common law jurisdictions still impose an "alter ego" limitation on the defense of others. It is called the "alter ego" rule because a defendant is placed **in the shoes** of the individual(s) being **attacked**. *State v. Gelinas*, 417 A.2d 1381 (R.I. 1980). A person in such a jurisdiction is only allowed to assert the defense of others to the extent that the others being defended are lawfully permitted to defend themselves. If the helper incorrectly perceives that another person lawfully is entitled to use self-defense, the helper cannot claim the defense of others. Thus, a **mistake** in defending another will **not** serve to exculpate the defendant. Instead, a premium is placed on guessing correctly (or at least informed guessing).

(a) EXAMPLE. Heavyweight Harry stumbled upon two individuals who appeared to be engaged in a lethal fight. One had pulled out a knife and was viciously attacking the other. Harry jumped in the way and killed the apparent "aggressor" with his bare hands. All of a sudden, he heard someone yell "cut!" Harry had mistakenly jumped into the filming of a movie. Under the "alter ego" limitation, Harry could not claim that he acted in defense of others, regardless of how reasonable Harry's mistake was. If the jurisdiction did not follow the "alter ego" limitation, however, Harry would be able to assert the defense of others if his mistaken belief in the need to use lethal force was reasonable under the circumstances.

---

(3) The Model Penal Code. [§401]

The Code permits individuals to protect others **without** any limitations regarding familial, employment status, or other restrictions depending on the defendant's relationship to the person(s) helped. [MPC §3.05.] The MPC does not recognize the "alter ego" rule, so a person can claim mistake in the defense of others as well. The person must still comply with the duty to retreat rule, however.

f. Defense of Property. [§402]

A person may use **non-lethal force** to protect her property from another person if she has a **reasonable belief** that force is **necessary** to protect that property from **imminent unlawful action**. *State v. Farley*, 587 P.2d 337 (Kan. 1978). A request to cease must occur prior to the use of such force.

A person defending **property** (no matter how prized the possession), generally **cannot use lethal force** to do so. There is one major **exception** to this rule, and that involves **defending one's home**, called defense of habitation. The policy supporting this exception is individuals' right to privacy within their own homes.

(1) Defense of Habitation. [§403]

While **deadly force** cannot be used to defend most types of property, it **can be used** to defend one's habitation. At early common law, deadly force could be used to protect against a forcible entry of a dwelling. *Commonwealth v. Emmens*, 157 Pa. Super. 495, 43 A.2d 568 (1945). In the later common law, a variation of this rule arose. Persons were permitted to defend their "castle" using deadly force when: (1) there was **reasonable apprehension** that **deadly force** was **necessary to prevent** an **attempted forcible entry**, which created (2) a **reasonable apprehension** that the assailant would (a) **commit a felony** once inside, or (b) **commit bodily harm** to an **occupant** of the dwelling. *Morrison v. State*, 212 Tenn. 633, 371 S.W.2d 441 (1963).

(a) EXAMPLE. Yarbar's house had been burglarized five days in a row. On the sixth day, he hid outside in the bushes waiting for the perpetrator to strike once again. Sure enough, almost at the exact same hour, the perpetrator broke in through the bathroom window and climbed out with Yarbar's color TV. Yarbar chased the thief and shot him dead. Yarbar cannot claim the defense of habitation under either the early or later common law because the intruder was neither in the process of forcibly entering the house, nor committing a felony inside when Yarbar shot him; instead, the victim had done his dirty work and had vacated the premises. Thus, Yarbar cannot claim the defense of habitation.

(b) EXAMPLE. Joan raised prized cows. Her competitor Ben tried to steal her favorite cow, Rose of Avalon, and Joan shot and killed Ben. Joan will not be able to claim defense of property, since the use of lethal force does not extend to protecting property such as Rose.

(2) Defense of Property with Mechanical Devices — e.g., Spring Guns. [§406]

Various types of mechanical devices have been used to protect real property. These devices range from silent alarm systems, to spotlights, to mechanically triggered guns, often called spring guns. These guns, and other devices that can inflict serious harm on intruders, are a highly **disfavored** method of "**self-help**" under both the common law and later statutes. *People v. Caballos*, 12 Cal. 3d 47, 116 Cal. Rptr. 233, 526 P.2d 241 (1974). Mechanical devices lack the human ability to bend to the particular circumstances; both their primary virtue and failing are that they work automatically and every time. Yet, at common law, mechanical devices were not completely banned. Spring guns and other automatic devices were permitted if, under the circumstances, the dweller of the house would have been privileged to use the gun in defense of habitation **had the dweller been present.**

(a) EXAMPLE. Mr. and Mrs. Alahandro decide to take a summer vacation. They lock up their house and place spring guns near all of the doors. Tony, a member of Mr. Alahandro's cub scout troop, decides to play a practical joke by placing three thousand rolls of toilet paper in the Alahandro's master bathroom. Tony uses a spare key given to him by Mr. Alahandro to enter the house. As he does so, he is shot and killed by the spring gun set nearby. The Alahandros likely would be guilty of criminal homicide if the common law rule applied. There was no forcible entry, because Tony lawfully had a key, so the use of lethal force under the circumstances likely would not have been permitted even had the Alahandros been present in the house. *State v. Barr*, 11 Wash. 481, 39 P. 1080 (1895).

(3) The Model Penal Code. [§408]

The MPC permits a person to use **non-deadly force** to protect his property against aggression so long as the person believes that: (1) the intruder's conduct is **unlawful**; (2) the intruder's conduct **affects property** the person possesses or is in his care; and (3) the **imminent use of force is necessary** to prevent or terminate the unlawful entry or the dispossession of personal property. [MPC §3.06.]

The MPC generally does not allow the use of **deadly force to protect** property. The MPC permits deadly force to be used against (1) **an intruder** who is believed to be either (a) **attempting to dispossess** the defendant of the **dwelling house**, or (b) **attempting** to commit a **dangerous felony** on the property such as arson, burglary, or robbery. These exceptions parallel the common law.

Mechanical devices, such as spring guns, are permitted only if: (1) that device is **not** known to cause a substantial risk of **serious bodily harm**; (2) the protective device is **reasonable** under the circumstances; and (3) the device is **customarily used** for such a protective purpose. If it is not customarily used, reasonable notice must be given about the device.

(a) EXAMPLE. The defendant rigs his house with a special alarm that drops acid rain from the trees on the property when it goes off. The MPC would not allow such a mechanical device because it may cause substantial bodily harm. While the defendant may believe that such a device is reasonable to protect his home, it certainly is not customary for it to be used for such a purpose. At a minimum, notice must be given about its use.

REVIEW PROBLEMS — DEFENSES AGAINST AGGRESSION

PROBLEM 1. "The Trap." The owner of a store which has the owner's living quarters attached to the rear of the same building has been the subject of several break-ins. He creates a trap for the unwary intruder by electrifying the grates in the ceiling of the store, intending to stun any intruder. Soon after the trap is set, an intruder breaks in and attempts to leave the premises through the ceiling. The intruder grabs the electric grate with both hands and is electrocuted. What crime if any did the store owner commit?

> **Answer:** The initial issue is whether the store owner has committed murder or manslaughter. In applying "**ARM**" (Act, Result and Mental state), the store owner did the act of electrifying the grate that was the cause-in-fact and proximate cause of the resulting death of the intruder. The store owner did not intend to kill or know that a death was practically certain to result from contact with the grate, so there was no specific intent to kill. However, the intentional act of setting up the trap may have been grossly reckless, evincing a mental state of gross indifference to human life. If so, the store owner met the elements of depraved heart murder. (If in setting up the grate, the store owner was reckless but not grossly reckless, he will be guilty of recklessness manslaughter.)

> If the store owner claims he acted in the defense of his property, the defense should fail. He was not defending his habitation with the trap — even though the habitation was connected — and thus, under the common law, deadly force could not be used to defend his property. If, however, the defendant was considered to be acting in defense of his habitation, the next issue would be whether the mechanical device was lawfully used. Under the common law, a mechanical device would be permitted only to the extent force would have been allowed had the defendant been present. Here, the deadly force was not used to prevent a forcible entry, since the intruder was leaving the store. The use of deadly force under such circumstances is consequently of doubtful legality if the common law rule is strictly applied.

PROBLEM 2. "Lisa, Lisa." Lisa is about to leave her apartment building when she sees a person breaking into the locked common hallway for residents. The intruder is yelling at her, "Here I come!" Fearing for her life, Lisa shoots at the intruder's leg, intending only to stun him. Instead, she had bad aim, and shoots the intruder in the heart, killing him instantly. Has Lisa committed any crime?

> **Answer:** Lisa meets the **ARM** elements (Act, Result, Mental state) for **intent to commit serious bodily harm murder**. She shot the bullet (the act) which actually and proximately caused the death (the result) of the intruder. She did not intend to kill the intruder, but her desire to shoot him in the leg likely constitutes an intent to commit serious bodily harm (the mental state).

> Lisa may claim defense of habitation, and possibly self-defense as well. Defense of habitation may succeed because there was a reasonable belief that force was necessary to prevent an attempted forcible entry, which created in Lisa a fear of death. The fact that the forced entry was of the hallway does not mean that Lisa can not protect her habitation; "habitation" means the entire residence, and not just the bedroom or living quarters. Here, the locked hallway is solely for residents, who would not have to wait to defend themselves until an intruder was knocking down their own apartment door.

Sum & Substance QUICK REVIEW of Criminal Law

Lisa arguably was entitled to use lethal force under the circumstances, because it reasonably appeared as if a forcible felony was being committed, with an intended violent felony against Lisa to follow (otherwise, why would the intruder yell at her and attempt to break-in?). Thus, Lisa's bad aim would not be considered excessive force under the circumstances.

A self-defense claim is less likely to be successful unless the facts show that the intruder was armed, or the infliction of serious bodily harm or death of Lisa was imminent. (The statement "Here I come!" is ambiguous, but certainly fright-inducing.) Lisa would not have to retreat under the "castle" exception, since she was in her own residence. (See Case Squibs section, *State v. Crawford*.)

g. The Necessity (or "Choice of Evils") Defense. [§410]

The necessity defense may be raised if: (1) an **emergency** occurs; (2) the emergency is **not** the **defendant's fault**; (3) the emergency creates a **reasonable expectation of imminent harm**; *State v. Kee*, 398 A.2d 384 (Me. 1979); (4) there is **no reasonable opportunity to avoid the injury except** by doing the **criminal act**; and (5) the **harm** from the injury **avoided outweighs** the **harm** from the **criminal offense committed**. *State v. Warshow*, 410 A.2d 1000 (Vt. 1980).

This defense is properly labeled the "choice of evils" defense, since the defendant **chooses** a **lesser evil** (which happens to be **a crime**) rather than a **greater evil** (such as **loss** of **life**, **limb** or **property**). *United States v. Contento-Pachon*, 723 F.2d 691 (9th Cir. 1984). The choices confronting the defendant present a **cost-benefit analysis**: which is the greater evil, for example, exceeding the speed limit, or allowing a wounded person to suffer further injury or perhaps die by following the speed limit? Sometimes, as this example illustrates, breaking the law is the lesser evil.

The necessity defense, also recognized in the law of torts, is like self-defense in that the defendant is protecting himself from an "attacker." In the necessity defense, however, the primary source of the coercion, the "attacker," is nature, and not another person. Thus, the necessity defense can be viewed as a "**justifiable emergency created by nature**."

At common law, the necessity defense was **not available** in several significant situations. It could not be used: (1) as a **defense to homicide**; (2) to justify stealing food or for other **economic reasons**; or (3) if the **legislature** has deliberately **decided** that the activity allegedly causing harm is more beneficial than the potential harm it may cause. This latter situation is called the "**legislative policy exemption**." If the legislature considered and then decided to legalize the disputed activity, courts will defer to the legislature's reasoned choice and prohibit the use of a necessity defense which would undermine the legislature's determination.

---

(1) EXAMPLE. Civil Disobedience. Members of the Jones Gang demonstrate against nuclear power at the local nuclear plant, and are arrested for trespass. Can the gang use the necessity defense to avoid conviction? In some jurisdictions, the answer has been yes, since the harm to be avoided, nuclear meltdown or a similar large-scale catastrophe, is far more weighty than the crime committed. *State v. Dorsey*, 395 A.2d 855 (N.H. 1978). Other courts, however, have not recognized the necessity defense in these circumstances, but have deferred to the "**legislative policy exemption**" instead. These Courts regard the legality of the nuclear plant operation as a deliberate policy choice by the legislature, preventing an independent, **de novo** judicial analysis of the competing values. If the legislature found nuclear power to be sufficiently safe to justify its use, this would preclude the use of the defense.

---

(2) Mistake in Necessity. [§411]

The mistake doctrine applies to the necessity defense in the same way it does to self-defense and other mistake in justification defenses. If a mistake in the facts occurs, that mistake must be **both honest and reasonable** to deserve an acquittal.

> **(a) EXAMPLE.** The first mate of a pleasure ship believes that the ship will sink unless passengers are thrown overboard. The mate throws overboard two passengers, a millionaire and his wife. If the first mate was mistaken in his belief, and there was no need to throw anyone overboard, he still could claim the defense of mistake in necessity if his mistake was both honest and reasonable. If the millionaire and his wife die as a result of being thrown overboard, however, the defense would not succeed. Under the common law, a **homicide could not be justified by necessity**, even if the defendants were stranded at sea in a lifeboat without any real hope of recovery.

(3) The Model Penal Code. [§413]

The MPC's definition of the necessity defense is similar to the common law. [MPC §3.02.] The MPC also contains its own **legislative policy exemption**, prohibiting the use of the defense if evidence exists that the legislature intended to exclude the defense in certain areas.

> **(a) EXAMPLE.** The defendant is arrested for trespass after a protest at what defendant thought was an artificial sweetener factory. The defendant claimed, "The sweeteners are killing us! Down with diet soda!" The factory turns out not to manufacture artificial products, just sugar. The defendant cannot assert the necessity defense even if the mistake in justification was both honest and reasonable. The legislative policy exception likely applies. The Food and Drug Administration has approved the use of artificial sweeteners, indicating that their benefits outweigh potential dangers. Thus, under the MPC, the necessity defense cannot be raised.

3. EXCUSE. [§415]

"Excuse" in the criminal law includes **insanity**, **duress**, and **entrapment**. An excuse operates differently than a justification but yields the same result. The excuse exonerates conduct that otherwise would be criminal. While the resulting acquittal is similar to that which occurs with "justifications," the two types of defenses have vastly different premises. Unlike a person who is justified in her conduct, a person who is excused from a criminal conviction did not, in committing the act, act efficiently (i.e., a greater harm was not avoided). The person is excused from responsibility, however, because society concludes that the person is **not blameworthy**; it would be improper to morally condemn the actor under the special circumstances that existed. Instead, one way to view excuses is that society treats the defendant in these situations almost as a victim.

a. Insanity. [§416]

The insanity defense is raised by a defendant who **admits to committing the offense**, but claims to have done so **as a result of a mental disease or defect**. The defendant asks, in essence, that his criminal conduct be excused because his insanity "made him do it." There are several different insanity tests. The major common law tests, discussed below in sections d and e are the **M'Naghten Rule** and the **Irresistible Impulse Test**. (A third test, the **Product Test**, required merely that the conduct be a product of a mental disease or defect, and was not widely adopted.) The MPC offers its own version of an insanity test, see Section C. While the common law and MPC tests differ, they all require that the defendant's actions result from a mental disease or defect.

(1) Relevant time. [§417]

The only time period that is relevant in judging a defendant's sanity for the purposes of the insanity defense is **the time at which the actus reus was committed**. Whether the defendant subsequently became sane or insane is irrelevant. Thus, any trial testimony about the defendant's sanity should relate back to the time of the incident in question.

(2) Waiver. [§418]

The issue of insanity is raised as an **affirmative defense** at trial. The significance of this statement is that the defense **can be waived**; a defendant who executes a proper waiver can plead not guilty, guilty, or even nolo contendere ("no contest").

(3) Punishment/Treatment. [§419]

Defendants found "not guilty by reason of insanity" are **not punished** and sent to prison, because they are not considered morally blameworthy. Yet, in many jurisdictions, such defendants are not released, either. Defendants found not guilty by reason of insanity can be **involuntarily committed** to a psychiatric hospital for treatment until such time as they are no longer dangerous as a result of their mental illness. The commitment period is **indefinite** and can last the committed person's entire natural life. Since the commitment is not considered punishment, but rather treatment, it can be of a longer duration than the maximum sentence a defendant might have received had he been found guilty of the offense(s) charged. In most jurisdictions, moreover, a criminally committed defendant (that is, a person committed after a finding of not guilty by reason of insanity in a criminal case), has the **burden of proof** in a release hearing to show she is no longer dangerous as a result of the mental disease or defect.

> **(a) EXAMPLE.** Sally is charged with shoplifting, a misdemeanor which has a maximum penalty of six months in jail. She raises an insanity defense and is found not guilty by reason of insanity. Sally likely will be committed to the psychiatric hospital, with a due process mandated review of her case every six months to determine if she can show she is no longer dangerous as a result of her mental illness. If committed, Sally potentially can be confined to

the hospital indefinitely, for a period of time far longer than the six month maximum jail sentence she could have received had she been found guilty. (Consequently, the insanity defense is most often asserted in cases involving serious penalties, such as murder prosecutions.)

(4) The M'Naghten Test. [§421]

The defendant will be found not guilty by reason of insanity if: (1) as a result of a **mental disease or defect** (generally a psychosis), the defendant either (2) (a) **did not understand the nature or quality of his actions or** (b) **did not know right from wrong.** *M'Naghten*, 8 Eng Rep. 718 (1843) (Decided by House of Lords upon certified answer from the Queen's Bench).

The **M'Naghten** test is based on a famous English case involving a man named Daniel M'Naghten, who intended to kill the Prime Minister of England, Peel. Instead, he killed Peel's Secretary, Drummond. As a result of testimony by several alienists (psychiatrists), the rule in M'Naghten's case was formulated. It was later borrowed by many American jurisdictions.

> **(a) EXAMPLE.** Jones squeezes someone to death while claiming that he is merely making lemonade. At trial, Jones will be found not guilty by reason of insanity if, as a result of his mental disease or defect, he did not understand the nature or quality of his behavior. Even if Jones had known he was squeezing a person's head and not just making lemonade, he could still be found not guilty by reason of insanity under the M'Naghten test if, as a result of his mental disease or defect, he did not know that squeezing a person's head was wrong (i.e., if a holy voice from Mars had informed the defendant that it was appropriate and even his duty to squeeze another).

(5) The "Irresistible Impulse" Test. [§423]

Other than M'Naghten, the most popular common law test was the irresistible impulse test. A defendant will be found not guilty by reason of insanity under this test if: (1) as a result of a **mental disease or defect**, (2) she had an **irresistible impulse preventing** her from **complying** with the **requirements of the law**. That is, she had irresistible impulses, not mere urges, causing her criminal behavior. *State v. Hartley*, 90 N.M. 448, 565 P.2d 658 (1977).

> **(a) EXAMPLE.** Sheila loved Almond Wonder candy bars, noting that they were "unbelievably scrumptious." She soon heard voices commanding her to steal them by the truckload. She knew this was wrong but she could not help herself. If prosecuted, Sheila could be found not guilty by reason of insanity under the irresistible impulse test because (1) as a result of a mental disease or defect, she lost touch with reality and began having hallucinations. This caused her to lose control over her conduct and consequently, (2) she was unable to resist the impulse to steal. (She would not meet the requirements of the M'Naghten Test, however, because, even though she acted as a result of a mental disease or defect, she knew both the nature and quality of her acts, as well as right from wrong; she simply could not follow the law.)

(6) Model Penal Code. [§425]

The MPC insanity test combines and broadens the irresistible impulse and M'Naghten tests. The Code permits an insanity defense if, (1) as a **result** of a **mental disease or defect**, a person lacks (2) **substantial capacity** (3) either to **appreciate the criminality** [wrongfulness] of the **conduct** or to **conform the conduct to the requirements of law**. [MPC §4.01.] The Code expands the M'Naghten test by substituting the word "appreciate" (appreciate criminality or wrongfulness) for "know" (know criminality or wrongfulness), and the word substantial ("lack substantial capacity") for an implicit all ("lacks [all] capacity"). The Code modifies the language used to describe the irresistible impulse test, moreover, stating "unable to conform ... conduct to the requirements of the law," instead of using the difficult to define term, "irresistible impulse."

> **(a) EXAMPLE.** R.J., after losing his job and becoming homeless, has recurring bouts with cyclical depressive and manic behavior. During one episode of manic activity, he comes to believe he is the President of the United States. He tries to storm past security to enter the White House, but is arrested and prosecuted for criminal trespass and resisting arrest. If he interposes an insanity defense and the MPC applies, R.J. will be found not guilty by reason of insanity if, as a result of his mental illness — likely a bipolar disorder, the modern psychological description of manic-depressive illness — R.J. lacked substantial capacity: (a) to appreciate that he hopped the White House fence and fought with the guards; or (b) to appreciate that what he did was wrong; or (c) to control himself to the extent that the law demanded.

(7) Guilty but Mentally Ill. [§427]

Some jurisdictions have become dissatisfied with choosing between verdicts of not guilty, guilty, and not guilty by reason of insanity. These jurisdictions have added one more choice, the verdict of guilty but mentally ill. While the precise formulation of the guilty but mentally ill verdict can vary from jurisdiction to jurisdiction, in substance it is very similar to a guilty verdict that automatically offers **psychiatric treatment** to the convicted defendant.

(8) Insanity Versus Incompetency to Proceed. [§428]

Insanity and incompetency to proceed are distinct concepts that often are confused with each other. The following comparison illustrates the differences.

(a) Insanity. [§428.1]

(1) Insanity is an **affirmative defense** raised at trial that can be waived.

(2) If successful, it results in a verdict of not guilty by reason of insanity and the defendant may be **confined indefinitely** for treatment in a psychiatric hospital.

(3) The defendant's insanity is measured only at the **time** of the **alleged incident** in question.

(4) Insanity requires a **mental disease** or **defect**.

(b) Incompetency to Proceed. [§428.2]

(1) The requirement of incompetency to proceed is constitutionally based, emanating from the due process clause of the Constitution. It **applies to any significant stage of the proceedings**, including those requiring the presence of the defendant, from pre-trial matters to the trial to post-trial proceedings such as sentencing. **Incompetency** to proceed **cannot be waived**; if the defendant is incompetent at any stage of the proceedings, all further proceedings are **void** until the defendant regains competency. (The incompetent defendant cannot agree to further proceedings by waiving an incompetency finding.)

(2) If the defendant is found incompetent to proceed and not likely to regain competency in the reasonably foreseeable future, she **cannot be detained indefinitely**, in the hospital or otherwise, but must be released. *Jackson v. Indiana*, 406 U.S. 715 (1972).

(3) The defendant's competency is measured as of the **time of the pre-trial**, **trial** and **post-trial proceedings**, not as of the time of the incident in question.

(4) Incompetency **does not require** that the defendant have a **mental disease or defect**. A defendant is incompetent if: (1) she is **unable to understand the nature of the proceedings** against her or (2) she is **unable** to **assist counsel with the defense**. *Dusky v. United States*, 362 U.S. 402 (1960). An incompetent defendant can become incompetent from amnesia or an incapacitating stroke.

b. Duress. [§429]

Duress is another defense based on coercion, namely coercion by another human being. Not all coercion by others to commit a crime qualifies for this defense at common law. There must be (1) a **threat of imminent death or serious bodily harm to the defendant or to a member of the defendant's family**, *United States v. Bailey*, 444 U.S. 394 (1980); (2) the coercion must be **by another human being**; (3) the **response** to such threats must be **reasonable**; and (4) the **situation** creating the coercion must **not be** the **defendant's fault**. *People v. Lovercamp*, 43 Cal. App. 3d 823, 118 Cal. Rptr. 110 (1975). At common law, duress could **not** be raised as a **defense to murder** where the defendant acted as a principal in the killing.

Duress can be compared to the necessity defense. The two defenses are both based on coercion, although the coercion in duress is caused by a human being, and not nature, as in the necessity defense. Both involve a choice of evils, and both are predicated on the belief that sometimes committing a crime is preferable to the alternative choice presented.

(1) Example of Duress. Bonnie is walking home from work when a man puts a gun to her head and says "Rob the convenience store across the street with this empty gun or you're dead. I'll be watching." If Bonnie commits the robbery and is prosecuted, she can claim **duress**. She was coerced to commit the crime by (1) a threat of death by (2) another human being. (3) Bonnie's response was certainly reasonable under the circumstances and (4) the situation creating the coercion was not her fault. Furthermore, she is not raising the defense to a murder charge, but to a robbery prosecution.

(2) The Model Penal Code. [§431]

The MPC not only recognizes duress as a defense, but also expands the common law definition. Duress occurs if the defendant is (1) coerced to commit an offense (2) by the use or threat of unlawful force against the defendant or any other person; and (3) a person of reasonable firmness in that situation would have been unable to resist. [MPC §2.09.]

Thus, (1) the coercion need not be restricted to threats of death or serious bodily harm. (2) The coercion can involve threats against anyone, not just against the defendant or the defendant's family. (3) The test to determine whether the coercion was sufficient to cause the defendant to commit a crime is an objective one, based on a person of "reasonable firmness" under the circumstances.

(a) EXAMPLE. Sarah, an auditor for a big accounting firm, is told by the boss that "if she doesn't lie on a particular audit, her best friends at the firm would 'feel it.'" Sarah can successfully assert the duress defense under the Model Penal Code if she is prosecuted for lying on the audit because (1) she was coerced by the boss to commit the offense, as a result of (2) the boss's threat of unlawful force against co-workers, which (3) likely would have been enough to coerce a person of reasonable firmness to lie.

The duress defense would not have been available to Sarah at common law since the threat was not one of serious bodily harm to either the defendant or a family member. Friends in the firm, unless also family members, would not qualify.

c. Entrapment. [§433]

Entrapment can be differentiated from other defenses because it focuses on the **fairness of police tactics** and not just on the culpability of the defendant. The essence of entrapment is that the police used unfair tactics to coerce a defendant into committing a crime. *People v. Tipton*, 78 Ill. 2d. 477, 401 N.E.2d 528 (1980). In one sense, entrapment can be viewed as a form of duress by the police.

(1) Tests for Entrapment. [§434]

There are two tests for entrapment: the **subjective** and the **objective** tests. *United States v. Russell*, 411 U.S. 423 (1973).

(a) The Subjective Test. [§435]

The subjective test is met if: (1) the **police**, or an **agent** of the police, such as a confidential informant, **originated** and **created** (i.e., **induced**) the crime; and (2) the **defendant** was **not predisposed** to committing such a crime. *Sorrells v. United States*, 287 U.S. 435 (1932). This approach penalizes the police only for using unfair methods to catch the unwary innocent. The linchpin of the test generally is the **predisposition** of the defendant to committing the crime. It allows the police much greater leeway with individuals who have criminal dispositions. (It is reasoned that individuals with a disposition towards criminality who are poised for another opportunity to strike, are less worthy of protection.) At trial, the defendant's **criminal record** is considered relevant to determining predisposition and admissible as substantive evidence (so long as not unduly prejudicial).

(b) The Objective Test. [§436]

This test asks whether (1) the offense is **created**, **originated** and **induced by the government** or its **agents**, creating a substantial risk that (2) a **reasonable law-abiding person** would have committed the crime. *People v. Barraza*, 23 Cal. 3d 675, 153 Cal. Rptr. 495, 591 P.2d 947 (1947). This test focuses exclusively on the governmental misconduct, and **not** whether the specific defendant was predisposed to commit the crime. This minority approach provides greater deterrence to unfair police methods, since no matter who is caught in the police net, the "fish must be thrown back" if the police did not play fairly. It also means fewer convictions.

(i) EXAMPLE. Stan, a former professional athlete, is pestered by an undercover police officer, Fran, to buy cocaine from the officer. After repeated cajoling and badgering, Stan caves in, saying "I'll buy it just to get you away from here." If Stan is prosecuted for the possession of cocaine, and the subjective test for entrapment applies, Stan's predisposition to commit the crime is a relevant issue. Thus, if his criminal background indicates he is predisposed, the unfairness of the police conduct will not prevent a conviction. If the objective test applies, the sole issue is whether the police conduct would have coerced a reasonable law-abiding person — not necessarily defendant Stan — to commit a crime. Thus, the focus is on the police methods used, and not the defendant's propensity for criminal activity.

Entrapment is very different from the setting of a police trap. Entrapment only can occur as a result of the police, or an agent of the police, "**manufacturing**" the commission of a crime. Surprising or trapping perpetrators in the act is not unfair, nor is it entrapment. Furthermore, entrapment applies only when the government, such as the police and their agents, does the entrapping, and not when private individuals do the coercing.

> **(ii) EXAMPLE.** Emma's friend Rebecca convinces her after much cajoling to help her rob the local convenience store. The police overhear the two discussing the matter, surround the building, and catch Emma and Rebecca in the act. Emma cannot claim entrapment. She was coerced by a private individual to commit the crime, and not by the police. The police merely caught her.

(c) The Model Penal Code. [§439]

The MPC adopts an **objective test** for entrapment. [MPC §2.13.] Evidence of the predisposition of the defendant to commit a crime is irrelevant. The Code further provides that entrapment is a legal issue to be tried to the court and not to the jury. (Note that the entrapment defense is not available when the crime charged includes an element of threatening or causing bodily injury, and the defendant is alleged to have done so to a third party.)

d. Infancy or Immaturity. [§440]

Under the common law, three separate age distinctions are made: (1) a **child under seven years** of age is **conclusively presumed** to be **unable** to commit a crime. (2) **Children between** the **ages** of **seven** and **fourteen** also are **presumed incapable** of committing a crime. However, such a presumption is **rebuttable**. (3) **No presumption of incapacity** to commit a crime exists for **children age 14 and over**.

> **(1) EXAMPLE.** Rambo, Jr., age 6, decides to blow up several buildings in the neighborhood "just for the fun of it." If he does so, he still cannot be convicted of committing a crime because of the conclusive (irrebuttable) presumption that he is incapable of committing a crime.

(2) The Model Penal Code. [§442]

The MPC sweeps away the different common law presumptions, and simply uses the age of 16 as the minimum age for treating a person as an adult capable of committing a crime.

e. Diminished Capacity. [§443]

The term "diminished capacity" has had many different meanings in the common law. It generally refers, however, to a **mental disease, defect, or abnormality that is not as severe as insanity**, but one that still affects a person's conduct. *People v. Wetmore*, 583 P.2d 1308 (Ca. 1978). In some jurisdictions, diminished capacity has been used to negate the mens rea for a crime. Jurisdictions are widely split on whether diminished capacity can serve as a defense. Some jurisdictions allow it as a defense, for example, but only to certain types of crimes.

(1) The Model Penal Code. [§444]

The MPC permits this defense for all crimes. The defense acts to **negate** the **mens rea** required for the particular crime charged. [MPC §4.02.]

REVIEW QUESTIONS — EXCUSES

PROBLEM 1. "April Fools." Harry is broke. He sees a street person sleeping with a $20 bill sticking out of his pocket. Harry believes that Jolly Roger, a force greater than mankind, has ordered him to take the money, so he does. After he grabs the money, the "street person" jumps up, flashes a police badge, and tells Harry he is under arrest. Has Harry committed any crimes?

Answer: Harry's conduct satisfied the elements of **larceny**. He took and carried away, without permission, the money of another, albeit a short distance, with the intent to permanently deprive the owner of that money by spending it. He probably has not committed robbery, however, because he took the money by stealth, and not by force or fear, since the alleged victim appeared to be asleep.

Harry may claim **entrapment** as a defense. Harry will contend that the police officer (1) induced Harry to commit the crime by pretending to sleep while a $20 bill was readily exposed "for the taking." If the **subjective test** applies, the second issue would be whether (2) Harry was predisposed to committing the crime. On this issue, Harry's prior criminal conduct would be pertinent. More information is necessary to resolve this question.

In contrast, if the **objective test** for entrapment applies, the second issue would be (2) whether a reasonable law-abiding person would have been induced to commit the crime as a result of the actions of the police. Answering this question is difficult, but a law-abiding citizen generally would not reach into someone else's pocket and take money, even if the money is protruding from the pocket.

Harry also may assert the **insanity defense**. If the **M'Naghten test** applies, Harry would claim that as the result of a mental disease or defect, he either (1) did not know right from wrong in committing the crime or (2) did not know the nature of his conduct. If the **irresistible impulse** test applies, Harry would argue that as a result of his mental disease or defect, he was (1) unable to conform his conduct to the requirements of the law. That is, Harry felt an irresistible impulse to take the money, in a way that was more than a mere urge.

OUTLINE

IX. PRACTICE MULTIPLE CHOICE QUESTIONS AND ANSWERS

Question 1

Al arrives home one day to find his wife Peg in bed with another man. Al takes out a gun and kills them both. Al is most likely guilty of which crime?

(A) Heat of passion manslaughter.

(B) Attempted manslaughter.

(C) Murder.

(D) No crime.

(E) Negligent homicide.

Question 2

Johnson, a petty thief, breaks into a house of another to steal some automobile parts. He lights a match to see where he is going, and unintentionally sets fire to some stored oil, causing the house to burn down. Johnson:

(A) Would be guilty of arson because the intent to break into the house would transfer to the intent to burn down the house.

(B) Would be guilty of arson because he acted negligently.

(C) Would not be guilty of arson if he only acted negligently.

(D) Would not be guilty of arson if he did not intend for the house to burn down.

Question 3

Joanne is charged with selling mislabeled pharmaceuticals. While Joanne agrees that she sold the drugs with an incorrect label, she said the mislabeling was a mistake. If selling mislabeled pharmaceuticals is considered to be a strict liability offense:

(A) Joanne's mistake will not be a defense.

(B) Joanne's mistake will be a defense only if it was honest and reasonable.

(C) Joanne's mistake will be a defense if it was honest.

(D) Joanne's mistake will be a defense, but only if she did not act recklessly.

Question 4

Barbara asked Suzanne if she could rent a floor of Suzanne's apartment building for the next month. Suzanne was aware that Barbara intended to use the apartments for prostitution. Suzanne said "yes" anyway, and charged Barbara extra because of the nature of the use. If **Suzanne** is charged with conspiracy to commit prostitution, which of the following is the most likely reason why:

(A) The intent to participate in a conspiracy can be inferred from knowledge of the criminal activity accompanied by a stake in the venture.

(B) The intent to participate in a conspiracy can be inferred from mere knowledge when a legal use occurs from the sale of legal goods or services.

(C) The intent to participate in a conspiracy can be inferred from mere knowledge of the criminal use of the goods or services.

(D) The intent to participate in a conspiracy generally must be express, and not implied, with the exception of cases involving "victimless" crimes such as prostitution.

Question 5

Kal, Mikey, J.B., Joel and T.C. go out on the town. They are grabbed by a young woman who exclaims "You are the son of Satan and the disciples of the temple all in one; I worship Thee!" After the woman grabbed them and would not let go, she was charged with battery. She most likely would be found not guilty by reason of insanity under the **M'Naghten** test if (choose the best answer):

(A) She did not know right from wrong.

(B) She could not control her conduct as a result of her mental illness.

(C) She did not know the nature of her acts as a result of her mental illness.

(D) Her conduct was a product of her mental illness.

Question 6

An English barrister named Leslie was on vacation in the United States. A starving adult bumped into the barrister, and picked the barrister's pocket to buy some bread. If charged with larceny, the starving adult:

(A) Cannot claim the necessity defense.

(B) Can claim the necessity defense, but only if the harm avoided was greater than the harm caused.

(C) Can assert the necessity defense, but only if it was not the adult's fault that the emergency occurred.

(D) Can claim necessity as a defense because the legislative policy exemption does not apply.

Question 7

Bo steals an automobile from the Pre-Owned Car Lot. Lila observes the crime in progress and throws Bo a pair of jumper cables to assist him, even though Lila was not asked to help or otherwise participate. While leaving the car lot, Bo shoots and seriously injures both the owner of the lot and an innocent bystander in order to successfully escape. Lila:

(A) Will be held liable for all foreseeable crimes in addition to the object crime of grand theft auto.

(B) Will be held liable for all crimes in furtherance of the grand theft auto crime.

(C) Will not be held liable for any crimes because she was only an accomplice before the fact.

(D) Will be held liable only for the object crime, grand theft auto.

Question 8

Farrah kills her husband Rick while he is sleeping. She raises the battered woman's syndrome as a defense at trial. If, immediately before the killing, the deceased husband exhibited contrition and loving behavior toward Farrah:

(A) This means that the battered woman's syndrome no longer exists.

(B) This behavior will be used to illustrate one of the phases of the battered woman's syndrome.

(C) This behavior has no bearing on whether the battered woman's syndrome exists.

(D) This behavior indicates a period of relative calm, which never exists in a battering relationship.

Question 9

Ann and Joanne decide to scalp tickets for the Cotton Bowl football game in Texas. While Ann and Joanne both believe it is unlawful to scalp tickets, there is no ordinance prohibiting them from doing so. If Ann and Joanne do scalp tickets, they could be convicted of:

(A) Attempted conspiracy to commit ticket scalping.

(B) Conspiracy to commit ticket scalping and ticket scalping.

(C) Attempted ticket scalping.

(D) No crime.

Question 10

Chuck Borris is told by a friend that his wife is having an affair. The friend tells Borris that his wife is in the upstairs bedroom of their home with her boyfriend, Dan. Chuck drives to the house and shoots through the living room window to try to scare his wife and the alleged boyfriend out of the house. Unbeknownst to Chuck, the alleged boyfriend was in the living room at the time. Dan was hit by the shot and slightly wounded. Chuck has committed which of the following crimes:

(A) Attempted manslaughter.

(B) Attempted murder.

(C) Intent to commit serious bodily harm murder.

(D) None of the above.

Question 11

Jane is married to Tom. Although Jane is aware that Tom is sexually assaulting Jane's daughter from a previous marriage, Jane does nothing. Jane is:

(A) Liable for sexual assault as an accomplice.

(B) Liable for sexual assault as a co-conspirator.

(C) Liable for sexual assault only if she has a legal duty to act.

(D) Liable for sexual assault if she actually was an eyewitness to an assault.

Question 12

When Jones returned home from visiting friends, he confronted an intruder who was exiting the house by the front door. As the intruder ran out the door, the intruder prepared to throw a knife directly at Jones' head. As he ducked, Jones pulled out a gun and fired at the intruder, killing him. The knife, which had just missed Jones, turned out to be made of plastic, although it looked genuine to even expert observers. Jones would most likely be found:

(A) Not guilty of criminal homicide.

(B) Guilty of heat of passion manslaughter.

(C) Guilty of murder because the knife missed him.

(D) Not guilty by reason of temporary capitation.

Question 13

Homer tells Marge that "If I were bigger, I'd punch you in the eye, right away!" Marge thereupon punches Homer in the nose, knocking him out. Marge:

(A) Cannot claim self-defense because the threat of physical harm was not imminent.

(B) Cannot claim self-defense because Marge was not threatened with deadly physical force.

(C) Cannot claim self-defense because she could have retreated.

(D) Would likely be successful upon a claim of self-defense.

Question 14

Dana shoots at Barb, intending to kill her. The gun, unbeknownst to Dana, is empty. Dana can be convicted of:

(A) Attempted murder if the lack of bullets is considered to be a factual impossibility.

(B) Attempted murder, but only if the lack of bullets is considered to be a legal impossibility.

(C) Attempted murder regardless of whether the lack of bullets is considered to be a factual or legal impossibility.

(D) Murder, because impossibility is too ambiguous.

Question 15

Proof beyond a reasonable doubt:

(A) Is required in criminal cases.

(B) Is required in the adjudicatory phase of juvenile proceedings.

(C) Is required in most civil cases.

(D) A and B above.

Question 16

Judy was riding along the highway on a snowy and blustery evening when she started looking down to fiddle with the radio. After trying every station, she glanced back towards the highway, where, to her surprise, there appeared to be a person flailing with his arms right in front of her on the road. Before she could slow down, she hit and killed the victim. That person had been robbed and left drunk and helpless on the road by Jones, who has been charged with murder. Which of the following is most likely to occur:

(A) A jury will find Jones not to have been a cause in fact of the victim's death.

(B) The jury will find Judy not to have been a cause in fact of the victim's death.

(C) If Judy's negligence is considered to be gross, she will be an intervening superseding cause, breaking the chain of proximate causation.

(D) Provided that Judy's conduct was inadvertent, she will be an intervening superseding cause, breaking the chain of causation.

Question 17

Tommy robbed the First National Federal City State Bank. He jumped into a cab driven by Carolyn, who was unaware of the robbery, and told her to drive as fast as she could to the other side of town. Carolyn did this excellently, and unwittingly helped Tommy evade the police. If Carolyn is charged with a crime for her participation in this robbery escape, she will be found, under the common law (5 choices):

(A) Guilty as a co-conspirator.

(B) Guilty as an accessory after the fact.

(C) Guilty as a principal in the second degree.

(D) Guilty under an accomplice theory of liability.

(E) Not guilty.

Question 18

Susanna hates her neighbor, Rosanna. One day, while Susanna is watering her vegetable garden, she sees Rosanna working nearby in her own vegetable garden. Susanna then takes the gardening hose, and under the pretense of spraying her own garden, deliberately sprays Rosanna with the hose. Rosanna becomes soaking wet and Susanna apologizes, although she is silently gleeful. At common law, Susanna has committed (choose the best answer):

(A) Assault.

(B) Battery.

(C) Aggravated assault and battery.

(D) Intentional infliction of emotional distress.

Question 19

Betty is invited to a late-night party thrown in the garden area of a sprawling estate. Betty is curious to see what the inside of the house looks like, so she breaks the lock on one of the basement windows and climbs through, desiring to "check it out." Upon entering the basement, she sees a baseball autographed by Jose Canseco and Dave Stewart, something she's always wanted. She puts the ball in her pocket and leaves the house. Betty has committed which common law crimes?

(A) Larceny only.

(B) Burglary and larceny.

(C) Burglary only.

(D) Burglary and robbery.

(E) Attempted larceny.

Question 20

Jean has blackout spells from a newly discovered disease called "nepolepsy." After learning about the sudden seizures she may have, she tells her friends, "I'll just drive home this once, and then give up driving altogether." On the way home, Jean suffers a seizure and, in an unconscious state, crashes into a person standing on the sidewalk, breaking his ankle. Jean would most likely be convicted of:

(A) No crime, because the blackout was involuntary.

(B) Battery, because the decision to drive was a negligent one.

(C) Assault with intent to kill, because the victim suffered a palpable injury.

(D) Attempted murder, if the victim almost died.

(E) Assault.

Question 21

Paul lights a fire with the purpose of burning down his enemy's house. Unbeknownst to Paul, Sarah has carelessly dropped a cigarette outside of the same house, causing a fire. Both Sarah's and Paul's fires burn down the house simultaneously. Is Paul guilty of arson?

(A) No, because Sarah is guilty of arson.

(B) Yes, because Paul need not cause the house burning, only intend it.

(C) Yes, because Paul's fire was a substantial factor in the house burning.

(D) No, because Paul can only be held liable if his fire was the sole cause of the house burning down.

Question 22

Sheri is charged with "negligently selling liquor to a minor at a public event." At trial, Sheri claims that she thought the minor had reached majority age. For Sheri to successfully use mistake in fact as a defense to this charge, that mistake:

(A) Need only be honest.

(B) Must be both honest and reasonable.

(C) Need not be honest or reasonable because the statute as framed is a strict liability offense.

(D) Need only be honest if this crime is considered to be a general intent offense.

Question 23

The defendant, an adult male, fired his gun at his neighbor's house, killing the neighbor. In which of the following situations would he be most likely convicted of manslaughter and not murder:

(A) Defendant was only trying to scare his neighbor by firing just above his neighbor's head.

(B) Defendant thought he was firing at his neighbor's brother and not his neighbor.

(C) Defendant simply intended to shoot at his neighbor's crowded dinner table and cause a little excitement.

(D) The defendant intentionally shot at his neighbor, honestly believing that the neighbor had picked up a rifle to shoot him first, when in fact the neighbor was just going to sweep the garage with a broom.

Question 24

George decided to protest the use of artificial sweeteners, claiming that they were extremely dangerous to humans. He and 50 other protesters were arrested for trespassing on the grounds of the Better-Sweet Artificial Sweetener Company headquarters. George asserts the defense of necessity at trial. This claim (choose the best answer):

(A) Would succeed even if George had invented and originally marketed the sweeteners, thereby creating the emergency situation.

(B) Would not succeed if the Food and Drug Administration had already considered the relative hazards that results from such artificial sweeteners, and had approved them after weighing the dangers.

(C) Would succeed even if there was a reasonable opportunity for George and his group to have engaged in a less intrusive alternative means of protest.

(D) Would succeed so long as the harm from the emergency situation equals the harm resulting from the criminal conduct.

(E) Would succeed no matter what the facts are.

Question 25

Three men and a dog are floating helplessly in a lifeboat at sea. Eeny, Meeney and Miney Moe are stranded along with their dog named Joe. Eeny says "let's get Miney Moe." Eeny takes his knife and approaches real slow. However, right before Miney Moe is knifed, he said "I have to go." Miney thereupon jumps overboard to avoid being knifed, and is eaten by sharks. Eeny can be convicted of:

(A) No crime, because people stranded in life boats are generally found not guilty by reason of insanity.

(B) Attempted murder.

(C) Murder.

(D) Simple assault.

(E) No crime, because Eeny did not kill Miney, Miney jumped overboard on his own.

Question 26

Dex decides to order 100 pizzas for his friend Lex as a prank. Dex is prosecuted for engaging in "conduct constituting a public mischief," a common law crime. If this prank, after the fact, is considered a public mischief, and Dex is convicted, on appeal his conviction should be: (Choose the best answer)

(A) Overturned because he did not engage in any mischief.

(B) Overturned because such a prosecution constitutes retroactive crime creation in violation of due process of law.

(C) Overturned because such a prosecution is a bill of attainder.

(D) Overturned because the mischief, if there was any mischief at all, was private and not public.

(E) Affirmed.

Question 27

Mortimer and O'Hara were sailing their sloop, John B., from the Bahamas to Miami. As they pulled into the Port of Miami, they were arrested and charged with possessing two tons of marijuana contained in the hold of the ship. Which of the following contentions made by O'Hara would most likely lead to an acquittal? (Assume the jury would believe the facts claimed by the defendant):

(A) He was not in actual possession of the narcotics.

(B) It wasn't his idea to sell the narcotics; instead, he was just a minor pawn in the operation.

(C) He did not honestly know that the hold of the ship contained narcotics of any kind.

(D) He thought there were only twenty pounds of marijuana, not two tons in the hull.

(E) While he was aware the marijuana was in the hull, he wasn't the only person with access to the hold of the ship and the marijuana.

Question 28

Phaedrus asked his friend Jackson to steal some cigarettes for him from the local convenience store. Jackson refused, so Phaedrus slapped him several times and asked again. When he again refused, he hit Jackson even harder. Phaedrus then said "Well? Are you ready to take the cigarettes now? It's just going to get worse." Jackson nodded weakly in agreement. If Jackson is charged with larceny, the most likely basis for acquittal would be:

Sum & Substance QUICK REVIEW of Criminal Law

(A) Not guilty by reason of insanity.

(B) Battered person syndrome.

(C) Duress.

(D) Entrapment.

Question 29

Assume for the purposes of this question that Jackson, from the preceding question, was followed into the convenience store by an undercover police officer. The officer befriended Jackson, and asked him what he was doing in the store. He told the officer about the planned theft, and in response the officer volunteered to stand guard. Jackson said okay. After the theft was successfully completed, the undercover officer arrested Jackson. Would Jackson be able to assert successfully the defense of entrapment?

(A) Probably, even if he was predisposed towards committing the crime.

(B) Probably, because the police officer used deception to arrest him.

(C) Probably, because the police officer originated and induced the crime.

(D) Not likely.

Question 30

Porsche parked her luxury car at the Day's Off Car Lot. After leaving her car and her car keys in the care of the parking attendant, one Ferris Boolah, she left. Ferris then drove away in the car, intending to keep it. Ferris is caught on the outskirts of town with the car. He can be convicted of which crime?

(A) Embezzlement.

(B) Attempted larceny.

(C) Larceny.

(D) Attempted embezzlement.

(E) False pretenses.

Question 31

After Lana observed Harry with another woman, she attacked him with her fists, knocking him over onto the marble floor in conduct constituting aggravated battery. As she did this, a hand gun still inside her purse discharged. It pierced Harry's heart, killing him. If Lana is charged with felony murder as a result of the aggravated battery, which is a felony:

(A) She would be convicted because aggravated battery is an inherently dangerous felony.

(B) She would be convicted because the death was directly caused by her harmful conduct.

(C) She would be acquitted because aggravated battery is not an inherently dangerous felony.

(D) She would be acquitted because the underlying felony is not independent.

Question 32

Cruise put a gun to the head of Costner, saying "if you don't kill Eastwood, Costner, you will die immediately." If Costner kills Eastwood as a result of the threat:

(A) Costner, under the common law, could successfully use the duress defense because the threat was imminent.

(B) Under the common law, Costner could successfully use the necessity defense because the threat was one of serious bodily harm.

(C) Under the common law, Costner could successfully use the duress defense because Costner appeared to have no reasonable chance to escape.

(D) Under the common law, Costner could not use the duress defense successfully.

Question 33

The defendant is charged with assault with intent to commit rape. If the defendant honestly but unreasonably believed the victim had consented to his advances, the defendant should be:

(A) Acquitted because assault with intent to commit rape is a specific intent crime.

(B) Acquitted because assault with intent to commit rape is a general intent crime.

(C) Acquitted because he could not have completed the act of rape.

(D) Convicted.

Question 34

The Terrible Terrorist Troupe, TTT, threatens to blow up an elementary school unless the students free two political prisoners. If the students free the prisoners, the students may be able to claim:

(A) Duress.

(B) Necessity.

(C) Entrapment.

(D) Insanity.

Question 35

Katie, after a workout, gets an irresistible urge for a Mounds Bar, which as everyone knows is indescribably delicious. Katie sews a special hidden pocket inside her sweat pants and goes to the all night convenience store. As she is about to enter the store, she is arrested. Katie would most likely be convicted of:

(A) Conspiracy to commit larceny.

(B) Attempted larceny.

(C) Larceny.

(D) No crime.

Question 36

Roy, Amy, and Emma decide to rob the local bank. Roy goes out and buys fourteen yards of rope, two guns, and ammunition, as well as masks and costumes, all of which are to be used in the robbery. Amy is immediately arrested on another charge and is thrown in jail. On the date agreed upon Roy and Emma are to meet in front of the bank. Roy shows up, but Emma doesn't, since she decides to go and watch a movie instead. Roy then robs the bank and is apprehended as he escapes. Emma can be charged with:

(A) Conspiracy only.

(B) Solicitation only.

(C) Conspiracy and attempted bank robbery.

(D) Conspiracy and bank robbery.

(E) None of the above.

Question 37

Assuming the same facts as above, Amy can be charged with:

(A) Solicitation to commit bank robbery.

(B) Conspiracy to commit bank robbery only.

(C) Conspiracy to commit bank robbery and bank robbery.

(D) No crime, since she was in jail when it occurred.

Question 38

Assuming the same facts as above, Roy can be charged with:

(A) Only bank robbery, since the conspiracy fell apart.

(B) Bank robbery and conspiracy.

(C) Bank robbery, conspiracy, and attempted bank robbery.

(D) No crime.

(E) A and C.

Question 39

Jim and Joan go fishing. Joan jumps in for a swim and suggests to Jim that he join her. Jim says he doesn't know how to swim. Joan responds by ridiculing Jim, calling him a chicken and suggesting that he is a real baby if he doesn't jump in and cool off. Jim does and starts to drown. Joan watches him while he in fact does drown. Joan can be convicted of which crime?

(A) Solicitation.

(B) Homicide.

(C) Deception.

(D) Intentional infliction of emotional distress.

(E) No crime.

Question 40

Arnold the "Terminator" is told that his wife Maria is having an affair. He is told that she is in the upstairs bedroom with her boyfriend. Arnold drives to the house and shoots at the living room window, trying to scare out Maria and her boyfriend. Unbeknownst to Arnold, Maria's boyfriend had walked downstairs to the living room, and was hit by the shot and slightly wounded. Arnold can be convicted of which crime?

(A)   Homicide.

(B)   Attempted murder.

(C)   Solicitation.

(D)   None of the above.

Question 41

Lenny, known as "The Big Man," was showing off his muscles at the Keg North Bar and Grill. As an audience developed, The Big Man began to act in a rowdy manner for his fans. Jimmie entered the bar and The Big Man began to tease him. Unbeknownst to The Big Man, Jimmie had a weak heart. The Big Man approached Jimmie and pretended to punch him. The Big Man intentionally missed him, hitting the wall instead. Jimmie, very scared, had a heart attack and died. The Big Man can most likely be convicted of which of the following:

(A)   Attempted murder.

(B)   Depraved heart murder.

(C)   Manslaughter.

(D)   Felony murder.

(E)   No crime.

Question 42

Jane hates her neighbor. One evening she decides to burn her neighbor's house down, forcing her neighbor to move. Unbeknownst to Jane, the neighbor's sister was in the house at the time it burned and she died. Jane is charged with both arson and felony murder. Jane is convicted of felony murder but acquitted on the arson charge. The felony murder conviction should be:

(A)   Reversed because felony murder requires proof of intent, and there was no intent to kill here.

(B)   Reversed because felony murder requires the conviction of a felony, and there was no underlying felony conviction here.

(C)   Reversed because felony murder requires an independent felony, and arson is not independent.

Question 43

Gary Creamer and Allen Coffee were neighbors who quarreled constantly about the picket fence which separated their property. One day during a particularly vicious argument, Creamer reached across the fence and grabbed Coffee by the arm, scratching him. Unbeknownst to Creamer, Coffee was a hemophiliac who subsequently bled to death as a result of the scratches. Creamer can be held liable for:

(A)   Intent to kill murder.

(B)   Depraved heart murder.

(C)   Manslaughter.

(D)   Only assault.

(E)   No crimes.

Question 44

The Miami Dolphins were playing the Jets. A fan of the Jets, Gaston Snow, decided to put Dan Marino out of action. Gaston fired his Saturday night special revolver at Marino during the second half intending to hit him in the thigh. Instead Gaston struck Josephine Namath, who was at the game as a spectator, killing her. Gaston has committed:

(A)   Murder.

(B)   Manslaughter.

(C)   Assault.

(D)   No crime.

Question 45

Sarah was given a new rifle for her 24th birthday. She decided to try it out by shooting out some of the windows in planes about to take off. She does not miss a single window from a distance of a hundred yards. In the process, she kills ten people. Sarah has committed:

(A)   Intent to kill murder.

(B)   Felony murder.

(C)   Depraved heart murder.

(D)   Manslaughter.

(E)   None of the above.

Question 46

Mr. A is sexually assaulted by Mr. B. Mr. B tells everyone in town about it causing Mr. A to become doubly upset. Mr. A goes out and buys a gun, and three days after the assault shoots and kills Mr. B. Mr. A has committed:

(A) Intent to kill murder because he desired to achieve the death of Mr. B.

(B) Intent to kill murder because there was sufficient cooling off time after the assault.

(C) Intent to kill murder because there was unreasonable and inadequate provocation.

(D) Manslaughter.

(E) None of the above.

ANSWERS TO THE MULTIPLE CHOICE QUESTIONS

Answer to Question 1.

(A) is the correct Answer.

Heat of passion manslaughter is the unlawful intentional killing of another person while subject to (1) actual, (2) reasonable, and (3) legally adequate provocation without (4) a reasonable opportunity to cool off. Killing his wife and her lover upon suddenly finding them in bed together actually provoked Al, and such provocation was reasonable under the circumstances and legally adequate. Choice (B) is incorrect because the victims died. (C) is incorrect because the mitigating circumstances will reduce this crime from murder to manslaughter. Since Al's conduct is still culpable and no defenses exist that would fully exonerate him, (D) is incorrect. Negligent homicide, (E), generally involves a negligent mental state. Here Al acted intentionally, and is likely guilty of a more heinous crime.

Answer to Question 2.

(C) is the correct Answer.

Because malice includes purposeful, knowing and reckless behavior, but not negligence, negligent conduct cannot constitute arson, regardless of the degree of negligence. (A) is incorrect because intent is not transferred from one crime to another. (B) is wrong because arson is limited to malicious conduct, not negligence. (D) is erroneous since malice includes recklessness, and Johnson still would be acting with malice if he acted recklessly, albeit unintentionally.

Answer to Question 3.

(A) is the correct choice.

Strict liability crimes afford no mistake of fact defense to the person charged with the violation, since a mistake of fact only negates the mens rea. With a strict liability offense, there is no mens rea to be negated. Choices (B) (C) and (D) are incorrect for the same reason.

Answer to Question 4.

(A) is the correct Answer.

Suzanne had knowledge of the criminal venture and impliedly became a participant by obtaining a stake in the venture, namely the increased rent. (B) is incorrect since prostitution is not a "legal use" of the apartment rental. (C) is faulty because the mere knowledge that a crime will be committed is generally insufficient. (D) is an incorrect statement of the law. A conspiracy can be either express or implied, without any limitation based on whether the crime is "victimless."

Answer to Question 5.

(C) is the correct choice.

Under the M'Naghten test, a defendant is not guilty by reason of insanity if, at the time of the act, the person was laboring under a major mental disease or defect causing the person (1) not to know the nature or quality of the act performed, or (2) not to know that the act performed was wrong. (A) is incorrect because the defendant's inability to know right from wrong must result from a mental disease or defect. (B) is amiss because the defendant's inability to control her actions is not covered by the M'Naghten test, but rather by the irresistible impulse test. (D) is erroneous as well because whether the conduct is a "product" of the mental illness is not pertinent to the M'Naghten test.

Answer to Question 6.

(A) is the correct Answer.

The necessity defense is not available to avoid economic hardship. Thus, the starving adult cannot successfully claim that she was acting under a "choice of evils." (B), (C), and (D) are all incorrect because they assume the defense is available.

Answer to Question 7.

(D) is the correct choice.

An accomplice may be held liable for the object crime, and thus (D) is the correct Answer. (A) is incorrect because, pursuant to the common law, Lila, as an accomplice, will at most be held liable for foreseeable homicides in addition to the object offense. The rule on vicarious liability for accomplices is much more restrictive than the extended liability applicable to co-conspirators. No homicides occurred in this case. (B) is faulty because it states the rule for conspiracy liability, not accomplice liability. Lila was not involved in a conspiracy because there was no agreement between Bo and Lila. Answer (C) is incorrect because Lila assisted at the crime scene, not before the fact, making her a principal in the second degree and liable for the commission of the object crime.

Answer to Question 8.

(B) is the correct Answer.

Contrition is one of the phases of the battered woman syndrome, which is an ongoing cycle of psychological and/or physical domination most often of a wife by her husband. The cycle involves an escalating abuse of the wife followed by a phase of contrition and a period of calm. (A) and (C) are wrong because contrition is one part of the battering cycle. (D) is wrong because the period of calm follows the contrition phase in the battered woman syndrome.

Answer to Question 9.

(D) is the correct choice.

This is a case of true legal impossibility, where the object offense — ticket scalping — is lawful. Thus, attempts to do a lawful act by lawful means are also lawful, regardless of whether the actors subjectively believe the acts are unlawful. Thus, (A), (B), and (C) are incorrect.

Answer to Question 10.

(D) is the correct Answer.

Since Borris did not intend to hurt anyone, and was unaware that anyone was in the living room when he shot, he did not act purposefully or knowingly with an intent to harm. Consequently, he cannot be found guilty of (A), (B), or (C), all of which require the specific intent to harm another. (Note that (A), attempted manslaughter, is not generally recognized as a crime under the common law.) Borris can be found guilty of aggravated battery, because his intent to scare constitutes the conscious disregard of a substantial and unjustifiable risk, which is reckless behavior.

Answer to Question 11.

(C) is the correct Answer.

Jane's omission is not a crime unless Jane had a legal duty to act. A legal duty may arise from a special relationship such as parent-child, but the scope of the duty depends on the circumstances. As a result, (A), (B), and (D) are incorrect statements since Jane did not assist (and therefore is not an accomplice), or agree (and is therefore not a conspirator). Although statutes are being enacted to the contrary, at common law she is not liable simply because she was an eyewitness.

Answer to Question 12.

(A) is the correct Answer.

Jones acted in self-defense because the intruder threw a knife which Jones honestly and reasonably believed to be real (even the experts were deceived). Thus, Jones' mistaken justification would be valid because his mistake was both honest and reasonable. Jones cannot claim defense of habitation because the intruder was exiting the house at the time of the confrontation, not forcibly entering it. (B) is incorrect because the provocation of the thrown knife transforms this case into self-defense and complete exoneration. (C) is incorrect because whether the knife struck the defendant is irrelevant to whether Jones can assert a self-defense claim. (D) is incorrect because "temporary capitation" is a made-up term and has no legal significance.

Answer to Question 13.

(A) is the correct Answer.

The word "if" indicates that Homer was not making an imminent threat of harm, a necessary predicate to a self-defense claim. Choice (B) is incorrect because a threat of deadly physical force is not necessary to invoke the self-defense doctrine. The duty to retreat does not apply to non-deadly force situations, and thus (C) is amiss. Answer (D) contradicts choice (A), and thus is incorrect.

Answer to Question 14.

(A) is the correct Answer.

Factual impossibility (where the crime cannot be completed due to some unforeseen physical or factual condition) is not a defense to an attempt crime; legal impossibility (where the attempt, had it been completed, would not have been a crime) is a defense. Thus, (B) and (C) are both incorrect statements of law. Answer (D) is incorrect because no one was killed.

Answer to Question 15.

(D) is the correct Answer, reflecting that both choices (A) and (B) are accurate.

(A) is accurate because proof beyond a reasonable doubt is the well-accepted standard of proof in all criminal proceedings. (B) is also true because, according to the United States Supreme Court in *In Re Winship*, 397 U.S. 358 (1970), this standard is required for adjudications of delinquency in juvenile proceedings as well. Thus, (D) is the best choice. (C) is incorrect because civil cases require either clear and convincing evidence or a preponderance of the evidence.

Answer to Question 16.

(C) is the correct answer.

Gross negligence, as compared to simple negligence, acts as an intervening superseding cause, breaking the chain of proximate causation. (A) is wrong because Jones was a cause in fact of the victim's death — "but for" Jones leaving the victim on the road in the condition the victim was in, the victim would not have been killed at that particular time. (B) is wrong because, by hitting the victim with her car, Judy also was a cause in fact of the victim's death. (D) is an incorrect statement of the law. Mere inadvertent behavior is not an intervening superseding cause which breaks the chain of causation.

Answer to Question 17.

(E) is the correct choice.

In order to be found guilty as an accomplice, the accused must have the necessary act and mental state. Carolyn assisted Tommy in escaping apprehension, thus committing the act required of an accessory after the fact. She did not intend to assist Tommy in committing a crime, however, and thus is not guilty because she did not have the requisite mental state of intentional assistance. Instead, she was an "innocent instrumentality." Choices (A)-(D) are thus incorrect.

Answer to Question 18.

(B) is the correct answer.

Battery is the harmful or offensive touching of another person. The touching need not be physical, so the spraying of water on another constitutes an offensive touching. Battery is a general intent crime, and the mens rea required is purpose, knowledge, recklessness, or negligence ("PKRN"). Susanna sprayed the water on Rosanna purposefully and consequently meets both the mens rea and actus reus elements of battery. Assault, on the other hand, is either the intentional creation of fear of an imminent battery, or an attempted battery. Here, the attempted battery type of assault by Susanna occurred, but it merges into the completed battery offense. Thus, (A) and (C) are incorrect. (D) is wrong because the intentional infliction of emotional distress is a tort, not a common law crime.

Answer to Question 19.

(A) is the correct choice.

Burglary is the breaking and entering of the dwelling house of another at nighttime with the intent to commit a felony therein. At the time Betty broke into and entered the house, she was not intending to commit a felony therein, just "to look around." Since Betty lacked the necessary mental state, she did not commit a common law burglary. This eliminates choices (B), (C) and (D). Betty took the baseball without permission, intending to keep it. This constitutes an actual, not attempted, larceny, so choice (E) is incorrect.

Answer to Question 20.

(B) is the correct answer.

A person who knows she is subject to seizures may be held responsible for injuries that the person negligently, recklessly, or intentionally causes. Jean's decision to drive knowing she may suffer a seizure was likely reckless, because she consciously disregarded a substantial and unjustifiable risk of harm. (A) is wrong since Jean voluntarily made the reckless decision to drive the car. Choices (C), (D) and (E) are incorrect statements since Jean did not intend to harm anyone.

Answer to Question 21.

(C) is the correct choice.

Arson is the malicious burning of the dwelling house of another. When two simultaneous causes occur, courts use the "substantial factor" test. The question changes from "but for" Paul's act, would the house have burned down? "Was Paul's act a substantial factor in the house burning down?" The answer to this question is yes. Answers (A), (B), and (D) are incorrect statements of law.

Answer to Question 22.

(B) is the correct Answer.

"Negligently selling liquor to minors" is a general intent offense because it requires negligence at a minimum. While this type of offense often is stated without a mens rea requirement, it is important to carefully read the definition given. Since the offense is framed here as a general intent crime, a mistake of fact must be both honest and reasonable. Answer (B) describes the correct standard, while (A), (C) and (D) provide incorrect rules.

Answer to Question 23.

(D) is the correct choice.

In (D), the defendant actually believed that the use of lethal force was necessary to defend himself. That belief was unreasonable, however, since the neighbor had picked up a broom with which to sweep the garage. Because the defendant's mistake was honest but unreasonable, this would be imperfect justification manslaughter. If the defendant's mistaken belief in the need for self-defense was reasonable as well as honest, it would have been mistaken self-defense and a complete defense to a criminal homicide charge. (B) is incorrect because it still presents a case of murder — the intent to kill a person is still present. (A) and (C) are examples of depraved heart murder.

Answer to Question 24.

(B) is the correct Answer.

(B) describes the legislative policy exception to the necessity defense, where the legislature previously has balanced the burdens and the benefits of a particular activity, leading the courts to hold the defense in abeyance regarding that activity. In essence, the courts are refusing to second-guess the legislature by recognizing a legislative policy exemption.

In order for the necessity defense to be successful, the harm caused by the protestor must be less than the harm caused by the Better-Sweet Company. Thus, (C), (D) and (E) are incorrect because the harm caused by the company in these answer choices apparently does not outweigh the harm caused by the protesters. (A) is wrong because George cannot create an emergency situation and then rely on the necessity defense.

Answer to Question 25.

(C) is the correct Answer.

Eeny committed murder. Eeny's act of approaching Miney with the knife was the actual and proximate cause of Miney Moe's death. Even though Eeny did not stab Miney Moe, "but for" Eeny's actions, Miney would not have jumped overboard. Proximate cause existed because it was reasonably foreseeable that Eeny's approach with a knife could provoke Miney to jump overboard. Lastly, Eeny's mental state at the time was purposeful — to kill Miney. Thus, Eeny met all of the "ARM" elements (**A**ct, **R**esult and **M**ental state), of murder. Answer (A) is not a correct statement of fact (see the famous case of *Regina v. Dudley and Stephens*, Case Squib Section) and (B) and (D) are lesser included offenses within Answer (C). Answer (E) contradicts the correct causation analysis.

Answer to Question 26.

(B) is the best Answer.

(B) reiterates the Principle of Legality; specifically, the principle of legality requires in part that crime creation must not be retroactive. This principle is embodied in the due process clause and the prohibition of ex post facto laws in the Constitution. (The ex post facto clause essentially prohibits the legislature from enacting retroactive laws.) (A) is wrong because it is not the sole issue, and it is in any event debatable whether ordering 100 pizzas is behavior constituting a public mischief. (C) is wrong because Dex was not somehow singled out and punished without a trial, the requirement for bills of attainder. (D) is wrong because there is no such offense as a private mischief. (E) is wrong because it contradicts (B), and the behavior by Dex was not clearly prohibited when the actus reus occurred.

Answer to Question 27.

(C) is the correct Answer.

In order to be found guilty of possession, the defendant must (1) exercise dominion and control over the thing possessed, with (2) the opportunity to dispossess, having (3) knowledge of the thing possessed. If O'Hara did not know that the hold of the ship contained marijuana, he would not have the requisite "knowing" mental state required for the crime of possession. (A) is incorrect because possession may be actual or constructive. Any person involved in a crime is subject to punishment as an accomplice if the assistance is provided intentionally. O'Hara would be culpable despite playing a minor role, so (B) is incorrect. Further, the amount of narcotics of which the defendant had knowledge is immaterial to whether the crime was committed, so (D) is incorrect. The involvement by others does not affect O'Hara's criminality, and thus (E) is incorrect.

Answer to Question 28.

(C) is the correct Answer.

Duress requires a (1) threat of imminent serious bodily harm to the defendant or to a family member (2) by another human being (3) with a reasonable response (4) in a situation that was not the defendant's fault. Phaedrus's coercive conduct provides Jackson with a duress defense, particularly after physical abuse commenced. Answer (A) is incorrect because Jackson was not insane at the time he stole the cigarettes. (B) is wrong because there is no evidence of the cycles necessary to establish the battered person syndrome. (D) is wrong because a police or a government agent has to create and induce the crime in an entrapment situation.

Answer to Question 29.

(D) is the correct choice.

The entrapment defense may be used when the police originate and induce the crime. Here, the crime was originated by Jackson; the police only offered to help after Jackson formulated the idea. This requirement exists in both the subjective and objective tests. The use of deception by the police officer is likely permissible in this case. Answers (A), (B), and (C) are thus incorrect.

Answer to Question 30.

(A) is the correct Answer.

Embezzlement is the fraudulent conversion of the property of another by a person who has lawful possession of the property. (B) and (C) are incorrect since Ferris had lawful possession and did not engage in a trespassory taking as required for larceny. (D) is incorrect since he actually did embezzle the car. (E) is incorrect since he did not obtain title to the property by a fraudulent misrepresentation of material fact.

Answer to Question 31.

(D) is the correct choice.

To be found guilty of felony murder, the death must be directly caused by the felony, the felony must be an inherently dangerous one, and the felony must be independent of murder, meaning it must not be a lesser included offense. Here the felony is aggravated battery, which is a lesser included offense of murder, and therefore not a proper felony upon which to base a felony murder conviction.

(A) is incorrect because while aggravated battery is an inherently dangerous felony, Lana would still be acquitted of felony murder because the felony is not independent. The same is true for (B). (C) is also incorrect because while aggravated battery is an inherently dangerous felony, it is the lack of independence that causes the acquittal.

Answer to Question 32.

(D) is the correct choice.

Under the common law, Costner could not use the duress defense successfully. At common law, the duress defense is not available to murder.

Answers (A), (B) and (C) all assume that the necessity defense can be asserted in this situation, and therefore are all incorrect.

Answer to Question 33.

(A) is the correct choice.

He should be acquitted because assault to commit rape is a specific intent crime. A mistake in a specific intent crime need only be honest to negate the mens rea.

Answer (B) is an inaccurate statement of the law. There is not enough information to determine whether C is incorrect, and therefore it is not the best choice. Answer D is simply incorrect — there will not be a conviction.

Answer to Question 34.

(A) is the correct choice.

Duress occurs where there is coercion by another person, causing the defendant to commit the crime charged. Here, the coercion was by the Terrible Terrorist Troupe, other persons.

Answer (B) is incorrect, because the necessity defense generally applies when the basis of the coercion is nature, such as a hurricane. Answer (C) is incorrect because entrapment focuses on the unfairness of police tactics, and that is not relevant to this question. Answer (D) is also irrelevant here, since the students did not act based on a mental disease or defect.

Answer to Question 35.

(B) is the correct choice.

The major issue in this question is whether defendant has committed an overt act and has gone far enough towards the commission of the crime for the act to be manifest or symbolic of the perpetrator's attempt. Because there was a hidden pocket sewn inside the defendant's sweat pants, the defendant's actions appear to have crossed the threshold for an attempt charge.

Answer (A) is incorrect because there was no evidence of a conspiracy here. Answer (C) is incorrect because Katie was arrested before she completed the crime. Answer (D) is wrong because it contradicts the correct answer, which is (B).

Answer to Question 36.

(D) is the correct choice.

Even though Emma did not participate in the robbery, as a conspirator she will be held liable for all crimes in furtherance of the object crime. This is called the Pinkerton Rule. At common law, the conspiracy charge does not merge with the substantive offense, and therefore Emma can be convicted of both conspiracy and bank robbery.

Answers (A), (B), (C) and (E) all are incorrect statements of the law.

Answer to Question 37.

(C) is the correct choice.

Amy can be charged with the same crimes as Emma, conspiracy to commit bank robbery and bank robbery. Simply because Amy is in jail does not mean she will not be held responsible for crimes in furtherance of the conspiracy. She is a conspirator, along with Roy and Emma, and will be held responsible for Roy's actions in committing the bank robbery.

Answers (A), (B) and (D) incorrectly state the law.

Answer to Question 38.

(B) is the correct choice.

Roy is the perpetrator of the robbery and a member of the conspiracy, and can be held responsible for both.

All of the other answers are incorrect conclusions.

Answer to Question 39.

(E) is the correct choice.

Unless Joan has a legal duty to act, her omission in watching Jim drown violates a moral duty, but not a legal one. Based on case law, Jim jumped in on his own and is solely responsible for his conduct.

Answer (A), solicitation, is incorrect because Joan did not ask Jim to commit a crime for her. Joan has not committed homicide since her act is not likely the proximate cause of Jim's death. Answer (C) does not state a common law crime. Answer (D) offers a tort, but not a crime.

Answer to Question 40.

(D) is the correct choice.

Since Arnold did not intend to harm Maria's boyfriend, he at most acted recklessly.

He did not commit homicide, answer (A), since no one was killed. There was no attempted murder either, answer (B), since Arnold did not act with the intent to kill anyone. Answer (C), solicitation, does not fit the facts of this question.

Answer to Question 41.

(C) is the correct choice.

The Big Man did not attempt to kill anyone, and therefore answer (A) is incorrect. He likely did not commit depraved heart murder either, since his conduct was probably not grossly reckless, even though it may have constituted simple recklessness, so (B) is incorrect. Answer (D) is incorrect, because even if the Big Man had committed a felony assault, it would not be an independent felony qualifying for felony murder. Answer (E) is incorrect, because at the very least, the Big Man committed an intent to scare assault.

Answer to Question 42.

(B) is the correct choice.

There was no underlying felony conviction here. Once Jane is acquitted of the arson charge, she cannot be convicted of felony murder.

(A) and (C) do not provide a similarly valid rationale.

Answer to Question 43.

(C) is the correct choice.

Answer (A) is incorrect because there was no intent to kill here, and while the scratch may have constituted a battery, it was likely not grossly reckless as required for depraved heart murder. Answer (D) is likely incorrect because, while there was a battery, the resulting death will probably increase the crime to manslaughter. Answer E is incorrect, because at the very least, there was an unlawful purposeful touching of another human being, which constitutes a battery.

Answer to Question 44.

(A) is the correct choice.

The defendant, Gaston Snow, intended to seriously injure another individual. Even though the defendant had bad aim and hit a different person, the defendant meets all of the requirements for attempt to seriously injure a human being. Therefore, the conduct likely constitutes intent to seriously injure another murder.

Answer (B), manslaughter, is the second logical choice. Answers (C) and (D) are only applicable if the conduct is not murder or manslaughter, which would be unlikely.

Answer to Question 45.

(C) is the correct choice.

Sarah's actions evidence a gross indifference to human life, meeting the requirements for depraved heart murder. In essence, she acted with gross recklessness.

(A), (B), (D), and (E) are not as valid.

Answer to Question 46.

(B) is the correct choice.

Intent to kill murder is correct because there was sufficient time to cool off after the assault. Based on case law, a reasonable person would have cooled off several days after such an event.

Answer (A) is incorrect. Even though there was an intent to kill, the defendant may still be eligible for the partial defense of heat of passion manslaughter. Answer (C) is incorrect because there was adequate provocation. Answer (D) is incorrect because defendant likely will not qualify for heat of passion manslaughter under the circumstances of this case. Answer (E) is also wrong. The defendant will be convicted of intent to kill murder in all likelihood.

X. PRACTICE ESSAY QUESTIONS

Question 1

The following story is sad but thankfully untrue. It is also a criminal law examination question.

"The Beginning"

One cold, miserable winter day four wide-eyed and innocent college juniors, Adam, Bill, Carl, and Don (nicknamed A, B, C, and D, respectively), decided to travel south to Fort Lauderdale for adventure. After all, they figured, what could it hurt? And adventure is what they found.

"Anna" was the name of the featured entertainer at the group's first stop in South Florida, "The Cabaret." The impressionable Adam soon fell madly in love with Anna and began to argue with the bartender, Zach (nicknamed "Z") about her.

A, B, C, and D eventually left the bar after each had consumed several beers. The group entered their car to leave. Adam drove. It was his car, and, after all, what could it hurt? Coincidentally, Zach, the bartender, was leaving as well. Because of the design of the parking lot, Zach's car and the boys' car blocked each other's path to the exit. One of the cars would have to back up. Neither driver — Adam or Zach — budged.

Instead, Adam and Zach resumed their argument. During the renewed hostilities, Zach yelled at Adam, "You probably didn't even fight in 'Nam, chicken!" With a flash, Adam saw with astonishing vividness the helicopters and death of Vietnam all around him, as if it were yesterday. He even saw the look on his dying Vietnamese girlfriend's face. The clarity of these recurrent nightmares always scared him.

This time, Zach's instigating pushed Adam deeper into Vietnam. Zach screamed, "Anna's no good, and you're not even good enough for her." Adam knew then that he had to rescue Anna from the enemy Zach. This time he would succeed, unlike his failed attempt to rescue his Vietnamese girlfriend. Adam didn't care if they convicted him and threw him in prison. He could stand it.

Zach pierced Adam's thoughts with another verbal barrage, and soon the two were face to face. Zach sneered: "You don't scare me, farm boy. Come on!" Zach then spit in Adam's face and made several menacing gestures at him. Adam just stood there, his face contorted with pain and rage.

Carl became infuriated and disgusted by the delay. He jokingly shouted to Adam, "Just run him over; let's get out of here." Adam returned to his car, yelled "All right!" and then thought to himself, "You'd kill me Zach if I didn't kill you first. It's you or me, Kid. Sorry but I'm not going to be the one to die." Adam then deliberately ran over Zach, killing him.

"The Middle"

The boys decided to rent a condominium in a multiple building complex. All of the condominium units looked alike, and the units were not clearly numbered. One night Bill drove home alone, intending to turn in early. After all, what could it hurt? When Bill tried the key to the condominium door, it did not work. The failure of the key to open the door was due to the fact that this particular unit was two floors above the boys' unit. Bill thought, however, that the other guys were just playing games. So he pried open a side window with a screwdriver and climbed on through.

Bill was upset and angry about the joke his friends had apparently played on him, so he decided to seek revenge. He saw some cash on the dresser and some jewelry that looked like it belonged to Carl, the member of the group with the most eccentric taste. Bill gathered up the cash and jewelry and went to leave, planning on spending the money and hocking the jewelry in a pawn shop.

As Bill turned to leave, he saw a cockroach. Bill hated cockroaches. Upon seeing this one, he instinctively jumped backwards, knocking over an oil lamp burning low in the living room. The noise woke up the rightful occupant of the condominium, Edie Edison (nicknamed "E").

Edie went to investigate. She arrived in time to observe Bill in the living room near the front door carrying her cash and jewelry. Edie yelled "Stop!"

Bill was extremely startled. He didn't believe that some person he'd never seen before, probably a friend or relative of one of the guys, was yelling at him like that. So Bill ignored Edie.

Then Edie picked up a heavy tire iron, swung it over her head, and charged Bill with the iron poised in an attack position. Bill, an expert in karate, decided to teach this "wild woman" a lesson. Before Edie could swing the iron, Bill gave Edie an unnecessarily vicious kick in the stomach, sending her flying across the room. Edie's head hit the wall and she died instantly.

Meanwhile, the oil lamp that Bill had accidentally knocked over had set the curtains on fire, and the whole condominium unit became an inferno. Bill managed to stumble out of the unit to safety.

"Towards the End"

Later that evening in another part of town, Carl and Don learned that Bill had been arrested and detained at the County Jail. Carl and Don started walking toward the jail. This way, they would save taxi fare. Carl wondered where they were going to get the $150 to bail Bill out of jail. That wasn't in the budget, and they just didn't have that kind of money.

Their path took them through a part of town where there had been an unusual number of recent thefts and robberies, particularly purse snatchings. The twosome soon came across a sleeping drunk lying with an open bottle of very smelly Southern Comfort whiskey in his hand. Carl couldn't believe their luck. Sticking out of the person's pocket were two $100 dollar bills.

Don saw the money as well, but wasn't as excited. Carl suggested to Don that "We should liberate that money, don't you think?" Don responded without enthusiasm, saying "I'm not sure it would be right, Carl."

"Look Don, I could make you take it, you know? And you know what kind of harm could come to you if you don't. I've been caught stealing twice before, but there's no way we're going to get caught tonight. I tell you what, all you have to do is look around and make sure no one is coming. What do you say?"

"Well, I could use the money, I guess. Okay."

Carl kicked the drunken individual to make sure he was still sound asleep, and then "liberated" the two $100 bills.

As Carl and Don started walking away, the "bum" jumped up and pointed a snub-nosed automatic gun at his assailants. "Merry Christmas! This is the police! Put your hands up!" he yelled while flashing his badge.

Discuss all possible crimes committed by A, B, C, and D and any possible defenses they may assert.

Question 2

"Twas the night before Christmas, and all through the house, not a creature was stirring, not even a mouse..."

Boredom for even the town's mice was nothing new for Lake Woebechobee. Yet it was anything but boring this Christmas eve. On this night, the sleepy little hamlet located seven miles northwest of Ft. Lauderdale played host to some most unwelcome visitors, the notorious Arthur "St. Nicholas" Deco and friends. The Art Deco Gang took up residence at the only residence in town for paying guests — the Hyatt Regency Governor's on the far end of Main Street.

Minutes after unpacking, gang member Bobbi Blitzen took a stroll outside of the hotel in the crisp night air. Bobbi noticed a Salvation Army Santa attempting to do a good deed — open the door of someone else's parked car to turn its lights off. The man, dressed in a Santa outfit, was fiddling with the door just as the car's owner, Halley Comet, walked out of the Governor's Bar. Blitzen, noticing the frightened look in Comet's eyes and a properly registered .47 magnum pistol sticking out of Comet's pocket, mischievously commented "Looks like a dangerous thief to me!" Comet, upon hearing this, said "I know the law allows me to use lethal force in this situation just like the John Howard and Prentice Rasheed cases!" He then pulled out the gun and shot at the Santa's shoulder. Comet was a terrible shot and the bullet erroneously pierced the Santa's heart, killing him instantly.

Later that evening in the Governor's bar, Art "St. Nick" Deco struck up a friendship with Donder Dosannah Dannah, a very naive nineteen-year-old geology student (who, for example, pondered such things as whether he would get wet if he went for a swim in melted dry ice; and why do humming birds hum?). They were joined in the bar by Moose Springstream, the multi-talented gang enforcer and accountant. Art and Moose decided to play a joke on Donder. They told him that to be a member of their gang, Donder must complete an initiation ritual. Donder was reluctant to join, but after several minutes of cajoling, finally agreed. The ritual Art and Moose thought up consisted of Donder making a fire in the fireplace of Mr. O'Leary's Rooming House. Unbeknownst to Donder, the fireplace at O'Leary's was a fake one and the fire would undoubtably spread if lit. While Art and Moose knew of this danger, they really didn't care one way or the other about what happened after Donder lit the fire. However, since they were going to this much trouble to play a joke, Art and Moose decided that while the joke was in progress and everyone was preoccupied with Donder, they would knock out a side window of the building and grab a couple of the Sony television sets from within the house.

Donder walked to the door of O'Leary's at 9 p.m. on Christmas eve carefully juggling two ten gallon cans containing a highly flammable kerosene-gasoline mixture — which he knew he had better not drop — as well as three logs, ten packs of matches and a flashlight. He informed the proprietor, Mr. O'Leary, that he was Fireplace Inspector Clousseau sent to inspect the fireplace. The proprietor, recognizing this as a joke, refused to let him in. Springstream and Deco, seeing that their plan was in trouble, went to the door to convince the proprietor to let Donder in. Art and Moose began to argue with the proprietor when Art exploded, punching Mr. O'Leary viciously in the face. O'Leary slowly raised himself off of the ground and started to say "Go ahead, make my day" when Art pulled out a gun for which he had a valid permit and prepared to hit O'Leary on the shoulder with the gun butt to subdue him. As he was in the process of swinging his arm over his head towards O'Leary, the gun accidently discharged, killing Vanna Viktum, who was nosily looking out her window in the house across the street. Upon hearing the gun shot, a frightened Donder accidentally dropped the kerosene, igniting the house. The house began to burn to the ground. Moose then sneaked around the side and smashed a window, taking several television sets from the burning house.

What are the potential criminal liabilities and defenses of the parties? Explain.

NOTE: (1) ASSUME THAT ALL CRIMES ARE FELONIES.

(2) THE COMMON LAW APPLIES WITH THE EXCEPTION OF THE FOLLOWING STATUTES:

STATE STATUTE 776.031.

USE OF FORCE IN DEFENSE OF OTHERS.

A person is justified in the use of force, except deadly force, against another when and to the extent that he reasonably believes that such conduct is necessary to prevent or terminate such other's trespass on, or other tortious or criminal interference with, either real property other than a dwelling or personal property, lawfully in his possession or in the possession of another who is a member of his immediate family or household or of a person whose property he has a legal duty to protect. However, he is justified in the use of deadly force only if he reasonably believes that such force is necessary to prevent the imminent commission of a forcible felony.

STATE STATUTE, 776.06.

FORCIBLE FELONY.

"Forcible felony" means treason, murder, manslaughter, sexual battery, robbery, burglary, arson, kidnapping, aggravated assault, aggravated battery, aircraft piracy, unlawful throwing, placing or discharging of a destructive device or bomb, and any other felony which involves the use or threat of physical force or violence against any individual.

Question 3

Maria Misguided was a student at the Highlight College of Law. One evening, as Maria was about to leave the school, she reached down to pick up her compact umbrella and go home. She reached for the umbrella, but mistakenly grabbed Susie's large beach umbrella instead. As Maria walked away with the umbrella, a little bag dropped out of it. Maria picked it up and exclaimed "Why, cocaine!" Maria then shoved the cocaine in a hollowed out space under the school steps "for safekeeping," and continued to walk home.

Later that week, Maria became restless. She called up her friend Sam Sluggo, who was a member of the same gun club as Maria. "Hey, Sam," she said, "could you send me an extra thousand rounds of ammo this month since I am going to knock off a local bank?" Sam said "Sure, my pleasure; but that will cost you extra!" Maria received the ammo, and decided to steal her neighbor's rifle for additional firepower. That night, she broke into her neighbor's house. Just before taking the gun, however, she changed her mind and left the house undetected.

The next day, Maria proceeded to the local bank, the Southeast Bank of Barnett. Maria walked into the bank and approached the teller's window. She realized, however, that while she had remembered the gun and the robbery note, she had forgotten the ammo. As she turned around to get the ammo from the car, she tripped. The gun fell out of her pocket and discharged, killing Teller Number Three.

Meanwhile, in another part of town, Sam Sluggo was having a drink at the local watering hole, Governor's Bar and Grill. Sluggo soon became embroiled in an argument with another patron. The other patron, Vinnie the Victim, told Sluggo "You are really a nogoodnik. As a matter of fact, you are a bad, rotten, horrible person." Before Sluggo responded, he saw his wife, Mrs. Susie Sluggo, from whom he was separated (although they maintained the same residence, bank accounts, and tax return status as man and wife). When his wife's head was turned, he picked her pocket and took her wallet, which contained $347. While Sluggo was picking the pocket, Vinnie continued to yell insults. Suddenly, he spit at Sam, hitting him in the foot, and threw a beer all over him. Sam, believing it was the patron sitting next to Vinnie — Bobbie Badluck — who had spit at him and thrown the beer, pulled a knife and stabbed her, killing her.

As Sluggo was leaving the bar, his friend Al — who was in the bar at the time of the killing but who had not observed the fatal events — offered him a ride home, saying, "Don't worry, be happy." Sluggo accepted the ride graciously. As Sluggo later left the car, Al told him "You can call me Al, anytime you want."

What, if any, crimes have the surviving participants in the above fact situation committed? Explain.

In addition to the common law crimes, the following statute also applies:

Drug trafficking.

    1. Except as otherwise authorized in chapter 23:

    (a) Any person who knowingly sells, purchases, manufactures, delivers or transports a controlled substance into this state, or has actual or constructive possession of any such controlled substance, is guilty of a felony in the first degree.

    (b) For the purposes of this section, a controlled substance is any drug which has the potential for abuse and has restricted or no medical benefits. As proscribed in section 23.02, such drugs are cocaine, heroin, marijuana, methamphetamine, and morphine.

    (c) In compliance with section 23.03 (1)(a), a controlled substance is in the constructive possession of an individual when such an individual exercises dominion and control over the substance.

QUESTION 4: "O.P.M."

Horace Debussy Jones's company, O.P.M., was faltering badly, and he needed a new infusion of money immediately. Since no bank would give Horace a loan, he knew he would need not one but several dastardly plans by which to keep his company afloat.

One fine sunny June morning, Horace awoke with a start. This would be the day he would make his money. He realized he would first need transportation. So he went to the nearby Jaguar automobile showroom, and test drove a brand new Jaguar convertible. When the salesperson left the car to obtain some paperwork, Horace quickly drove away without the salesperson knowing what had occurred. Horace put the top down, and drove around for a while, until he realized he needed gas. Although he knew he had no cash, he did have a fake $50 bill, which he used to pay for a full tank of gas. Soon he drove to a wealthy suburb of the city, where he saw an elderly lady walking six poodles. Horace jumped out of his car and said to the woman, "Give me your money or I'll blow up your home." Horace knew that what rich people hated most was the prospect of being poor. The woman gave Horace $30,000 in jewelry, and Horace fled.

By now it was getting dark out. Horace passed a well-dressed man and stopped his car just behind the man. Horace picked up a rock and hit the man over the head, knocking him unconscious. Horace then leafed through his pockets, and took a billfold with $20,000 in it.

Horace stopped at a nearby house, admiring what appeared to be several priceless paintings inside. It was dark, and becoming cooler. It was dinner time as well. Horace had an idea. He ran to the nearby pizza restaurant, and then returned to the house. He rang the doorbell, and when the butler answered, said that he was delivering five pizzas courtesy of the neighbors. The butler was bewildered by this turn of events, but permitted Horace to bring the pizza into the pantry, especially since, the pepperoni and mushrooms smelled quite good. As soon as Horace entered the pantry, he ran upstairs to steal one of the priceless works of art. To his surprise, the "paintings" were simply holographic projections on the wall. There were no actual paintings at all.

As Horace was about to climb out of the upstairs window with great disgust, he noticed a young adult woman sleeping in the adjacent bedroom. He went over to her, gave her a big kiss, and jumped out of the window into the thorny rose bushes below. Scratched and empty-handed, he ran away as fast as he could to the screams of the now wide awake woman in the background.

He returned to his Jaguar, and drove away. Soon, he saw a house with an open window. He stopped his car and approached the house. Mischievously, he threw a lighted match onto its beautiful wooden living room floor. He then returned to the Jaguar and drove home. The entire floor of the house became scorched and caved in as a result of small fires. The house, however, did not burn down.

When Horace returned home, he dumped the jewelry and money on the bed, thinking about how rich he would one day be. He sighed and said, "O.P.M., 'Other People's Money'; the name is certainly true to form."

What crimes, if any, has Horace committed?

QUESTION 5: "The New Ninja Turtles"

In a remote area of Fort Lauderdale, Florida, considerably west of the Turnpike, a small neighborhood existed. In it was a club for youths in their twenties called the New Ninja Turtles Club. The "founding fathers" of this club included Leonardo (L), Raphaelo (R), Donatella (D), and Bo (B). A motto of the club was "Liberty, fraternity and pizza!"

Raphaelo, the daring one, decided one day to steal some money from the home of the richest person in South Florida. After thinking through the possibilities — Don Johnson? Bebe Rebozo? Jackie Gleason's nephew? — he hit upon a choice which would make a statement — Gloria Estefan! Raphaelo approached Bo and asked Bo if he wanted to serve as a lookout during the theft. Bo answered, "Bo knows baseball, Bo knows football, and Bo knows tennis, but Bo doesn't know lookouts! I won't do it for you; no way!" After Bo said this, Raphaelo looked kind of sad, so Bo added, "But I do know a quick exit away from the Estefan residence." Bo then proceeded to tell Raphaelo about the special getaway.

When Bo walked away, he saw a frog and jumped. "Boy," he said, "I hope no one else learns that I hate frogs with a passion!" Two minutes later, Bo was startled when a huge green thing came teetering out of the woods about twenty feet away from Bo. "Yuck! A giant six foot frog!", Bo screamed. He took out his gun and shot immediately at the "frog," killing it with a single shot. Bo turned to run away. Within seconds, he had a sinking feeling when it dawned on him that it was not a frog after all that he had shot, but actually a man dressed up as a Leprechaun. "I guess that makes sense," Bo thought, "since this is St. Patrick's Day."

Meanwhile, Raphaelo had asked Donatella to be the getaway driver for the Estefan heist, and Donatella agreed. Raphaelo believed that if he entered the mansion at 4:56 p.m., it would be sufficiently dark out to sneak in undetected. Technically, at that time it was still daytime. At precisely 4:52 p.m., Raphaelo opened the basement window with his "thief" brand crow bar and entered the mansion. As Raphaelo tiptoed towards the bedroom, Emilio (E), Gloria's husband, heard him. Emilio calmly picked up his gun, which he called "Sweet Music," and went into the room where the noise had come from. Emilio, thinking that the intruder was a crazed fan of Gloria's, yelled to Raphaelo to "get out." When Raphaelo did not move, Emilio yelled "now!" Raphaelo turned and ran for the front door while Emilio chased him, yelling "The music is gonna get you!" Emilio fired a warning shot in Raphaelo's direction, but well away from his person. The butler, Mr. Gilbert, thought a gun fight was occurring, ran upstairs, and arrived just in time to accidentally step in front of Emilio's second warning shot. Mr. Gilbert was immediately killed by the bullet. Raphaelo and getaway driver Donatella escaped.

That evening, the New Ninja Turtles gathered at their clubhouse to play cards, with each hand worth no more than $5.00. After the players drank several beers, Donatella started taunting Leonardo because Donatella was winning most of the hands; she knew Leonardo was a sore loser with a bad temper. Donatella said, "You big lug, you're a loser!" Donatella then called him a chicken. A frustrated Leonardo said, "Oh, yeah?" and winged a card at Donatella, hitting her in the nose. Raphaelo was getting tired of this bickering, so he said, "Leonardo, you mealymouthed turtle, you've ruined the game." This statement infuriated Leonardo even further, and he retorted "Okay, you and I, Raphaelo, head to head, one hand of black jack." Raphaelo responded that he did not want to play. Leonardo pointed out that Raphaelo did own that "fake rolex watch worth three bucks," that Leonardo had always wanted. Raphaelo still did not want to play, but Leonardo, after standing up — all 6' 8" of him — made it very clear that Raphaelo had no choice. The two played for Raphaelo's watch, which, unbeknownst to everyone, was a valuable fake rolex indeed — worth $295.95 as a limited edition fake. Just as the two finished the hand, the police burst in and arrested Leonardo, Raphaelo, and Bo. Raphaelo looked at Donatella and said "What's the matter with her, why don't you arrest her too?" Donatella just looked at him coolly, flipped out her police badge indicating she was an undercover police officer, and said "Book 'em."

What possible crimes have been committed by Raphaelo, Leonardo, and Bo? Explain. Please note that the common law applies unless instructed to the contrary. In addition to the common law crimes, the following statute also applies:

§849.08 gambling — whoever plays or engages in any game at cards, keno, roulette, faro, or any other game of chance, at any place, by any device whatever, for money or other thing of value, shall be guilty of a misdemeanor of the second degree if such single round, hand, or game exceeds $10.00 in value.

SHORT ANSWER QUESTIONS

1. The victim met Dennis in a bar, where the two had numerous drinks. When Dennis offered to drive her home, she accepted. On the way home, the victim became unconscious from the excessive amount of alcohol she drank. Dennis, knowing that the victim was utterly senseless and incapable of consenting to intercourse at the time, pulled the car over and had intercourse with her anyway. Has Dennis committed the crime of rape?

2. Rita Alexander was shopping in front of the local department store. As she crossed the street in front of the store, Ray Patton swiftly grabbed her purse, throwing her arm back "a little bit." Patton then fled with the purse. In fact, the purse was gone before Rita Alexander even realized what had happened. Is this purse snatching a robbery?

3. Michael Angelo picked Raphael's pocket. Raphael discovered what occurred after the fact, and confronted the perpetrator, with the result that the perpetrator hit Raphael in the face. Has a robbery occurred?

4. Sara walked up to her victim, Jillian, and his her over the head with a blunt object, knocking her unconscious. Sara then proceeded to pick the pocket of Jillian. Has Sara committed a robbery?

5. Blue sold Green her car in exchange for a diamond ring that Green falsely represented to be a priceless family heirloom. It was a fake. What crime has Blue committed?

6. Fred had this great scheme going. He would walk into an auto show room and test drive a care with a salesperson. After he and the salesperson returned to the lot, and the salesperson left the car to obtain paper work, Fred would surreptitiously drive away without the salesperson watching. He would never return, having intended to steal the car all along. What crime has Fred committed?

7. Wild Scheme No. 3078: The defendants would pretend to find a pocket book containing several thousand dollars. They would offer to divide the money up with the victim once it is reported if the victim would give them $100 to show his good faith. When the victim would turn over the money, the defendant would disappear. What crime have the defendants committed?

8. After a busy night at the checkout counter at Publix, Cashier No. 7 took the receipts, pocketed half, and deposited the other half with the Publix supervisor. The Publix attendant has committed what crime?

9. Scam No. 3,400,700: Dwayne drove his T-bird into the gas station and said "Fill 'er up." He did not intend to pay for the gas, and after the tank was full and the cap put back on, he drove away while the attendant was not looking. What crime has Dwayne committed?

10. Thurston sees that his neighbor's back window is partially opened and that no one is home. Thurston moves the window open slightly and slips in through the window intending to take his neighbor's signed Picasso painting. He could not find the painting and slipped out through the same window just before dawn. Has Thurston committed a crime?

11. Malicious Mel walked up to Jane who was sitting on a horse. Without her permission he leans over and kisses her and then whips the horse, causing it to bolt and Jane to fall. Has Mel committed a crime?

12. Peter Pyromaniac decided to fool around on the floor of a friend's house, placing all sorts of candles and matches on the floor to see if he could burn it without creating an actual fire. The entire floor became scorched, but the house did not burn down (although small fires were caused). What crime, if any, has Peter committed?

Suggested Analysis to the Essay Questions

Answer to Question No. 1

The first issue is whether Adam can be held liable for running over and killing Zach with his car. **Murder** requires the unlawful killing of another human being with malice aforethought. Adam did the act of running Zach over, causing his death. Adam's act was both the actual and the proximate cause of the death, since it directly killed Zack without any intervening cause. Adam deliberately ran Zach over, meeting the mental state element of malice, since "deliberately" indicates purposefulness.

Adam may be able to raise several defenses. He may be able to raise the defense of **voluntary intoxication**. Voluntary intoxication is a defense to a specific intent crime. If Adam can show that his intoxication negated the mental state required for intent to kill and gross recklessness murder, he would escape a murder conviction and instead be liable for manslaughter, a general intent crime to which voluntary intoxication is not a defense. In this case, Adam's intent to kill apparently was not negated by his intoxication. (It may even have been exacerbated by it.) He would not escape a murder conviction as a result.

Adam also may be able to claim **insanity**. Adam's flashbacks to Vietnam may indicate a major mental disease or defect. To meet the M'Naghten test, Adam must show that, as a result of his mental disease or defect, he either did not know right or wrong in committing the acts in question, or did not know the nature or quality of his acts. It does not appear that Adam was still under the influence of his flashbacks to the Vietnam era when he ran Zach over in the car. Thus, this defense likely is not available.

Adam also may be able to claim **heat of passion manslaughter**. To meet the heat of passion manslaughter test, Adam would have to show that he acted under (1) actual provocation, which was (2) legally adequate; that he (3) acted reasonably, and he did not have (4) adequate time to cool off. Here, the facts indicate that Adam was actually very angry at Zach since Adam's face was "contorted with pain and rage." The conduct by Adam was legally adequate, since Zach made both a menacing gesture at him, indicating a possible **assault**, and spit in Adam's face, which would be a **battery**, defined as the unlawful touching of another human being. It was a battery because the spitting was likely offensive, meeting the test for unlawfulness, namely harmful or offensive. The next provocation element would be whether Adam's response was reasonable under the circumstances. If a reasonable person in his situation would have responded in the same manner, then Adam meets this element. The combination of events, particularly the spitting in the face, likely would provoke an average reasonable person (although it is questionable if the circumstances were sufficiently provocative to kill). Lastly, it further appears that Adam did not have an opportunity to reasonably cool off, since he immediately responded to the provocation, without any significant time lapse.

Adam possibly could claim **self-defense**. Self-defense, using lethal force, may occur if Adam reasonably believed that he was being threatened with imminent serious bodily harm or death. There is no factual support, however, for such a belief. While Adam yelled "You'd kill me Zach, if I didn't kill you first. It's you or me, Kid," there is no indication that Zach was in fact about to strike or harm Adam in any way. Thus, no self-defense exists on these facts. However, if Adam was mistaken, he still could claim self-defense if his **mistaken justification** was both honest and reasonable. While his mistake may have been honest — he may have actually believed that Zach was going to kill him if he did not kill Zach first — there is no indication that under the circumstances a reasonable person would believe that lethal force, or force of any type, was appropriate. Therefore, Adam at most can claim imperfect justification manslaughter, provided that he can show his unreasonable belief was at least honest.

Carl may be charged with murder, but in the capacity of an **accomplice**. If Carl committed **solicitation** — a form of accomplice liability — when he shouted to Adam "Just run him over; let's get out of here," he may be held liable for the object offense, murder. To be guilty of solicitation, a person must encourage, entice, cajole, demand, ask, etc. another to commit a crime for that person, with the intent that the other person commit the crime. Carl met the act requirement, since he did encourage Adam to run Zach over. The facts show that Carl only half-jokingly shouted that statement to Adam, and thus it is questionable as to whether Carl really intended for Adam to commit the murder. The key is the description "half-joking" — did he seriously intend the result, and if only partially, how much?

"The Middle"

Bill may be charged with **burglary**, which in common law is the breaking and entering of the dwelling house of another at nighttime with the intent to commit a felony therein. While Bill did break and enter another person's dwelling, namely that person's condominium, Bill did not intend to commit a felony therein, since he honestly believed he was climbing into his own house. Therefore, he did not commit a burglary.

Bill may be charged with **larceny** as a result of picking up the cash and jewelry that looked like it belonged to his friend Carl. To commit larceny at common law, there must be a trespassory taking and carrying away of the personal property of another with the intent to deprive them of that property permanently. Bill did not have permission to gather the other's cash and jewelry, and thus took it trespassorily. He did take and carry the items away, albeit for a short distance. He admitted that it was not his own property; thus it belonged to another. His intent to deprive them of it permanently existed as a result of his decision to spend the money and hock the jewelry. If hocking jewelry, presumably in a pawnshop, is not sufficient to intend to permanently deprive another of property, then he would not be guilty of larceny of the jewelry.

Bill may be charged with **murder**. Murder is the unlawful killing of another human being with malice aforethought. Bill committed the actus reus by kicking Edie in the stomach. The kick in the stomach directly led to Edie's death when she hit the wall, thus meeting the actual and proximate cause requirements. Bill also apparently intended to hurt Edie seriously, thus meeting the intent to commit serious bodily harm requirement of malice.

Bill may claim **self-defense**. Self-defense using lethal force requires a reasonable belief of imminent, serious, bodily harm or death. Bill can claim that he did have such a belief when Edie swung a heavy tire iron over her head and "charged ... with the iron poised in an attack position." The facts indicate, however, that Bill, an expert in karate, gave Edie an unnecessarily vicious kick, indicating that the force used to defend himself was excessive. If so, Bill will not be able to rely on self-defense.

The **duty to retreat** may apply. Under this doctrine, an individual who is faced with using self-defense to lethal force must retreat if she can knowingly do so with complete safety. One exception to this rule is if the person attacked is lawfully in his or her own home. Bill may claim that he reasonably mistook the other's condo for his own home, and therefore reasonably believed that he was not required to retreat.

Finally, Bill may be charged with **arson**, which at common law is the malicious burning of the dwelling house of another. Here, Bill committed the act of burning the dwelling house of another when he knocked over an oil lamp that set fire to the curtains and the entire condominium. He likely would not be guilty of maliciously doing so unless his "accidental" toppling of the oil lamp constituted recklessness, which is the minimum standard available for malice. His "accidental" behavior could be reckless, negligent, or non-negligent. Additional information is needed to clarify the situation.

"Towards the End"

Carl and Don may be charged with **larceny**. Larceny is the trespassory taking and carrying away of the personal property of another with the intent to deprive them of it permanently. When Carl took the two $100 bills, he did not have permission to do so. It was the personal property of another, and he intended to keep the money and deprive the other of that property permanently. Therefore, Carl committed larceny. Don could be charged with larceny as an **accomplice** since he provided intentional assistance by serving as a lookout. He also stated in response to Carl's question that he "could use the money," indicating he intentionally aided and abetted Don in stealing the money.

Carl and Don can both claim **entrapment**. The entrapment defense is defined either subjectively or objectively. The subjective test requires that the police originate and induce the crime and that the defendant not be predisposed towards committing the crime. The objective test asks whether a reasonable law-abiding citizen would have been induced by the police tactics to commit a crime. Here, the crime was originated and induced by the undercover police officer. If the subjective test applies and Carl and Don were predisposed towards committing the crime, they still could be found guilty. If the objective test applies, the question is whether the police tactics would have induced a reasonable person to take the money. The answer is not likely, since a reasonable law-abiding person could clearly see that the money belonged to another. Yet, realistically, money hanging out of a sleeping person's pocket may be very tempting, even to a reasonable person.

Carl could be found guilty of **battery** on the undercover police officer. Battery is the unlawful touching of another person. Carl kicked the police officer, constituting the touching, and did so deliberately, which meets the minimum mental state of negligence.

Both Carl and Don could be charged with **conspiracy** to commit larceny. They agreed to take the money from the undercover police officer, constituting the actus reus of conspiracy, and they had the intent to take the money as well as the intent to agree. If a conspiracy existed, Don may be held liable for the battery under the **Pinkerton** rule. The battery may be considered in furtherance of the object crime of larceny and reasonably foreseeable under the circumstances.

Finally, Don may be able to claim **duress** as a defense. Duress occurs when the defendant is coerced into committing a crime by a threat of serious bodily harm or death to the defendant or a family member. The defendant's response must be reasonable, and the situation giving rise to the duress cannot be the defendant's fault. Whether Don can claim duress depends on whether Carl's statement to Don "And you know what kind of harm can come to you if you don't [take the money]" indicates that there might be serious bodily harm if Don does not comply with Carl's coercion. It can be reasonably construed as such a threat under the circumstances, and Don's response appears reasonable as well. Finally, while Don was voluntarily walking with Carl, he does not appear to be culpable in creating the duress situation. If Don can raise duress as a defense, he can assert it in response to the conspiracy, the larceny, and the battery charges.

Answer to Question No. 2

Comet

When Comet shot and killed "Santa," he could be found guilty of **manslaughter**. Manslaughter is the unlawful killing of another human being without malice aforethought. Manslaughter is divided into two major categories: voluntary manslaughter, in which there is usually an intent to kill; and involuntary manslaughter, in which the death is generally accidental.

Comet committed the act of shooting "Santa," which had the actual and proximate result of killing him ("instantly"). Comet also had a purposeful mental state in shooting "Santa," as indicated by his statement that he was justified by law in using lethal force. By shooting at Santa's shoulder, his intent was to seriously injure him.

Comet may raise the defense of **protection of property** to justify his conduct. Lethal force is not permitted to defend property, however, unless it is one's habitation, (which it was not), or in prevention of a forcible felony such as robbery. (See statute 776.031.) The theft of the auto does not qualify as a forcible felony, since under the applicable statute, 776.031, auto theft is not one of the enumerated crimes.

Comet also may assert a **mistake in the law** (i.e., that he was permitted to use lethal force under the circumstances), as a defense. While he did make a mistake, ignorance of the law is generally not a defense to criminal conduct. There is no indication that Comet falls within one of the limited exceptions, such as reliance on an official but erroneous interpretation of the law, so his mistake will not exonerate his actions.

Comet might raise the defense of **voluntary intoxication**. Voluntary intoxication acts to negate the mens rea. Here, the facts state that Comet shot the Santa after exiting the Governer's Bar. There is no indication of how much alcohol Comet consumed, if any. Whether alcohol consumption negated Comet's mens rea for the specific intent crime of intent to commit serious bodily harm murder is a question of fact.

Blitzen

By encouraging Comet to shoot the Santa ("Looks like a dangerous thief to me!"), Blitzen may be charged with **solicitation**, and through **accomplice liability**, murder. Solicitation (and accomplice liability), requires the act of entering, encouraging, demanding, asking, etc. another person to commit a crime for the solicitor, with the intent that the other person commit the crime. While Blitzen committed the act of encouraging Comet, it does not appear Blitzen had the requisite intent because he spoke "mischievously." Thus, he probably would not be found guilty of solicitation or murder as an accomplice.

Art and Moose

Art and Moose might be charged with **solicitation**. Solicitation occurs when a person requests, encourages, entices, demands, asks, etc. another to commit a crime for the solicitor, with the intent that the other person commit the crimes. No solicitation likely occurred, however, because the person solicited must be aware that he or she is being asked to commit a crime, and not be duped as was Donder. Since Donder was tricked into committing a crime, he will be viewed as an innocent instrumentality.

Art and Moose are guilty of **conspiracy**. A conspiracy is an agreement between two or more persons to commit a crime (or, as commonly described, to do either an unlawful act or a lawful act by unlawful means), with two intents — an intent to agree and an intent to commit the object crime. (At common law, no overt act in furtherance of the conspiracy was necessary to satisfy the actus reus element.)

Art and Moose agreed that while the "joke" was in progress they would commit a **burglary** knocking out a window of the building where others reside at night to steal television sets from within O'Leary's house. It appears that Art and Moose both intended to agree and to commit the burglary and larceny at the time of the agreement.

Art can be charged with **battery** for punching Mr. O'Leary in the face. Battery is the unlawful touching of another person. Art punched O'Leary intentionally (the facts say "viciously"), meeting the negligence minimum required for battery at common law. He met the unlawful touching actus reus as well when he hit O'Leary harmfully.

Moose may be held liable for Art's **battery** under a **conspiracy** liability theory if the battery is in furtherance of the conspiracy. Under the circumstances, the punch may have permitted Donder to gain entry into O'Leary's rooming house, furthering the aims of the conspiracy. If so, Moose is also guilty of battery.

Art may have **assaulted** O'Leary when Art pulled out a gun and prepared to hit him. An "intentional scaring" form of assault requires the intentional creation of the imminent apprehension of a battery. When Art pulled the gun, it was with the intent to subdue O'Leary. It can be inferred that scaring O'Leary into submission was included within that thought.

Since Art swung the gun over his head towards O'Leary, he committed the actus reus of creating the imminent apprehension of the commission of a battery (it can be assumed that O'Leary would be frightened by observing a gun about to hit him). An attempted battery type of assault may apply as well. Art was in the process of hitting O'Leary, and this would likely be close enough to the completion of the crime to constitute the requisite act, a "substantial step" under the applicable statute 5.01. All that remained to occur was for Art's arm to come crashing down on O'Leary.

When Art accidentally killed Vanna Viktum, he may have committed **felony murder**. A felony murder occurs when there is a killing during the commission or attempted commission of a felony; (provided that the killing directly results from the felony and that the felony is inherently dangerous and independent of murder).

The underlying felony here is the **assault** of O'Leary. (Since Art had a valid permit for the gun, it would not be unlawful possession of a firearm as in the cases **Goodseal** and **Underwood**. (See Case Squibs Section.)) Vanna was killed during the commission of the assault, which may or may not be a felony depending on whether it is categorized as a simple assault (a misdemeanor), or an aggravated assault (a felony). If it is a felony, the death of Vanna was a direct result. It was reasonably foreseeable that a loaded gun being swung over a person's head, under the circumstances, could accidentally discharge and hurt someone seriously. An assault also is inherently dangerous in the abstract, since a reasonable person could be sufficiently frightened to suffer a heart attack or jump into harm's way (i.e., into traffic) as a result. Generally, however, an assault is not considered independent of murder; here, however, there are special circumstances. The assault was not of the victim Vanna, but of someone else. Therefore, while an assault of Vanna would be a lesser included offense of Vanna's murder, an assault of O'Leary generally would be considered independent of **any** crime committed against Vanna. A felony murder charge is consequently permissible.

Moose may be guilty of the **felony murder** of Vanna if, under a conspiracy theory, the accidental death was in furtherance of the conspiracy (i.e., reasonably foreseeable). That would depend on the scope and nature of the agreement, and whether there was any contemplation of the use of, or knowledge about, weapons. Liability would be questionable.

Moose committed **burglary** and **larceny** as a result of the theft of the television sets. He committed a burglary when he broke the side window and entered the rooming house (a dwelling of others), on Christmas eve (at nighttime) with the intent to steal the television sets (likely felony larceny). He committed larceny when he actually took and carried away the sets without permission, intending to steal them.

Art would be held liable for **burglary** and **larceny** as well conspiracy since burglary and larceny were the object crimes of his and Moose's criminal enterprise. Art and Moose also may have committed arson by sending Donder to O'Leary's to light a fire. (In using Donder as an innocent instrumentality, they did not commit solicitation because Donder was duped into acting, and was not consciously aware of the criminal nature of the activity as required.)

Arson is the malicious burning of the dwelling house of another. By sending Donder, Art and Moose caused O'Leary's boarding house to be burned down. Whether they acted maliciously is a difficult question, since it is unclear from the facts whether they intended Donder to actually light a fire, or whether they were just playing a prank. Even if they were joking, sending Donder may very well have been reckless, since they were consciously aware of the risk of a fire if a false fireplace was lit, and that risk certainly could be considered substantial and unjustifiable if Donder had gained entry into O'Leary's.

If Donder's unanticipated conduct in dropping the kerosene-gasoline mixture is viewed as an intervening factor that absolves Art and Moose of responsibility for the fire (this is debatable), Art and Moose could still be prosecuted for **attempted arson**. Whether they intended for Donder to light the fire or were just joking again would be crucial to the mens rea analysis. The act required by the applicable statute, 5.01, would be a substantial step. When Donder brought the tools of the arson to the scene of the crime, this likely fell within one of the examples provided in the statute, 5.01(2)(f), of a substantial step.

Donder

Donder would not be guilty of either **conspiracy** or attempted arson because, as an innocent instrumentality, it appears that he was duped into furthering Art and Moose's criminal enterprise. Donder may be prosecuted for **arson**, however. He performed the act of burning down O'Leary's boarding house. He also arguably had the minimum mental state of recklessness due to the way he was "juggling...a highly flammable kerosene-gasoline mixture" among other things. The facts say that "he knew he had better not drop" the flammable liquid, thus indicating a conscious awareness of the risk of fire. A reasonable person might find that risk to be both substantial and unjustifiable in light of the potential severity of the consequences. If the risk was substantial and unjustifiable, Donder would have acted recklessly and, can be found guilty of arson at common law.

Answer to the Question No. 3

Maria Misguided

Maria Misguided can be charged with **larceny**, which at common law is the trespassory taking and carrying away of the personal property of another with the intent to permanently deprive them of that property. Maria took and carried away without permission Susie's large beach umbrella, intending to keep it for herself at the time she did it. Thus, Maria appears to have met all of the elements of larceny.

However, Maria may claim **mistake in fact**, since she believed the umbrella was hers. Since larceny is a specific intent crime, Maria's mistake need only be honest, which it may or may not have been (more facts are needed). If her mistake was honest, she likely will be found not guilty of larceny.

Maria can be charged with the **possession of cocaine**. To be guilty of possession, Maria must knowingly exercise dominion and control over the thing possessed, having had an opportunity to dispossess it. Here, Maria meets the knowledge requirement by virtue of her exclamation "Why, cocaine!" When she places the cocaine under the school steps, she is still exercising dominion and control over the contraband, although her possession is constructive and not actual. Constructive possession means that she controls the thing, but it is not on her person or within arm's reach. Maria also had an opportunity to dispossess the contraband, but it does not appear that she abandoned it; but rather that she is storing it for a subsequent pickup. Thus, Maria is likely guilty of the possession of cocaine.

Maria may held be liable for **conspiracy** with Sam Sluggo once she requested an extra thousand rounds of ammunition with which to rob a local bank. The question of whether a conspiracy exists depends on whether Sam, a lawful supplier, is considered to be a participant. Sam will be a participant if he has a stake in the outcome. It appears that since Sam is selling Maria extra ammunition, the question exists as to whether the increased volume of sales is attributable to Maria's intended unlawful activity. If Sam is knowingly benefiting from Maria's criminal enterprise (he does say to Maria that it will "cost you extra!") a conspiracy may exist.

Burglary at common law is the breaking and entering into the dwelling house of another at nighttime with the intent to commit a felony therein. Here, Maria broke and entered into her neighbor's house at night time with the intent to steal her neighbor's gun. If stealing the gun is a felony, she has committed burglary. The fact that she did not take the gun is irrelevant to the burglary charge, which is complete once she breaks into the house.

Sum & Substance QUICK REVIEW of Criminal Law

An **attempted bank robbery** occurs if there is an overt act towards the commission of the bank robbery along with an intent to commit the robbery. Maria appeared to intend to commit the robbery of the bank by virtue of her robbery "tools," including the gun and robbery note. She likely met the overt act requirement when she walked into the bank with the robbery note and the gun, an unequivocable act symbolic of an imminent robbery. The fact that she decided to go and get the ammunition prior to the robbery does not constitute an abandonment, but a simple revision of her plans. Thus, Maria is likely guilty of attempted robbery.

Felony murder requires a killing during the commission of a felony or attempted felony. The attempted felony here was robbery, and the killing of Teller Number Three occurred during the commission of the attempted robbery. With felony murder at common law, however, several limitations existed. The death must be a direct result of the felony, the felony must be inherently dangerous, and the felony must be independent of murder. Here, the death was both actually and proximately caused by the felony — it was reasonably foreseeable that when Maria carried a loaded gun into the bank for the purpose of robbing it, someone could get seriously injured. In addition, armed robbery is certainly an inherently dangerous offense to human life. Finally, robbery is not a lesser included offense of murder, and therefore it stands as independent. Maria thus can be convicted of felony murder. She can also be charged with depraved heart (gross recklessness) murder, but the prosecutor would have to prove malice — specifically gross recklessness. A felony murder charge would offer an easier route for the prosecutor, since no malice need be proven.

Sam Sluggo

Sluggo will be guilty of **conspiring** with Maria to rob the bank if, as explained above, he had a stake in the outcome. If Sluggo is a co-conspirator, under the <u>Pinkerton</u> Rule, he will be held liable for all acts in furtherance of the conspiracy. Thus, reasonably foreseeable acts in furtherance of the conspiracy may include Maria's burglary of her neighbor's house to obtain additional fire power, and the killing of Teller Number Three.

Sluggo can be charged with **larceny** for picking his wife's pocket of $347. Larceny is the trespassory taking and carrying away of the personal property of another with the intent to deprive the other of that property permanently. Sluggo certainly did not have permission to take his wife's wallet with the money, and he did take it and carry it away with the intent to keep it permanently. However, at common law, a person is deemed incapable of stealing property from a co-owner. While Sluggo and his wife are separated, they did maintain the same bank accounts, and thus it is likely that Sluggo was already a co-owner of the money he took. If Sluggo does happen to meet all the elements of larceny, he may claim that he was so intoxicated the specific intent required for the crime was negated. This issue would be a question of fact for the factfinder.

Heat of passion manslaughter is a partial defense to an intentional killing. It requires that the defendant be actually and reasonably provoked, and that the provocation be legally adequate. Furthermore, the defendant must not have cooled off; the provocation must provoke a sudden response. Here, the provocation of Vinnie spitting at Sam, hitting him in the foot, and throwing a beer all over him, was legally adequate. Vinnie's actions constituted a battery, and surpassed the "mere words are not enough" limitation. Under the circumstances, it was reasonable for Sam to act the way he did, and it certainly appeared that Sam was actually provoked. Sam's mistake, however, will not be a defense unless it was honest and reasonable. More facts will be necessary to answer this issue.

Al

An **accessory after the fact** knowingly assists a person who has committed a crime in escaping or avoiding apprehension. Here Al did commit the act of assisting Sluggo escape or avoid apprehension. However, it does not appear that Al had the requisite mental state, since he was unaware that several potential crimes occurred inside the bar. Therefore, Al will likely be found not guilty of any crimes.

Answer to the Question No. 4

When Horace walked into the automobile dealer and drove away in the car after test driving it, he committed larceny by trick. Larceny is the trespassory taking and carrying away of the personal property of another with the intent to deprive the other of that property permanently. The trespassory element can be satisfied by fraud or chicanery. The fraud must result only in a change of possession but not title.

Because Horace fraudulently induced the car dealer into letting Horace take a test drive, he obtained possession through fraud. This trickery satisfied the "trespassory taking and carrying away" element of larceny. Since Horace intended to permanently deprive the automobile dealer of the car, Horace satisfied the intent to permanently deprive element as well. Note that Horace would have committed false pretenses if he had obtained the title to the car through trickery.

When Horace paid for the gas with counterfeit money, he committed the crime of false pretenses. This statutory crime requires the following elements: (1) There must be false representation of a material fact; (2) causing the victim; (3) to pass title to his property to the defendant; (4) who knows that the representation is false, but still; (5) intends to defraud the victim. In some jurisdictions, this crime is called "swindling." It is different from larceny by trick, a form of the common law crime of larceny, because it requires that title, and not merely possession, pass from the victim to the defendant. Here, Horace obtained title to the gasoline — that is ownership — and not merely possession through his trickery.

When Horace informed the elderly lady that he would blow up her home if she did not give him money, he committed a robbery. Robbery is defined as larceny from a person or that person's presence by force or fear. The larceny here was the stealing of the woman's jewelry, without permission, with the intent to deprive her of that jewelry permanently. The threat to her home was sufficient to satisfy the "by force or fear" element.

When Horace hit the man on the sidewalk over the head with an object and then picked the man's pocket, he again committed <u>robbery</u>. If the defendant uses any means of force to render the victim unconscious or otherwise helpless, whether by a violent blow or by other means such as administering drugs or alcohol involuntarily, a robbery has occurred. Thus, when Horace rendered his victim unconscious and took the money from the man's billfold without permission he committed robbery.

When Horace entered the house by tricking the butler into believing that Horace was a pizza delivery person, he committed the crime of <u>burglary</u>. Burglary is defined at common law as the breaking and entering of the dwelling house of another at night-time with the intent to commit a felony therein. (Modern statutory definitions have broadened the crime of burglary greatly.) The breaking and entering element was satisfied when Horace tricked the butler into allowing Horace into the house. Any trick used to enter the house under false pretenses, such as an allegation that he is a policeman investigating a crime or something equally outlandish, would satisfy the breaking element. The dwelling house of another element is also met, since this house was occupied by other persons. The facts state that it was at nighttime. When Horace entered, he intended to steal priceless art that he thought was hanging in the house, which would have been a felony. Thus Horace met all of the elements of burglary once he entered the house by tricking the butler into believing he was a pizza delivery person.

When Horace went to steal the art, he may have committed <u>attempted larceny</u>. An attempt crime requires an overt act plus the intent to commit the crime. Horace had the intent to commit larceny, and he did come very close to committing the crime itself. Thus, depending upon how the overt act is defined, Horace likely met the attempted larceny requirement. However, Horace may assert the defense of impossibility. It was impossible for Horace to steal the art, since it was only a holographic representation. Horace would assert the defense of legal impossibility; that is, had the act been completed, it would not have been a crime. Horace would claim that it was impossible to steal a holograph. The state would counter, claiming that it was factual impossibility, which is not a defense to an attempt crime. Factual impossibility occurs when, but for an unforeseen factual or physical circumstance, a crime would have been completed. The state would argue that but for the unforeseen fact that the walls contained holographs, and not the real art, Horace would indeed have stolen one of the paintings and committed larceny. In all likelihood, a court would find Horace not guilty of attempted larceny.

A dissimilar result likely would be reached when Horace kissed the sleeping occupant in her bedroom. This kiss likely would be a <u>battery</u>. A common law battery is defined as the unlawful (harmful or offensive) touching of another human being. Here, Horace touched the woman by kissing her. Since the kiss occurred without permission, it undoubtedly would be considered offensive. Further, because Horace kissed the woman intentionally, he satisfied the mens rea of negligence required for a battery.

Horace also may be found guilty of <u>arson</u> for setting the house on fire as he was driving home. Arson is defined at common law as the malicious burning of the dwelling house of another. The facts indicate that it was a house, and it can reasonably be inferred that it was a dwelling occupied by another person. Horace set the fire intentionally, and the facts support this by suggesting he was acting "mischievously." The only issue is whether a house that does not burn down can still be considered arson. Under the common law, arson simply requires a scorching or burning, and not; a complete burning down of the dwelling house. Subsequently, Horace is likely guilty of arson as well.

Answer to the Question No. 5

RAPHAELO

When Raphaelo asked Bo to help him steal money from the, Estefans' house, he may have committed <u>solicitation</u>. Solicitation is the asking, enticing, encouraging, requesting, etc. another person to commit a crime, with the intent that the other person commit the crime. Here, Raphaelo had the intent that Bo commit a crime. There was no solicitation, however, because solicitation can only occur if the solicitee is asked to be the principal in the crime. Here, Bo was asked to assist Raphaelo. No solicitation has occurred.

Did Raphaelo commit <u>conspiracy</u> when he asked Bo to help him steal money from the Estefan house? The answer is no, since conspiracy requires an agreement between two or more persons to commit a crime with the intent that they agreed and the intent to commit the crime. Here, Bo refused Raphaelo's request, and thus there was no agreement.

When Donatella agreed to be the getaway driver for the Estefan heist, there may have been a <u>conspiracy</u>. (See definition above.) However, Donatella turned out to be an undercover police officer, and may not have intended to commit the crimes charged. If the unilateral theory of conspiracy governs, a defendant can be found guilty even though he conspired with an undercover police officer. If the bilateral approach governs, and it takes two or more persons to intend to commit the crime, then Raphaelo may not be found guilty of conspiracy.

When Raphaelo broke into the house, he may not have committed a <u>burglary</u>. A burglary at common law requires a breaking and entering of a dwelling house of another at nighttime with the intent to commit a felony therein. Raphaelo did break into the Estefan mansion, which was the dwelling house of another, and he did intend to commit a felony inside, that is, larceny. However, there is a question as to whether it was nighttime. The facts say that it was not nighttime (and, by inference, not dark outside). Therefore, no common law burglary occurred. However, Raphaelo may still be found guilty of attempted burglary, since he did appear to commit an overt act and had the concurrent intent to commit a burglary. Even if charged with attempted burglary, Raphaelo may raise the defense of impossibility. If his failure to successfully burglarize the house was deemed to be legal impossibility, it would be a defense to the attempted burglary charge. If it was deemed to be factual impossibility, however, it would be no defense. In all likelihood, a court would find that this situation was factual impossibility, and but for the unforeseen occurrence that it was daylight and not nighttime, there would have been a conviction.

If there was an attempted burglary, Raphaelo may be held liable for the death of the butler under a <u>felony murder</u> theory. A felony murder is a killing that occurred during the commission of a felony or an attempted felony. Several felony murder limitations exist: (1) there must be a direct link between the felony and the killing; (2) the felony or attempted felony must be inherently dangerous; and (3) the felony must be independent of murder. These prerequisites are satisfied in this case. The death was directly and proximately caused by the break in of the house. Burglary is considered to be an inherently dangerous crime, since it is reasonably foreseeable that people may die or be seriously injured during the course of a burglary. Finally, burglary is independent of murder, since it is not a lesser included offense.

Since the defendant or co-defendants did not do the killing, but one of the victims did, a special test governs. If a nondefendant such as a bystander or a victim kills someone other than the perpetrators of a crime, the defendants will only be held liable if the proximate cause theory applies. Under the wide open proximate cause theory, defendants are held liable for all killings that occur during the course of a felony. The rationale is that the defendants set the wheels in motion, and should be held responsible for any reasonably foreseeable harm. If the limited proximate cause theory applies, the defendants would be liable only for any deaths caused to non-defendants. Under the limited proximate cause approach, defendants are not liable if a bystander or victim actually kills one of the defendants.

BO

When Bo offered to provide a shortcut for the getaway, he became an <u>accomplice</u>. An accomplice is someone who aids and abets in the commission of a crime, with the intent to do so. When Bo gratuitously assisted Raphaelo in the crime by offering a special getaway with the intent to assist, he met the actus reus requirement. His intention of assisting can be inferred. As a result, Bo becomes liable for the object crime with which he assisted, and in some jurisdictions, any deaths that are reasonably foreseeable in furtherance of the object crime. Since there was no agreement between the two, no conspiracy occurred.

When Bo shot the "giant frog" he in fact killed a person, and he may be liable for <u>murder</u>. Murder is the unlawful killing of another human being with malice aforethought. This could not be considered, however, intent to kill murder, since Bob did not intend to kill a human being, nor even to seriously injure one. Bo was mistaken about the nature of the "animal" and his mistake likely would be considered unreasonable. Therefore, Bo would most likely be guilty of negligence/recklessness manslaughter.

LEONARDO

When Leonardo hit Donatella in the nose with the card, he likely committed a battery. Battery at common law is the unlawful (harmful or offensive) touching of another human being. He did touch Donatella with the card — he need not touch her with his person — and the touching was likely harmful or offensive as required. Finally, Leonardo acted intentionally, and thus met the negligence minimum required for battery.

There are two tests for entrapment, an objective and a subjective one. The objective one focuses on the tactics of the police and looks to see whether those tactics induced and created the crime, as well as whether those tactics persuaded a reasonable person of ordinary intelligence to commit such a crime. If the subjective test applies, the court looks to see if the defendant was predisposed to commit the crime in addition to whether the police tactics created or initiated the crime. Here, the question is whether Donatella created the battery, and whether she would have induced a reasonable person to commit the crime. Donatella's taunting of Leonardo would not likely be sufficient to attribute the creation of the crime to her, and the entrapment defense would likely fail.

The facts indicate that the card players drank several beers, and Leonardo may try to claim intoxication as a defense to the battery charge. Intoxication is a defense to a specific intent crime. Since battery is a general intent crime, intoxication would not be a defense. The voluntary intoxication is itself unreasonable, thus satisfying the minimum negligence requirements for the mental state of a battery.

A conspiracy requires an agreement between two or more persons along with the intent to agree and the intent to commit the crime. Here, Leonardo agreed with the others to play cards and surely intended to play. Thus, since more than the two individuals necessary for conspiracy agreed to play, the two conspirators would not be protected by Wharton's Rule (which requires that a conspiracy charge be based on more than the minimum number of individuals required to commit the crime).

The statutory crime of gambling does not appear to require any mental state. The tradition in the common law, however, is to imply a minimum culpability, generally negligence, when a mental state has been omitted. Thus, negligence can be implied in the statute on gambling as the minimum mental state required. Strict liability often applies, however, to valuing stolen goods. Thus, the degree of the crime would depend on the objective value of the watch.

ANSWERS TO SHORT ANSWER QUESTIONS

1. Although rape is traditionally defined as "the carnal knowledge of a woman by force and against her will," the "by force" part of the definition has been interpreted to include without the victim's consent. A woman who is unconscious cannot consent, and thus Dennis has committed rape.

2. A robbery requires the use of force or a threat of imminent force. Historically, a simple purse snatch or a sudden taking of other property from a person of another has not been considered to involve sufficient force to constitute a robbery. Instead, without sufficient violence, the crime is generally considered to be larceny from the person. See *People v. Patton*, 76 Ill. 2d 45 (1979). This conclusion, however, is the subject of some dispute. In *Commonwealth v. Jones*, 283 N.E.2d 840 (Mass. 1972), the Supreme Judicial Court of Massachusetts decided that purse snatching alone can satisfy the "force" element.

3. No. A robbery will only occur if the violence or fear occurs during the taking. For example, if the pick-pocket jostles the victim or there is a struggle over the property, a robbery will have occurred.

4. Yes. If the defendant uses any means of force to render the victim unconscious or otherwise helpless, whether by a violent blow or other means such as administering drugs or alcohol involuntarily, a robbery will have occurred.

5. Blue has committed the crime of false pretenses, which originated not in the common law but by statute. It contains the following elements: (1) there must be a false representation of a material fact (2) causing the victim (3) to pass title (and not just possession) of his property to the defendant, (4) who knows that the representation is false, but still (5) intends to defraud the victim. This crime has been called in some jurisdictions "swindling" and is different from larceny by trick, a form of the common law crime of larceny, because false pretenses requires that title pass from the victim to the defendant, and not merely possession as in larceny by trick.

6. Larceny by trick. Because Fred intended to take the car all along, the fact that he obtained possession, but not title, through fraud makes the crime a form of larceny, and not false pretenses.

7. Because title is obtained to the money, and not merely possession, this would constitute false pretenses, and not larceny by trick.

8. The attendant has committed embezzlement, not larceny. The major difference between larceny and embezzlement is that in embezzlement, the property was initially and lawfully possessed by the defendant. With respect to larceny, the property is either fraudulently or unlawfully obtained initially; that is, there is a trespassory taking of the property.

There is a distinction between possession and custody in the law. An employee who is given property to use by her employer, such as a sales person who is given the use of a car, is considered to be in custody of that car, and not in possession of it. If an employee is given property by a third person, such as when a supermarket checkout person is given money in exchange for purchasing food, the checkout person is considered to be in possession of that property.

9. Dwayne's actions constitute larceny by trick, and not false pretenses or embezzlement, because Dwayne is considered to have only possession of the gas until he pays for it. That is, the title to the gas is considered not to pass until payment is made. Thus, for example, if Dwayne has paid for the gas with counterfeit money at the time of the transaction, the crime would be false pretenses because he would have fraudulently obtained title to the gas, and not just possession. See *Hufstetler v. State*, 37 Ala. App. 71, 63 So.2d 730 (1953).

10. Thurston has committed burglary. "Breaking" does not require an actual physical breaking of the property of the house of another, simply that any act or physical force be used to remove an obstruction to entering. Thus, if the defendant unlatches an unlocked door, opens a partially opened door, or even tricks a person into opening the door through false premises — for example, the perpetrator claims he is a policeman, pizza delivery person, etc. — this would constitute the breaking element. It is not a sufficient breaking, however, if the defendant enters through a completely open window and does not touch that window, walks through a completely open door, or enters the home as a guest-invitee. In many jurisdictions today, the breaking element is no longer required.

11. Mel has committed two different crimes of battery. When he kissed Jane without her permission, this likely would constitute the intentional offensive touching that would suffice for the crime. The second battery occurred when Mel whipped the horse causing Jane to fall. There need not be actual and direct touching of the victim by the defendant. The harmful touching such as the whipping may be indirect.

12. Peter has committed the crime of arson. Arson simply requires a scorching or burning, and not a complete burning down of the house. The fire was set intentionally, however, meeting the malice requirement and easily surpassing the "gross recklessness" minimum for arson.

XI. CASE SQUIBS

PRINCIPLE OF LEGALITY

Rex v. Manley, 1 K.B. 529 (Court of Criminal Appeal 1933).

This case offers a fine illustration of the problem of judge-made law. Elizabeth Manley was charged in England with two counts of filing false statements to the police. Both statements involved similar alleged attacks. The court found that her conduct was punishable under the criminal law as a public mischief. The court concluded that public mischief was an actionable offense, and that the waste of time caused by the false reports and the exposure of others to suspicion of committing a crime warranted her conduct being considered a public mischief.

However, it is arguable that while Manley's conduct may have been offensive and injurious to the community, there was no prior notice that her conduct was in fact unlawful. There also were no ascertainable standards for determining what exactly constituted a public mischief. Thus, there is a strong argument that this case was wrongly decided.

Commonwealth v. Donoghue, 63 S.W.2d 3, 250 Ky. 343 (Ct. App. 1933).

This case provides an American illustration of judicial crime creation. The defendant, along with two others, was charged with conspiracy to engage in usury. At the time of the alleged crime, usury was not a criminal offense in Kentucky. The court held that because in this case there was a "nefarious plan" for gross usury, and not simply an isolated instance of it, a criminal charge of conspiracy to commit usury was warranted. While the result may have been justifiable, the process again illustrated the problems with judicial crime creation. The court made the defendant's action a crime only because those actions were believed post hoc to be heinous; there was no prior warning or notice, or any articulated standard by which to judge the criminality of the conduct. Instead, this kind of retroactive crime creation provides an incentive for police and prosecutors to unilaterally expand the potential conduct that may be criminal, in the hope that a judge or jury will decide later, after the fact, that the conduct is criminal under public mischief.

CONSTITUTIONAL LIMITATIONS

Parker v. Levy, 417 U.S. 733, 94 S.Ct. 2547 (1974).

This case stands for the proposition that laws which are otherwise void for vagueness on their face in violation of the due process clause can be saved through narrowing constructions of the law. Dr. Howard Levy was a captain in the army stationed at Fort Jackson during the Vietnam War. He engaged in various statements of opposition to the war, including public statements to enlisted men. As a result of his public statements and his refusal to establish a training program, he was court martialed in violation of various articles of the Uniform Code of Military Justice. Two of these articles provided that military personnel would be punished for "conduct unbecoming an officer and a gentleman," and for "all disorders and neglects to the prejudice of good order and discipline in the armed forces." The Supreme Court concluded that the broad face of these provisions had been sufficiently narrowed to survive a void for vagueness challenge. Subsequent constructions limited the applicability of these provisions to provide fair notice and warning of what would be prohibited under these articles. The dissent argued that even the numerous narrowing constructions of these articles could not sufficiently narrow language such as "an officer and a gentleman." While laws may be vague, this case illustrates that laws must not be excessively vague. The test for whether vagueness is excessive includes subsequent narrowing interpretations of the law.

Kolender v. Lawson, 461 U.S. 352, 183 S.Ct. 1855 (1983).

This case addressed the constitutionality of a "stop and identify" statute. The United States Supreme Court found California's law requiring a person to "stop and identify" himself or herself with "credible and reliable" identification void for vagueness in violation of the due process clause. The Court concluded that too much power rested in law enforcement personnel to determine whether an alleged violator has sufficiently identified himself to avoid arrest under this provision.

Papachristou v. City of Jacksonville, 405 U.S. 156, 92 S.Ct. 839 (1972).

This case illustrates the extreme difficulty of creating sufficiently concrete laws when attempting to prevent harms well in advance of when they occur. This difficulty is particularly apparent in vagrancy statutes. The Jacksonville statute declared in part, "rogues and vagabonds, or dissolute persons who go about begging, common gamblers, persons who use juggling or unlawful games or plays, common drunkards, common nightwalkers, common pilferers, common thieves or pickpockets . . . shall be considered vagrants and subject to criminal penalty." The United States Supreme Court found this statute to be void for vagueness because it lends itself to the danger of unbridled police discretion in its enforcement. Here, the principle of legality stands not so much for fair warning, notice, or ascertainable standards, but as a limitation on the dangers of excessive power in the hands of law enforcement.

Keeler v. Superior Court of Amadora County, 2 Cal. 3d 619, 87 Cal. Rptr. 481, 470 P.2d 617 (1970), overruled, **People v. Carlson**, 112 Cal. Rptr. 321 (1974) (Keeler was overruled by statute to include "unborn fetus").

This case illustrates how the judiciary is limited not only in creating criminal law, but in interpreting existing statutory criminal law as well. The petitioner was charged with murder after killing the unborn, viable fetus of his pregnant ex-wife. The issue before the court was whether the killing of a fetus fell within the California definition of murder, which prohibited the unlawful killing of a human being with malice aforethought. The court held that an unborn but viable fetus is not a human being within the meaning of the statute because the legislature did not intend for the law to include feticide. The Court reviewed the legislative history to discern the legislature's intent. The Court concluded that to judicially interpret the law to include feticide as murder would violate the principle of legality and the petitioner's due process rights. While the petitioner in this case deserved to be punished for what he did, the rule of law requires that criminal law be created only with prospective application so as to provide fair warning and notice. Thus, the "legally correct" decision involved no judicial extension of the statute.

THE ACTUS REUS

Jones v. United States, 308 F.2d 307 (D.C. Cir. 1962).

This case illustrates the principle that a person cannot be found guilty of a crime for omitting to act unless the person has a legal duty to do so. The appellant was charged with manslaughter for failing to take care of a friend's child. The child died of malnutrition, primarily as a result of neglect, shortly after being removed from the appellant's house by the police. The jury convicted the appellant, but the District of Columbia Circuit Court of Appeals reversed. The Appeals Court found that the trial judge failed to properly instruct the jury as to legal duty. The judge did not indicate to the jury that to convict a defendant for failing to act, a legal duty to act was required, whether originating in statute, a status relationship, a contract, or the voluntary assumption of care and seclusion. This case further illustrates the principle that some appeals are often won not because the jury erred in interpreting the evidence, but rather because the judge erred in instructing the jury.

People v. Beardsley, 150 Mich. 206, 113 N.W. 1128 (1907).

This case illustrates how courts often strictly construe potential duty to act situations. The defendant had an affair with the victim one weekend while the defendant's wife was out of town. The two drank quite a lot, and the victim, without the defendant's consent, took morphine. At the end of the weekend, when the defendant's wife was expected to return, the defendant moved the unconscious victim out of his house to the room of a friend who was to look after her. The victim died several hours later, never reviving. The Michigan Supreme Court reversed the defendant's conviction, reasoning that no legal duty to aid the victim existed on the part of the defendant.

Barber v. Superior Court of Los Angeles County, 147 Cal. App. 3d 1006, 195 Cal. Rptr. 484 (2d D.C.A. 1983).

This case illustrates the difficulties that arise when the legal duty requirement confronts advances in medical technology. The victim was in a hospital in a vegetative state with severe brain damage. Several defendants, who were the victim's doctors, "pulled the plug," stopping all mechanical devices sustaining the victim's life, including hydration and nourishment. The family of the victim had previously consented to the doctors' actions. The doctors were charged with murder, but the appellate court reversed, determining that their conduct was merely an omission to continue treatment. The court ruled that the doctors had no legal duty to continue essentially futile treatment when there was no prognosis for a reasonable possibility of return to "cognitive and sapient life." Significantly, the court's characterization of "pulling the plug" as an omission paves the way for the medical community and families to hasten the death of loved ones who are in a persistent vegetative state.

VOLUNTARY ACTS

Robinson v. California, 370 U.S. 660, 82 S.Ct. 1417, 8 L.Ed. 2d 758 (1962).

This case stands for the proposition that an individual cannot be prosecuted for an illness or a status which requires no act in the jurisdiction. The appellant was convicted of violating a California statute that made it a crime "to be addicted to the use of narcotics...." The United States Supreme Court reversed, finding that convicting the appellant for an illness that may be contracted innocently or involuntarily, without an act in the jurisdiction, was cruel and unusual punishment in violation of the Constitution. This rationale created as many questions as it resolved, since it was unclear as to whether it was the lack of an act altogether, the lack of a voluntary act, or the nature of the act — i.e., one resulting from an illness — or a combination of all three, that motivated the Court's decision.

Powell v. Texas, 392 U.S. 514, 88 S.Ct. 2145 (1968).

This case clarified the holding of *Robinson v. California*. A Texas statute made it a crime to be found drunk in public. The defendant argued that he could not be convicted of such an offense because his appearing drunk in public resulted from chronic alcoholism. The Supreme Court rejected this claim, finding that "appearing in public" constituted a voluntary act. The Court in *Powell* interpreted *Robinson* to mean that a state could not punish solely a "mere status," but that the inclusion of a voluntary act makes the criminalization of conduct permissible. Thus, the Supreme Court permitted the prosecution of an addict for a voluntary act, and steepened the slippery slope of exempting from the criminal laws all conduct that is arguably a derivative of an illness or addiction.

People v. Decina, 2 N.Y.2d 133, 133 N.E.2d 799 (1956).

This case illustrates the rule that a person may be prosecuted for committing an involuntary act in the course of culpable voluntary conduct. The defendant suffered an epileptic seizure while driving, killing several bystanders. He was convicted of negligent homicide while driving a motor vehicle. The prosecution was upheld on appeal because the culpable act was the defendant's voluntary decision to drive knowing that he could suffer an epileptic seizure, not the seizure itself. While this rule makes sense, it raises a question about the meaning of negligence and whether the defendant technically operated the vehicle negligently in the manner forbidden by the statute.

MENS REA

Regina v. Faulkner, 13 Cox Crim. Cases 550 (Ire. 1877).

This case examines the definition of malice in the criminal law. Defendant, a seaman, entered the cargo area of his ship to steal rum. After quenching his thirst, he lit a match to see better, and unintentionally set the ship on fire. He was tried and convicted for "feloniously, unlawfully, and maliciously" setting fire to the ship. On appeal, the court reversed his conviction. It held that "malice" did not mean wicked or perverse disposition, and that the intent to steal did not "transfer" to become an intent to burn. That is, the defendant is not considered to have acted maliciously simply because he was attempting to commit some other crime at the time he lit the match that caused the fire.

Regina v. Cunningham, 41 Crim. Ap. 155 (English Court of Criminal Appeals 1957).

Like *Faulkner* above, this case stands for the proposition that legal "malice" does not equal ill will or spite, and that it does not transfer from the commission of one criminal act to another. In the unusual facts of this case, the defendant stole the contents of a gas meter located in the basement of a house occupied by his prospective in-laws, a house soon to be occupied by himself and his new bride. As a result of stealing the contents of the gas meter, gas leaked into the neighboring "flats" and nearly asphyxiated a sleeping neighbor. The trial judge instructed the jury that malice means ill will or wickedness. On appeal, the court reversed, stating that malice is either purposeful, knowing, or reckless behavior, quite separate from ill will. This case is distinguishable from *Faulkner* in that malice was defined in *Faulkner* to include negligent conduct as well.

Morissette v. United States, 342 U.S. 246, 72 S.Ct. 240 (1952).

This case illustrates the proposition that statutes written without a mens rea requirement will be construed as containing the mens rea requirement of negligence, unless the legislature clearly intended to the contrary. Morissette took what he believed to be abandoned bomb casings from a remote area in Michigan for eventual sale to help meet expenses after a hunting trip. He was convicted of "unlawfully, willfully, and knowingly" stealing and converting property of the United States. The Supreme Court reversed, holding that the omission of a mental state requirement from the statute does not mean that Congress intended the crime to be a strict liability offense. The Court observed that the requirement of mens rea is a basic principle of the criminal law, and therefore a mental state would be implied. The Court added that if a mental state requirement exists, the defendant's claim that he believed the shells had been abandoned could be dispositive in the case. This case instructs that moral blameworthiness is an essential component of a criminal conviction. Unless the crime is intended by the legislature to be a strict liability offense, it will not be construed as such.

CAUSATION

People v. Kibbe, 35 N.Y.2d 407, 362 N.Y.S.2d 848, 321 N.E.2d 773 (Ct. App. 1974).

In this case, the New York Court of Appeals found that to hold a person criminally liable for a homicide, that person must be a sufficiently direct cause of death. The defendant and a cohort robbed the victim, who was quite drunk, and left him on a dark highway on a cold winter night in upstate New York. The victim's clothes were partially off, and his eyeglasses were left in the defendant's car. Shortly thereafter, the victim was run over by a driver unconnected to the robbery who did not observe the victim in time. The defendant's conviction was affirmed on appeal, with the court holding that the driver who caused the death of the victim did not commit an intervening act breaking the chain of causation. The actions of the defendant, rather, constituted a sufficiently direct cause of death. The victim's death was reasonably foreseeable either from being hit by a car, or, in the alternative, being exposed to the bitter cold.

New Jersey v. Farrad, 753 A.2d 648 (2000).

> In this case, the defendant walked into a "Roy Rogers Restaurant", placed a scarf over his face, approached the counter and reached into his pocket for a gun. Police officers standing outside the restaurant witnessed the entire event and apprehended the defendant before he could rob the restaurant. The court held that even though the defendant was arrested prior to committing a robbery, he took a "substantial step" in completing the crime. The act of approaching the counter and reaching for his gun went beyond mere preparation to commit robbery and constituted an "overt act," upon which an attempt crime could be grounded. Therefore, the defendant could be convicted of "attempt."

People v. Bowen and Rouse, 10 Mich. App. 1, 158 N.W.2d 794 (1968).

> This case focuses on the minimum act required to support a conviction for an attempt crime. The defendants were invited into the elderly victim's home and were caught in the home after apparently moving various items of jewelry for an eventual theft. The trial judge failed to instruct the jury on the necessity of convicting only on the basis of an overt act and not on an act constituting mere preparation. On appeal, the court held that entry into another's home with permission, without more, did not meet the overt act requirement for attempt. Instead, such conduct only constituted preparation. The court required a more conspicuous act to manifest the defendants' criminal intent for a conviction to stand and a jury instruction that adequately reflected this limitation on the type of act necessary for an attempt conviction.

People v. Pippin, 25 N.W.2d 164 (Mich. 1946).

> This case illustrates the distinction between an overt act, which is sufficient to convict on an attempt charge, and mere preparation, which is insufficient. In this case, the defendant was convicted of attempting to entice a thirteen-year-old boy into his car for the purpose of committing a lewd and immoral act. The defendant had previously been convicted of gross indecency. The Michigan Supreme Court reversed the conviction, holding that the defendant's act was nothing more than mere preparation.

People v. Jaffe, 78 N.E. 169 (N.Y. 1906).

> This case illustrates the concepts of legal and factual impossibility. It more narrowly stands for the proposition that one cannot be convicted of attempting to receive stolen goods if the goods received were not actually stolen. The New York Court of Appeals reversed the defendant's conviction of feloniously receiving stolen cloth. The defendant attempted to purchase cloth he believed to be stolen, which in fact was not. The Court of Appeals held that one cannot be convicted of attempting to receive stolen goods, if the act, had it been completed, would not be criminal. The court described this case as an example of legal impossibility, a defense to an attempt charge. The court contrasted this case with factual impossibility, where the act is not completed due to some unforeseen physical or factual condition (such as when a person attempts to pick an empty pocket). Factual impossibility is not a defense to an attempt charge.

People v. Valot, 33 Mich. App. 49, 189 N.W.2d 873 (Ct. App. 1971).

This case illustrates that a conviction for possession can occur when there is a constructive exercise of dominion and control over the thing possessed. The defendant was convicted of possessing marijuana in a hotel room. He was found lying in bed with several marijuana joints in somewhat close proximity scattered about the room. Although others were in the room at the same time, the defendant had registered for the room and had paid part of the rent. The court held that this was sufficient to hold the defendant liable for the marijuana found in the room. The interesting question raised in this case is how to distinguish who will be held responsible for contraband which is found among a group of people and not on anyone's person. The case demonstrates that anyone who appears to knowingly exercise dominion and control over the thing possessed, albeit constructively and jointly with others, can be held responsible.

People v. Burleson, 50 Ill. App. 3d 629, 8 Ill. Dec. 776, 365 N.E.2d 1162 (8 D.C.A. 1977).

This case illustrates that the number of existing conspiracies depends on the number of agreements made, not the number of crimes to be committed. The defendant and two others conspired to rob a local bank. After commencing with their plans, they decided to postpone the robbery because the area was crowded and potential interference existed. The co-conspirators tried again at a later date, but their efforts were foiled. The court found that two distinct conspiracies had occurred. The first conspiracy concerned the aborted initial intended date of the robbery. The second involved the agreement to try again at a later date. The court consequently held that two conspiracy charges could be lodged against the defendant, although under Illinois law a conspiracy conviction merged with a conviction for the object offense.

People v. Lauria, 251 Cal. App. 2d 471, 59 Cal. Rptr. 628 (Ct. App. 1967).

This case examines whether a supplier of lawful goods and services who knows that those goods and services will be used unlawfully, can be charged with conspiracy. The court held that generally, the mere knowledge that lawful goods or services are being put to an unlawful use is not enough to deem the provider a participant in a conspiracy. Instead, knowledge of the unlawful use of lawful goods and services plus an intent to further the illegal use are both required before a conspiracy conviction will be valid. The intent to further a criminal enterprise can be inferred when the seller has a stake in the outcome, as indicated by an inflated price of sale or an extra quantity sold, or where no legitimate use for the product(s) or service(s) exists. Furthermore, if the object crime is especially heinous, mere knowledge alone may be enough to support a conspiracy conviction.

Pinkerton v. United States, 328 U.S. 640, 66 S.Ct. 1180 (1946).

This seminal case sets forth the imputed liability theory — that is, liability for the acts of others—relating to crimes of conspiracy. The defendants were convicted of Internal Revenue Code violations and conspiracy. A defendant challenged the conviction on the substantive offense, claiming he could not be convicted because it was his co-defendant, not he, who committed the offense. The United States Supreme Court affirmed his conviction, holding that a conspirator is liable for the acts of co-conspirators performed in furtherance of the substantive crime. The co-conspirator's acts in furtherance of the conspiracy are imputed to the defendant.

United States v. Peoni, 100 F.2d 401 (2d Cir. 1938).

This case stands for the principle that accomplice liability will exist only for someone who assists another in the commission of an offense. The defendant, Peoni, was charged as an accessory to B's possession of counterfeit money after selling counterfeit bills to A, who then sold them to B. The court held that Peoni could not be held as an accomplice to B's possession of the money because Peoni in no way assissted B in his crime of possession. After Peoni sold the bills to A he did not know or control what A was going to do with the money or assist in B's gaining possession of the money and therefore cannot be held as an accomplice to B's possession.

HOMICIDE

Commonwealth v. Malone, 354 Pa. 180, 47 A.2d 445 (1946).

This case provides a poignant illustration of depraved heart murder. The defendant, a seventeen-year-old boy, played a game of "Russian Roulette" with a thirteen-year-old. The defendant pointed a gun at the head of the thirteen-year-old, and pulled the trigger. The thirteen-year-old was killed when the gun went off. The court found the defendant guilty of murder as a result of a "wicked, depraved, and malignant heart." It was irrelevant that the defendant may not have intended to kill. In other words, intentionally taking a grossly unreasonable risk of serious bodily harm to others is sufficient for a conviction of murder.

State v. Goodseal, 220 Kan. 487, 553 P.2d 279 (Kan. 1976).

This case illustrates the different tests used to determine whether a felony is sufficiently dangerous to support a felony murder conviction. The appellant was convicted of felony murder after the gun he was carrying during a shakedown accidentally discharged and killed the victim. The felony in question was the possession of a gun by a convicted felon. The defendant claimed that the felonious possession of a firearm is not inherently dangerous to human life, and therefore could not serve as a basis for felony murder. In rejecting this conviction, the appellate court considered both the nature of the offense in the abstract and the circumstances of its commission under the particular facts of this case. In using this "as applied to the circumstances" approach, the court found that since the appellant used the gun to scare the victim, the felony possession of the gun was inherently dangerous. As a result, his conviction was affirmed.

State v. Underwood, 228 Kan. 294, 615 P.2d 153 (1980).

In this case, the Supreme Court of Kansas reversed its earlier position in *Goodseal*. The Court overruled its conclusion that the unlawful possession of a firearm by a convicted felon is an inherently dangerous felony. The appellant was convicted of felony murder when he shot and killed a man in a brawl. The underlying felony for the felony murder charge was the unlawful possession of a firearm just as in *Goodseal*. On appeal, the Court decided that the determination of whether an underlying felony is inherently dangerous should be calculated only in the "abstract," and not in the "abstract plus the circumstances of the case." The Court reversed the conviction because it found that the unlawful possession of a firearm, when considered in the abstract, is not a felony inherently dangerous to human life.

Freddo v. State, 127 Tenn. 376, 155 S.W. 170 (1913).

This case explains the elements of heat of passion manslaughter. The defendant was raised by a proper Nashville lady and hated foul language of any kind. While working for the railway, he was called a foul name by a co-worker. The defendant became enraged, and hit the offender over the head with a steel bar, killing him. After a conviction for second degree murder, the Supreme Court of Tennessee concluded that this case did not meet the requirements for heat of passion manslaughter. The court advanced three elements for the heat of passion test: (1) actual provocation that was (2) legally adequate and (3) reasonable. Under the facts of the case, the court observed that the provocative words addressed to the defendant were not legally adequate because "mere words are not enough." The insult would have sufficed had it been accompanied by an assault of some kind. The court added that although the defendant was in fact provoked, he must be judged by the reasonable person test, not as a person who is especially sensitive to foul language.

People v. Casassa, 49 N.Y.2d 668, 427 N.Y.S.2d 769, 404 N.E.2d 1310 (1980).

This case illustrates the defense of "extreme emotional disturbance." The defendant sought to date the victim, but his advances were spurned. After becoming extremely upset, the defendant intentionally stabbed the victim to death. The defendant argued that his emotional disturbance should be considered a mitigating factor, reducing the crime from murder to manslaughter. The court concluded, however, that the defendant's actions were unworthy of mitigation because he was not reasonably provoked. The court affirmed Casassa's conviction for murder.

Essex v. Commonwealth, 228 Va. 273, 322 S.E.2d 216 (1984).

This case examines whether a killing by a drunk driver can be malicious under Virginia law, and thus constitute murder. The defendant, while driving drunk, unintentionally crossed the median in the road and caused a head-on collision, killing several people. The Court held that malice could not be inferred when a defendant unintentionally kills while driving drunk. In such a situation, a defendant could be convicted of recklessness manslaughter, at most. While the Court could have used a *People v. Decina* analysis (see above), and found that the culpable, reckless act was the deliberate decision to operate a car while drunk, the Court in this case chose not to similarly expand the time frame for determining culpability. Instead, it looked at the act that occurred at the precise time of the accident, and concluded that no implied malice existed. Many jurisdictions have dealt with the awkwardness that often arises in attempting to categorize unintentional killings resulting from drunk driving by creating a separate criminal statute — "driving under the influence" manslaughter.

In Re Winship, 397 U.S. 358, 90 S.Ct. 1068 (1970).

This case stands for the proposition that proof beyond a reasonable doubt is required not only in criminal cases, but in juvenile adjudications as well. A twelve-year-old boy was charged in New York State Court with stealing money. The question was whether, despite the civil nature of the juvenile adjudication, proof beyond a reasonable doubt was necessary for the juvenile to be adjudicated delinquent. The Supreme Court held that the civil label attached to juvenile proceedings was one of mere convenience, and was not dispositive of whether and in what form due process attached. The Court reiterated the importance of proof beyond a reasonable doubt in cases involving a deprivation of liberty, which may occur in both criminal cases and juvenile adjudications.

CASE
SQUIBS

Sandstrom v. Montana, 442 U.S. 510 (1978).

This case exemplifies the constitutional requirement that the state must prove every element of a crime beyond a reasonable doubt in a criminal case. Defendant was convicted of deliberate homicide which, under Montana law, requires the defendant to purposely or knowingly cause the death of another person. The judge instructed the jury by stating that "the law presumes that a person intends the ordinary consequences of his voluntary actions." The United States Supreme Court reversed the defendant's conviction. It found that the jury instruction improperly shifted the burden of proof away from the prosecutor by allowing the jury to presume facts that must be proved. Therefore, the instruction violated the defendant's right to due process of law.

Mullaney v. Wilber, 421 U.S. 684, 95 S.Ct. 1881 (1975).

This case stands for the proposition that a state must prove all of the elements of a crime beyond a reasonable doubt. The case concerned the State of Maine's penal law, which required the State to prove that a homicide was intentional and unlawful for a murder conviction. As part of the definition, the State included in the crime the absence of heat of passion. The Supreme Court held that the State could not presume a lack of heat of passion, but must prove it because it is so significant to the culpability level of the defendant. Consequently, Maine's presumption of the lack of heat of passion violated due process requirements, and improperly shifted part of the required burden onto the defendant.

Patterson v. New York, 432 U.S. 197, 97 S.Ct. 2319 (1977).

This case requires that, despite *Mullaney v. Wilber*, due process requires that a state need only prove, beyond a reasonable doubt, all of the elements of the crime charged. However, due process does not require the state to prove the nonexistence of all affirmative defenses. The New York penal law required a defendant to prove conduct occurring as a result of an extreme emotional disturbance, for which there was "a reasonable explanation or excuse," to reduce a murder charge to manslaughter. The Supreme Court affirmed the defendant's conviction, holding that this case was not controlled by *Mullaney*, and that the New York law did not deprive the defendant of due process. The Court focused on the fact that there was no presumption or implied acceptance of any of the elements of the crime charged. Thus, if a law indicates that the government has the burden of proof on a particular element, it cannot simply create a presumption or implication that the element exists. The government must prove the element completely, beyond a reasonable doubt.

DEFENSES NEGATING THE MENS REA

Director of Public Prosecutions v. Majewski, 2 ALL E.R. 142, House of Lords, 1976.

This case illustrates the proposition that intoxication is not a defense to a general intent crime. The defendant was prosecuted for "assault occasioning actual bodily harm." The defendant claimed in defense that the act was committed under a combination of drugs and alcohol, none of which had been medically prescribed. The court held that self-induced intoxication is not a defense to a crime satisfied by a mens rea requirement of recklessness. The court affirmed the conviction, concluding that the defendant's drunkenness was itself an act of recklessness.

United States v. Short, 4 U.S.C.M.A. 437, 16 CMR 11 (1954).

This case explores the situations in which a mistake of fact can be used as a defense to a specific intent crime. The defendant was convicted of assault with intent to commit rape. He alleged that he mistakenly believed that the victim consented to his advances. He requested a jury instruction stating that "[i]n order to constitute an offense, the accused must think the victim is not consenting because he must intend not only to have carnal knowledge of the woman, but to do so by force." This proposed instruction was not given. The court incorrectly concluded that for a mistake in fact to serve as a defense, it must be both honest and reasonable. The court confused the crime of rape, which is a general intent crime, with the crime actually charged, assault with intent to commit rape, a specific intent crime. As the dissenting justice correctly points out, with specific intent crimes, a mistake need only be honest for it to serve as a defense.

State v. Downs, 116 N.C. 1064, 21 S.E. 689 (1895).

Downs advances the famous maxim, "Ignorance of the law is no excuse." The defendants were convicted of selling liquor within two miles of a church. The defendants argue that they sought advice from counsel to determine if their sale of liquor would violate the law. Their attorneys advised them that their actions would not violate the law. The defendants acted on this advice. The court held that neither the defendants' ignorance, nor the ignorance of their attorneys regarding the law, excused them from criminal responsibility.

DEFENSE OF JUSTIFICATION

State v. Warshow, 138 Vt. 22, 410 A.2d 1000 (1979).

This case illustrates that the defense of necessity can be utilized only when an emergency exists and the legislature has not decided as a matter of policy that the risks of an activity are outweighed by its benefits. The defendants were charged with unlawful trespass when they protested at a nuclear power plant in Vermont. They wanted the dangers of nuclear power, including low-level radiation and nuclear waste, to cease, and claimed that these dangers outweighed and justified their criminal activity. The court disagreed. The majority held that the "specter of nuclear accident" did not justify the trespass, and the concurrence held that the legislature had previously made a deliberate policy choice that the benefits of nuclear power outweighed its risks.

Regina v. Dudley & Stephens, 14 Q.B.D. 273 (1884).

This case illustrates the traditional reluctance by courts to allow the necessity defense to a charge of murder. In this famous "lifeboat" case, the two defendants were ship-wrecked with a seventeen-year-old boy. The defendants killed the boy after eighteen days in the lifeboat without food or water. The defendants were rescued four days later. They argued that had they not killed the boy, they would have died. The court, however, disagreed with the defendants' reasoning and refused to allow them to assert the necessity defense. After a conviction, the defendants were sentenced to death. The sentence was later commuted to six months imprisonment.

Crawford v. State, 231 Md. 354, 198 A.2d 538 (Ct. App. Md. 1963).

This case offers a fine illustration of both self-defense and the defense of habitation. The defendant, a 42-year old disabled man, lived in a rooming house where he had been persistently badgered by two young men. One of the men had held a knife to him, demanded money, and threatened him with further harm. The two young men returned at a later time and attempted to break into the rooming house. One of the young men stood by the rear door to prevent escape, while the other attempted to break in through the front door. As the young man was in the process of breaking in, the defendant loaded a rifle, aimed it at the hand of the man breaking in, and fired. The gun jerked up as it discharged and killed the man. The defendant was convicted of manslaughter for using excessive force. On appeal, the court reiterated the rules for self-defense and defense of habitation using deadly force. The appellate court held that in circumstances where the defendant was in reasonable fear of being attacked in his own home, he lawfully acted in defense of his own habitation. The court consequently reversed the defendant's conviction.

Jahnke v. State, 682 P.2d 991 (Wyo. 1984).

This case offers a variation of the defense of the battered woman's syndrome, namely the battered child's syndrome. Defendant, age sixteen, shot and killed his father after waiting for him to return home. Defendant attempted to augment his self-defense claim at trial with evidence that he had been physically and mentally abused by his father. The judge disallowed the evidence, and defendant was convicted of manslaughter. The Wyoming Supreme Court affirmed the conviction, as well as the lower court's refusal to permit the testimony pertaining to the syndrome. It held that the deceased had not performed any act which would induce a reasonable person to fear for his life. As such, the syndrome testimony was deemed to be irrelevant.

State v. Kelley, 97 N.J. 178, 478 A.2d 369 (1984).

This case provides an instructive review of the defense of the battered woman's syndrome. The defendant was charged with criminal homicide for stabbing and killing her husband. She claimed that he had battered her for many years, commencing shortly after their honeymoon. She wished to offer the testimony of an expert psychologist who would state that she was suffering from battered woman's syndrome at the time she killed her husband. On appeal, the New Jersey Supreme Court reviewed the three stages of battered woman's syndrome: (1) minor battering; (2) acute battering; and (3) contrition; and then discussed whether the battered woman's syndrome could be raised in that jurisdiction as a defense. The Court held that expert testimony on the honesty and reasonableness of the defendant's belief that deadly force was necessary may be admissible at trial.

EXCUSE

M'Naghten's Case, 8 Eng. Rep. 718 (H.L. 1843).

This English case set the precedent for the insanity rules followed in many American jurisdictions. Daniel M'Naghten was a drifter with a history of paranoid mental illness and radical political views. He shot at a person he believed was the Prime Minister at that time, Robert Peel, but instead killed the Prime Minister's private secretary, Drummond. Seven alienists (i.e., psychiatrists) testified that M'Naghten was mentally ill, and a jury agreed. Subsequently, the appellate court fashioned the M'Naghten test, which determines that a person will be found not guilty by reason of insanity if that individual, as a result of a mental disease or defect, does not know either the nature and quality of the act or right from wrong.

Parsons v. State, 81 Ala. 577 2 So. 854 (1887).

This case illustrates the "irresistible impulse" test of insanity. The court stated that a defendant would be considered insane if "by reason of the duress of such mental disease, he had so far lost the power to choose between the right and wrong, and to avoid doing the act in question, as that his free agency was at the time destroyed . . . ." In effect, a lack of free will must be the cause of the defendant's act.

United States v. Bailey, 444 U.S. 394 (1980).

This case analyzes the duress defense. Clifford Bailey, along with two co-defendants, escaped from subpar jail conditions in the District of Columbia jail. They were subsequently apprehended and charged with escape. At trial, they claimed that the failure to instruct the jury on the duress defense was erroneous. The Supreme Court held that since the defendants failed to offer evidence of a "bona fide effort to surrender and return to custody as soon as the claim of duress or necessity had lost its course of force," a duress instruction was not proper. The court also noted that duress is an excuse that occurs when a defendant is under an unlawful threat of imminent death or serious bodily injury which causes the defendant to violate the criminal law.

Sorrells v. United States, 287 U.S. 435, 53 S.Ct. 210 (1932).

This case illustrates the subjective, or "predisposition," test for entrapment. The Supreme Court held that entrapment exists "when the criminal design originates with the officials of the government, and they implant in the mind of an innocent person the disposition to commit the alleged offense and induce its commission in order that they may prosecute." If a defendant is predisposed to committing the crime, a conviction will stand. The entrapment defense is thus for use by only the unwary innocent.

People v. Barraza, 23 Cal. 3d 675, 153 Cal. Rptr. 459, 591 P.2d 947 (1979).

This case presents an example of the objective test of entrapment. The defendant Barraza allegedly sold heroin to an undercover police agent. The defendant claimed entrapment. On appeal, the Supreme Court of California reversed the defendant's conviction, stating that the objective test for entrapment is the appropriate standard. The court adopted the objective approach to deter impermissible law enforcement activity. Thus, police activity that improperly causes a reasonable law-abiding citizen to commit a crime is subject to an entrapment defense.

DEADLY WEAPONS

People v. Aguilar, 945 P.2d 1204 Sup. Ct. Cal. (1997).

> D attacked a person rollerblading by hitting and kicking him repeatedly. D. was found guilty of assault with a deadly weapon. D appealed. Court held that a deadly weapon must be an object extrinsic to the body. Therefore, the D's hands and feet cannot be considered deadly weapons.

State v. Bennett, 493 S.E.2d 845 Sup. Ct. S.C. (1997).

> D appeals conviction where trial judge instructed jury that a hand or fist could be considered a deadly weapon for purposes of armed robbery. Court held that in some circumstances, a hand or fist could be considered a deadly weapon. Here, D was 9 inches taller and 100 pounds heavier than the victim. Given the size difference and the type of resulting injuries from the attack, the Court upheld the jury instructions.

CONSPIRACY

Miller v. State, Wyo. Sup. Ct. 955 P.2d 892 (1998).

> Supreme Court of Wyoming adopted the "unilateral theory" of conspiracy. Therefore, D can be prosecuted for conspiracy even if all the other parties to the conspiracy are government agents or are only feigning agreement. As long as the D believes he is conspiring to commit a crime it is irrelevant as to whether the other parties actually agree.

FELONY MURDER

People v. Lowery, 178 Ill.2d 462 (1997).

> This case stands for the principle that a felon can be convicted of murder for a death that results from the commission of a felony. Defendant attempted armed robbery. The intended victim fought back, gained control of the gun, and then fired at the fleeing defendant, accidentally killing another person. Defendant was convicted of felony murder. The fact that the victim might fight back and someone could get injured or killed during the commission of an attempted robbery — which is an inherently dangerous felony — was a foreseeable result of the crime. Therefore, the defendant was liable for any acts that arose during the commission of the felony.

YEAR AND A DAY RULE

Commonwealth v. Casanova, Mass. Sup. Jud. Ct., 708 N.E.2d 86 (1999).

> Defendant was charged with murder following the death of an individual which he had shot 6 years earlier. The injury affected the victim's ability to breathe and ultimately was using a ventilator to breathe. The Court had abolished the year and a day rule. Defendant urged the court to adopt another standard, however the Court refused. The Court found no violation of the Defendant's due process rights.

State v. Rogers, 992 S.W.2d 393 (1999).

Tennessee Supreme Court abolished the year and a day rule because the reasons that supported the rule in the past no longer exist. Medical technology: (1) allows life to be sustained years after the injury; (2) resolves medical causation issues; (3) determines the cause of death much more accurately. The Court refused to adopt another standard in place of the year and a day rule, stating that the state's burden of proving causation beyond a reasonable doubt is sufficient to satisfy due process.

ENTRAPMENT

People v. Watson, 990 P.2d 1031 (2000).

This case analyzes the entrapment defense. Police officers set up a "sting" operation in which they staged the arrest of a plainclothes officer and then left the car he was driving unlocked with the keys inside. The defendant was arrested later that day driving the car. The court held that the tactics used by the police to catch the defendant did not constitute entrapment. The conduct of the officers would not likely have induced a reasonable law-abiding citizen to commit the crime in question — car theft — and thus was not unfair.

XII. APPENDIX: SELECTED PROVISIONS OF THE MODEL PENAL CODE

Section 1.05. All Offenses Defined by Statute; Application of General Provisions of the Code

(1) No conduct constitutes an offense unless it is a crime or violation under this Code or another statute of this State.

(2) The provisions of Part I of the Code are applicable to offenses defined by other statutes, unless the Code otherwise provides.

(3) This Section does not affect the power of a court to punish for contempt or to employ any sanction authorized by law for the enforcement of an order or a civil judgment or decree.

Section 1.13. General Definitions

In this Code, unless a different meaning plainly is required:

(1) "statute" includes the Constitution and a local law or ordinance of a political subdivision of the State;

(2) "act" or "action" means a bodily movement whether voluntary or involuntary;

(3) "voluntary" has the meaning specified in Section 2.01;

(4) "omission" means a failure to act;

(5) "conduct" means an action or omission and its accompanying state of mind, or, where relevant, a series of acts and omissions;

(6) "actor" includes, where relevant, a person guilty of an omission;

(7) "acted" includes, where relevant, "omitted to act";

(8) "person," "he" and "actor" include any natural person and, where relevant, a corporation or an unincorporated association;

(9) "element of an offense" means (i) such conduct or (ii) such attendant circumstances or (iii) such a result of conduct as

(a) is included in the description of the forbidden conduct in the definition of the offense; or

(b) establishes the required kind of culpability; or

(c) negatives an excuse or justification for such conduct; or

(d) negatives a defense under the statute of limitations; or

(e) establishes jurisdiction or venue;

(10) "material element of an offense" means an element that does not relate exclusively to the statute of limitations, jurisdiction, venue or to any other matter similarly unconnected with (i) the harm or evil, incident to conduct, sought to be prevented by the law defining the offense, or (ii) the existence of a justification or excuse for such conduct;

(11) "purposely" has the meaning specified in Section 2.02 and equivalent terms such as "with purpose," "designed" or "with design" have the same meaning;

(12) "intentionally" or "with intent" means purposely;

(13) "knowingly" has the meaning specified in Section 2.02 and equivalent terms such as "knowing" or "with knowledge" have the same meaning;

(14) "recklessly" has the meaning specified in Section 2.02 and equivalent terms such as "recklessness" or "with recklessness" have the same meaning;

(15) "negligently" has the meaning specified in Section 2.02 and equivalent terms such as "negligence" or "with negligence" have the same meaning;

(16) "reasonably believes" or "reasonable belief" designates a belief which the actor is not reckless or negligent in holding.

ARTICLE 2. GENERAL PRINCIPLES OF LIABILITY

Section 2.01. Requirement of Voluntary Act; Omission as Basis of Liability; Possession as an Act

(1) A person is not guilty of an offense unless his liability is based on conduct which includes a voluntary act or the omission to perform an act of which he is physically capable.

(2) The following are not voluntary acts within the meaning of this Section:

(a) a reflex or convulsion;

(b) a bodily movement during unconsciousness or sleep;

(c) conduct during hypnosis or resulting from hypnotic suggestion;

(d) a bodily movement that otherwise is not a product of the effort or determination of the actor, either conscious or habitual.

(3) Liability for the commission of an offense may not be based on an omission unaccompanied by action unless:

(a) the omission is expressly made sufficient by the law defining the offense; or

(b) a duty to perform the omitted act is otherwise imposed by law.

(4) Possession is an act, within the meaning of this Section, if the possessor knowingly procured or received the thing possessed or was aware of his control thereof for a sufficient period to have been able to terminate his possession.

Section 2.02. General Requirements of Culpability

(1) Minimum Requirements of Culpability. Except as provided in Section 2.05, a person is not guilty of an offense unless he acted purposely, knowingly, recklessly or negligently, as the law may require, with respect to each material element of the offense.

(2) Kinds of Culpability Defined.

(a) Purposely.

A person acts purposely with respect to a material element of an offense when:

(i) if the element involves the nature of his conduct or a result thereof, it is his conscious object to engage in conduct of that nature or to cause such a result; and

(ii) if the element involves the attendant circumstances, he is aware of the existence of such circumstances or he believes or hopes that they exist.

(b) Knowingly.

A person acts knowingly with respect to a material element of an offense when:

(i) if the element involves the nature of his conduct or the attendant circumstances, he is aware that his conduct is of that nature or that such circumstances exist; and

(ii) if the element involves a result of his conduct, he is aware that it is practically certain that his conduct will cause such a result.

(c) Recklessly.

A person acts recklessly with respect to a material element of an offense when he consciously disregards a substantial and unjustifiable risk that the material element exists or will result from his conduct. The risk must be of such a nature and degree that, considering the nature and purpose of the actor's conduct and the circumstances known to him, its disregard involves a gross deviation from the standard of conduct that a law-abiding person would observe in the actor's situation.

(d) Negligently.

A person acts negligently with respect to a material element of an offense when he should be aware of a substantial and unjustifiable risk that the material element exists or will result from his conduct. The risk must be of such a nature and degree that the actor's failure to perceive it, considering the nature and purpose of his conduct and the circumstances known to him, involves a gross deviation from the standard of care that a reasonable person would observe in the actor's situation.

(3) Culpability Required Unless Otherwise Provided. When the culpability sufficient to establish a material element of an offense is not prescribed by law, such element is established if a person acts purposely, knowingly or recklessly with respect thereto.

(4) Prescribed Culpability Requirement Applies to All Material Elements. When the law defining an offense prescribes the kind of culpability that is sufficient for the commission of an offense, without distinguishing among the material elements thereof, such provision shall apply to all the material elements of the offense, unless a contrary purpose plainly appears.

(5) Substitutes for Negligence, Recklessness and Knowledge. When the law provides that negligence suffices to establish an element of an offense, such element also is established if a person acts purposely, knowingly or recklessly. When recklessness suffices to establish an element, such element also is established if a person acts purposely or knowingly. When acting knowingly suffices to establish an element, such element also is established if a person acts purposely.

(6) Requirement of Purpose Satisfied if Purpose Is Conditional. When a particular purpose is an element of an offense, the element is established although such purpose is conditional, unless the condition negatives the harm or evil sought to be prevented by the law defining the offense.

(7) Requirement of Knowledge Satisfied by Knowledge of High Probability. When knowledge of the existence of a particular fact is an element of an offense, such knowledge is established if a person is aware of a high probability of its existence, unless he actually believes that it does not exist.

(8) Requirement of Wilfulness Satisfied by Acting Knowingly. A requirement that an offense be committed wilfully is satisfied if a person acts knowingly with respect to the material elements of the offense, unless a purpose to impose further requirements appears.

(9) Culpability as to Illegality of Conduct. Neither knowledge nor recklessness or negligence as to whether conduct constitutes an offense or as to the existence, meaning or application of the law determining the elements of an offense is an element of such offense, unless the definition of the offense or the Code so provides.

(10) Culpability as Determinant of Grade of Offense. When the grade or degree of an offense depends on whether the offense is committed purposely, knowingly, recklessly or negligently, its grade or degree shall be the lowest for which the determinative kind of culpability is established with respect to any material element of the offense.

Section 2.03. Causal Relationship Between Conduct and Result; Divergence Between Result Designed or Contemplated and Actual Result or Between Probable and Actual Result

(1) Conduct is the cause of a result when:

(a) it is an antecedent but for which the result in question would not have occurred; and

(b) the relationship between the conduct and result satisfies any additional causal requirements imposed by the Code or by the law defining the offense.

(2) When purposely or knowingly causing a particular result is an element of an offense, the element is not established if the actual result is not within the purpose or the contemplation of the actor unless:

(a) the actual result differs from that designed or contemplated, as the case may be, only in the respect that a different person or different property is injured or affected or that the injury or harm designed or contemplated would have been more serious or more extensive than that caused; or

(b) the actual result involves the same kind of injury or harm as that designed or contemplated and is not too remote or accidental in its occurrence to have a [just] bearing on the actor's liability or on the gravity of his offense.

(3) When recklessly or negligently causing a particular result is an element of an offense, the element is not established if the actual result is not within the risk of which the actor is aware or, in the case of negligence, of which he should be aware unless:

(a) the actual result differs from the probable result only in the respect that a different person or different property is injured or affected or that the probable injury or harm would have been more serious or more extensive than that caused; or

(b) the actual result involves the same kind of injury or harm as the probable result and is not too remote or accidental in its occurrence to have a [just] bearing on the actor's liability or on the gravity of his offense.

(4) When causing a particular result is a material element of an offense for which absolute liability is imposed by law, the element is not established unless the actual result is a probable consequence of the actor's conduct.

Section 2.04. Ignorance or Mistake

(1) Ignorance or mistake as to a matter of fact or law is a defense if:

(a) the ignorance or mistake negatives the purpose, knowledge, belief, recklessness or negligence required to establish a material element of the offense; or

(b) the law provides that the state of mind established by such ignorance or mistake constitutes a defense.

(2) Although ignorance or mistake would otherwise afford a defense to the offense charged, the defense is not available if the defendant would be guilty of another offense had the situation been as he supposed. In such case, however, the ignorance or mistake of the defendant shall reduce the grade and degree of the offense of which he may be convicted to those of the offense of which he would be guilty had the situation been as he supposed.

(3) A belief that conduct does not legally constitute an offense is a defense to a prosecution for that offense based upon such conduct when:

(a) the statute or other enactment defining the offense is not known to the actor and has not been published or otherwise reasonably made available prior to the conduct alleged; or

(b) he acts in reasonable reliance upon an official statement of the law, afterward determined to be invalid or erroneous, contained in (i) a statute or other enactment; (ii) a judicial decision, opinion or judgment; (iii) an administrative order or grant of permission; or (iv) an official interpretation of the public officer or body charged by law with responsibility for the interpretation, administration or enforcement of the law defining the offense.

(4) The defendant must prove a defense arising under Subsection (3) of this Section by a preponderance of evidence.

Section 2.06. Liability for Conduct of Another; Complicity

(1) A person is guilty of an offense if it is committed by his own conduct or by the conduct of another person for which he is legally accountable, or both.

(2) A person is legally accountable for the conduct of another person when:

(a) acting with the kind of culpability that is sufficient for the commission of the offense, he causes an innocent or irresponsible person to engage in such conduct; or

(b) he is made accountable for the conduct of such other person by the Code or by the law defining the offense; or

(c) he is an accomplice of such other person in the commission of the offense.

(3) A person is an accomplice of another person in the commission of an offense if:

(a) with the purpose of promoting or facilitating the commission of the offense, he

(i) solicits such other person to commit it; or

(ii) aids or agrees or attempts to aid such other person in planning or committing it; or

(iii) having a legal duty to prevent the commission of the offense, fails to make proper effort so to do; or

(b) his conduct is expressly declared by law to establish his complicity.

(4) When causing a particular result is an element of an offense, an accomplice in the conduct causing such result is an accomplice in the commission of that offense, if he acts with the kind of culpability, if any, with respect to that result that is sufficient for the commission of the offense.

(5) A person who is legally incapable of committing a particular offense himself may be guilty thereof if it is committed by the conduct of another person for which he is legally accountable, unless such liability is inconsistent with the purpose of the provision establishing his incapacity.

(6) Unless otherwise provided by the Code or by the law defining the offense, a person is not an accomplice in an offense committed by another person if:

(a) he is a victim of that offense; or

(b) the offense is so defined that his conduct is inevitably incident to its commission; or

(c) he terminates his complicity prior to the commission of the offense; and

(i) wholly deprives it of effectiveness in the commission of the offense; or

(ii) gives timely warning to the law enforcement authorities or otherwise makes proper effort to prevent the commission of the offense.

(7) An accomplice may be convicted on proof of the commission of the offense and of his complicity therein, though the person claimed to have committed the offense has not been prosecuted or convicted or has been convicted of a different offense or degree of offense or has an immunity to prosecution or conviction or has been acquitted.

Section 2.08. Intoxication

(1) Except as provided in Subsection (4) of this Section, intoxication of the actor is not a defense unless it negatives an element of the offense.

(2) When recklessness establishes an element of the offense, if the actor, due to self-induced intoxication, is unaware of a risk of which he would have been aware had he been sober, such unawareness is immaterial.

(3) Intoxication does not, in itself, constitute mental disease within the meaning of Section 4.01.

(4) Intoxication which (a) is not self-induced or (b) is pathological is an affirmative defense if by reason of such intoxication the actor at the time of his conduct lacks substantial capacity either to appreciate its criminality [wrongfulness] or to conform his conduct to the requirements of law.

(5) Definitions. In this Section unless a different meaning plainly is required:

(a) "intoxication" means a disturbance of mental or physical capacities resulting from the introduction of substances into the body;

(b) "self-induced intoxication" means intoxication caused by substances which the actor knowingly introduces into his body, the tendency of which to cause intoxication he knows or ought to know, unless he introduces them pursuant to medical advice or under such circumstances as would afford a defense to a charge of crime;

(c) "pathological intoxication" means intoxication grossly excessive in degree, given the amount of the intoxicant, to which the actor does not know he is susceptible.

Section 2.09. Duress

(1) It is an affirmative defense that the actor engaged in the conduct charged to constitute an offense because he was coerced to do so by the use of, or a threat to use, unlawful force against his person or the person of another, which a person of reasonable firmness in his situation would have been unable to resist.

(2) The defense provided by this Section is unavailable if the actor recklessly placed himself in a situation in which it was probable that he would be subjected to duress. The defense is also unavailable if he was negligent in placing himself in such a situation, whenever negligence suffices to establish culpability for the offense charged.

(3) It is not a defense that a woman acted on the command of her husband, unless she acted under such coercion as would establish a defense under this Section. [The presumption that a woman, acting in the presence of her husband, is coerced is abolished.]

(4) When the conduct of the actor would otherwise be justifiable under Section 3.02, this Section does not preclude such defense.

Section 2.13. Entrapment

(1) A public law enforcement official or a person acting in cooperation with such an official perpetrates an entrapment if for the purpose of obtaining evidence of the commission of an offense, he induces or encourages another person to engage in conduct constituting such offense by either:

(a) making knowingly false representations designed to induce the belief that such conduct is not prohibited; or

(b) employing methods of persuasion or inducement which create a substantial risk that such an offense will be committed by persons other than those who are ready to commit it.

(2) Except as provided in Subsection (3) of this Section, a person prosecuted for an offense shall be acquitted if he proves by a preponderance of evidence that his conduct occurred in response to an entrapment. The issue of entrapment shall be tried by the Court in the absence of the jury.

(3) The defense afforded by this Section is unavailable when causing or threatening bodily injury is an element of the offense charged and the prosecution is based on conduct causing or threatening such injury to a person other than the person perpetrating the entrapment.

ARTICLE 3. GENERAL PRINCIPLES OF JUSTIFICATION

Section 3.01. Justification an Affirmative Defense; Civil Remedies Unaffected

(1) In any prosecution based on conduct which is justifiable under this Article, justification is an affirmative defense.

(2) The fact that conduct is justifiable under this Article does not abolish or impair any remedy for such conduct which is available in any civil action.

Section 3.02. Justification Generally: Choice of Evils

(1) Conduct which the actor believes to be necessary to avoid a harm or evil to himself or to another is justifiable, provided that:

(a) the harm or evil sought to be avoided by such conduct is greater than that sought to be prevented by the law defining the offense charged; and

(b) neither the Code nor other law defining the offense provides exceptions or defenses dealing with the specific situation involved; and

(c) a legislative purpose to exclude the justification claimed does not otherwise plainly appear.

(2) When the actor was reckless or negligent in bringing about the situation requiring a choice of harms or evils or in appraising the necessity for his conduct, the justification afforded by this Section is unavailable in a prosecution for any offense for which recklessness or negligence, as the case may be, suffices to establish culpability.

Section 3.04. Use of Force in Self-Protection

(1) Use of Force Justifiable for Protection of the Person. Subject to the provisions of this Section and of Section 3.09, the use of force upon or toward another person is justifiable when the actor believes that such force is immediately necessary for the purpose of protecting himself against the use of unlawful force by such other person on the present occasion.

(2) Limitations on Justifying Necessity for Use of Force.

(a) The use of force is not justifiable under this Section:

(i) to resist an arrest which the actor knows is being made by a peace officer, although the arrest is unlawful; or

(ii) to resist force used by the occupier or possessor of property or by another person on his behalf, where the actor knows that the person using the force is doing so under a claim of right to protect the property, except that this limitation shall not apply if:

(1) the actor is a public officer acting in the performance of his duties or a person lawfully assisting him therein or a person making or assisting in a lawful arrest; or

(2) the actor has been unlawfully dispossessed of the property and is making a re-entry or reception justified by Section 3.06; or

(3) the actor believes that such force is necessary to protect himself against death or serious bodily harm.

(b) The use of deadly force is not justifiable under this Section unless the actor believes that such force is necessary to protect himself against death, serious bodily harm, kidnapping or sexual intercourse compelled by force or threat; nor is it justifiable if:

(i) the actor, with the purpose of causing death or serious bodily harm, provoked the use of force against himself in the same encounter; or

(ii) the actor knows that he can avoid the necessity of using such force with complete safety by retreating or by surrendering possession of a thing to a person asserting a claim of right thereto or by complying with a demand that he abstain from any action which he has no duty to take, except that:

(1) the actor is not obliged to retreat from his dwelling or place of work, unless he was the initial aggressor or is assailed in his place of work by another person whose place of work the actor knows it to be; and

(2) a public officer justified in using force in the performance of his duties or a person justified in using force in his assistance or a person justified in using force in making an arrest or preventing an escape is not obliged to desist from efforts to perform such duty, effect such arrest or prevent such escape because of resistance or threatened resistance by or on behalf of the person against whom such action is directed.

(c) Except as required by paragraphs (a) and (b) of this Subsection, a person employing protective force may estimate the necessity thereof under the circumstances as he believes them to be when the force is used, without retreating, surrendering possession, doing any other act which he has no legal duty to do or abstaining from any lawful action.

(3) Use of Confinement as Protective Force. The justification afforded by this Section extends to the use of confinement as protective force only if the actor takes all reasonable measures to terminate the confinement as soon as he knows that he safely can, unless the person confined has been arrested on a charge of crime.

Section 3.05. Use of Force for the Protection of Other Persons

(1) Subject to the provisions of this Section and of Section 3.09, the use of force upon or toward the person of another is justifiable to protect a third person when:

(a) the actor would be justified under Section 3.04 in using such force to protect himself against the injury he believes to be threatened to the person whom he seeks to protect; and

(b) under the circumstances as the actor believes them to be, the person whom he seeks to protect would be justified in using such protective force; and

(c) the actor believes that his intervention is necessary for the protection of such other person.

(2) Notwithstanding Subsection (1) of this Section:

(a) when the actor would be obliged under Section 3.04 to retreat, to surrender the possession of a thing or to comply with a demand before using force in self-protection, he is not obliged to do so before using force for the protection of another person, unless he knows that he can thereby secure the complete safety of such other person; and

(b) when the person whom the actor seeks to protect would be obliged under Section 3.04 to retreat, to surrender the possession of a thing or to comply with a demand if he knew that he could obtain complete safety by so doing, the actor is obliged to try to cause him to do so before using force in his protection if the actor knows that he can obtain complete safety in that way; and

(c) neither the actor nor the person whom he seeks to protect is obliged to retreat when in the other's dwelling or place of work to any greater extent than in his own.

Section 3.10. Justification in Property Crimes

Conduct involving the appropriation, seizure or destruction of, damage to, intrusion on or interference with property is justifiable under circumstances which would establish a defense of privilege in a civil action based thereon, unless:

(1) the Code or the law defining the offense deals with the specific situation involved; or

(2) a legislative purpose to exclude the justification claimed otherwise plainly appears.

ARTICLE 4. RESPONSIBILITY

Section 4.01. Mental Disease or Defect Excluding Responsibility

(1) A person is not responsible for criminal conduct if at the time of such conduct as a result of mental disease or defect he lacks substantial capacity either to appreciate the criminality [wrongfulness] of his conduct or to conform his conduct to the requirements of law.

(2) As used in this Article, the terms "mental disease or defect" do not include an abnormality manifested only by repeated criminal or otherwise antisocial conduct.

ARTICLE 5. INCHOATE CRIMES

Section 5.01. Criminal Attempt

(1) Definition of Attempt. A person is guilty of an attempt to commit a crime if, acting with the kind of culpability otherwise required for commission of the crime, he:

(a) purposely engages in conduct which would constitute the crime if the attendant circumstances were as he believes them to be; or

(b) when causing a particular result is an element of the crime, does or omits to do anything with the purpose of causing or with the belief that it will cause such result without further conduct on his part; or

(c) purposely does or omits to do anything which, under the circumstances as he believes them to be, is an act or omission constituting a substantial step in a course of conduct planned to culminate in his commission of the crime.

(2) Conduct Which May Be Held Substantial Step Under Subsection (1)(c). Conduct shall not be held to constitute a substantial step under Subsection (1)(c) of this Section unless it is strongly corroborative of the actor's criminal purpose. Without negativing the sufficiency of other conduct, the following, if strongly corroborative of the actor's criminal purpose, shall not be held insufficient as a matter of law:

(a) lying in wait, searching for or following the contemplated victim of the crime;

(b) enticing or seeking to entice the contemplated victim of the crime to go to the place contemplated for its commission;

(c) reconnoitering the place contemplated for the commission of the crime;

(d) unlawful entry of a structure, vehicle or enclosure in which it is contemplated that the crime will be committed;

(e) possession of materials to be employed in the commission of the crime, which are specially designed for such unlawful use or which can serve no lawful purpose of the actor under the circumstances;

(f) possession, collection or fabrication of materials to be employed in the commission of the crime, at or near the place contemplated for its commission, where such possession, collection or fabrication serves no lawful purpose of the actor under the circumstances;

(g) soliciting an innocent agent to engage in conduct constituting an element of the crime.

(3) Conduct Designed to Aid Another in Commission of a Crime. A person who engages in conduct designed to aid another to commit a crime which would establish his complicity under Section 2.06 if the crime were committed by such other person, is guilty of an attempt to commit the crime, although the crime is not committed or attempted by such other person.

(4) Renunciation of Criminal Purpose. When the actor's conduct would otherwise constitute an attempt under Subsection (1)(b) or (1)(c) of this Section, it is an affirmative defense that he abandoned his effort to commit the crime or otherwise prevented its commission, under circumstances manifesting a complete and voluntary renunciation of his criminal purpose. The establishment of such defense does not, however, affect the liability of an accomplice who did not join in such abandonment or prevention.

Within the meaning of this Article, renunciation of criminal purpose is not voluntary if it is motivated, in whole or in part, by circumstances, not present or apparent at the inception of the actor's course of conduct, which increase the probability of detection or apprehension or which make more difficult the accomplishment of the criminal purpose. Renunciation is not complete if it is motivated by a decision to postpone the criminal conduct until a more advantageous time or to transfer the criminal effort to another but similar objective or victim.

Section 5.02. Criminal Solicitation

(1) Definition of Solicitation. A person is guilty of solicitation to commit a crime if with the purpose of promoting or facilitating its commission he commands, encourages or requests another person to engage in specific conduct which would constitute such crime or an attempt to commit such crime or which would establish his complicity in its commission or attempted commission.

(2) Uncommunicated Solicitation. It is immaterial under Subsection (1) of this Section that the actor fails to communicate with the person he solicits to commit a crime if his conduct was designed to effect such communication.

(3) Renunciation of Criminal Purpose. It is an affirmative defense that the actor, after soliciting another person to commit a crime, persuaded him not to do so or otherwise prevented the commission of the crime, under circumstances manifesting a complete and voluntary renunciation of his criminal purpose.

Section 5.03. Criminal Conspiracy

(1) Definition of Conspiracy. A person is guilty of conspiracy with another person or persons to commit a crime if with the purpose of promoting or facilitating its commission he:

(a) agrees with such other person or persons that they or one or more of them will engage in conduct which constitutes such crime or an attempt or solicitation to commit such crime; or

(b) agrees to aid such other person or persons in the planning or commission of such crime or of an attempt or solicitation to commit such crime.

(2) Scope of Conspiratorial Relationship. If a person guilty of conspiracy, as defined by Subsection (1) of this Section, knows that a person with whom he conspires to commit a crime has conspired with another person or persons to commit the same crime, he is guilty of conspiring with such other person or persons, whether or not he knows their identity, to commit such crime.

(3) Conspiracy With Multiple Criminal Objectives. If a person conspires to commit a number of crimes, he is guilty of only one conspiracy so long as such multiple crimes are the object of the same agreement or continuous conspiratorial relationship.

(4) Joinder and Venue in Conspiracy Prosecutions.

(a) Subject to the provisions of paragraph (b) of this Subsection, two or more persons charged with criminal conspiracy may be prosecuted jointly if:

(i) they are charged with conspiring with one another; or

(ii) the conspiracies alleged, whether they have the same or different parties, are so related that they constitute different aspects of a scheme of organized criminal conduct.

(b) In any joint prosecution under paragraph (a) of this Subsection:

(i) no defendant shall be charged with a conspiracy in any county [parish or district] other than one in which he entered into such conspiracy or in which an overt act pursuant to such conspiracy was done by him or by a person with whom he conspired; and

(ii) neither the liability of any defendant nor the admissibility against him of evidence of acts or declarations of another shall be enlarged by such joinder; and

(iii) the Court shall order a severance or take a special verdict as to any defendant who so requests, if it deems it necessary or appropriate to promote the fair determination of his guilt or innocence, and shall take any other proper measures to protect the fairness of the trial.

(5) Overt Act. No person may be convicted of conspiracy to commit a crime, other than a felony of the first or second degree, unless an overt act in pursuance of such conspiracy is alleged and proved to have been done by him or by a person with whom he conspired.

APPENDIX

(6) Renunciation of Criminal Purpose. It is an affirmative defense that the actor, after conspiring to commit a crime, thwarted the success of the conspiracy, under circumstances manifesting a complete and voluntary renunciation of his criminal purpose.

(7) Duration of Conspiracy. For purposes of Section 1.06(4):

(a) conspiracy is a continuing course of conduct which terminates when the crime or crimes which are its object are committed or the agreement that they be committed is abandoned by the defendant and by those with whom he conspired; and

(b) such abandonment is presumed if neither the defendant nor anyone with whom he conspired does any overt act in pursuance of the conspiracy during the applicable period of limitation; and

(c) if an individual abandons the agreement, the conspiracy is terminated as to him only if and when he advises those with whom he conspired of his abandonment or he informs the law enforcement authorities of the existence of the conspiracy and of his participation therein.

OFFENSES INVOLVING DANGER TO THE PERSON

ARTICLE 210. CRIMINAL HOMICIDE

Section 210.0. Definitions

In Articles 210-213, unless a different meaning plainly is required:

(1) "human being" means a person who has been born and is alive;

(2) "bodily injury" means physical pain, illness or any impairment of physical condition;

(3) "serious bodily injury" means bodily injury which creates a substantial risk of death or which causes serious, permanent disfigurement, or protracted loss or impairment of the function of any bodily member or organ;

(4) "deadly weapon" means any firearm, or other weapon, device, instrument, material or substance, whether animate or inanimate, which in the manner it is used or is intended to be used is known to be capable of producing death or serious bodily injury.

Section 210.1. Criminal Homicide

(1) A person is guilty of criminal homicide if he purposely, knowingly, recklessly or negligently causes the death of another human being.

(2) Criminal homicide is murder, manslaughter or negligent homicide.

Section 210.2. Murder

(1) Except as provided in Section 210.3(l)(b), criminal homicide constitutes murder when:

(a) it is committed purposely or knowingly; or

(b) it is committed recklessly under circumstances manifesting extreme indifference to the value of human life. Such recklessness and indifference are presumed if the actor is engaged or is an accomplice in the commission of, or an attempt to commit, or flight after committing or attempting to commit robbery, rape or deviate sexual intercourse by force or threat of force, arson, burglary, kidnapping or felonious escape.

(2) Murder is a felony of the first degree [but a person convicted of murder may be sentenced to death, as provided in Section 210.6].

Section 210.3. Manslaughter

(1) Criminal homicide constitutes manslaughter when:

(a) it is committed recklessly; or

(b) a homicide which would otherwise be murder is committed under the influence of extreme mental or emotional disturbance for which there is reasonable explanation or excuse. The reasonableness of such explanation or excuse shall be determined from the viewpoint of a person in the actor's situation under the circumstances as he believes them to be.

(2) Manslaughter is a felony of the second degree.

Section 210.4. Negligent Homicide

(1) Criminal homicide constitutes negligent homicide when it is committed negligently.

(2) Negligent homicide is a felony of the third degree.

Section 210.5. Causing or Aiding Suicide

(1) Causing Suicide as Criminal Homicide. A person may be convicted of criminal homicide for causing another to commit suicide only if he purposely causes such suicide by force, duress or deception.

(2) Aiding or Soliciting Suicide as an Independent Offense. A person who purposely aids or solicits another to commit suicide is guilty of a felony of the second degree if his conduct causes such suicide or an attempted suicide, and otherwise of a misdemeanor.

Section 211.1. Assault

(1) Simple Assault. A person is guilty of assault if he:

(a) attempts to cause or purposely, knowingly or recklessly causes bodily injury to another; or

(b) negligently causes bodily injury to another with a deadly weapon; or

(c) attempts by physical menace to put another in fear of imminent serious bodily injury.

Simple assault is a misdemeanor unless committed in a fight or scuffle entered into by mutual consent, in which case it is a petty misdemeanor.

(2) Aggravated Assault. A person is guilty of aggravated assault if he:

(a) attempts to cause serious bodily injury to another, or causes such injury purposely, knowingly or recklessly under circumstances manifesting extreme indifference to the value of human life; or

(b) attempts to cause or purposely or knowingly causes bodily injury to another with a deadly weapon.

Aggravated assault under paragraph (a) is a felony of the second degree; aggravated assault under paragraph (b) is a felony of the third degree.

Section 213.4. Sexual Assault

A person who has sexual contact with another not his spouse, or causes such other to have sexual contact with him, is guilty of sexual assault, a misdemeanor, if:

(1) he knows that the contact is offensive to the other person; or

(2) he knows that the other person suffers from a mental disease or defect which renders him or her incapable of appraising the nature of his or her conduct; or

(3) he knows that the other person is unaware that a sexual act is being committed; or

(4) the other person is less than 10 years old; or

(5) he has substantially impaired the other person's power to appraise or control his or her conduct, by administering or employing without the other's knowledge drugs, intoxicants or other means for the purpose of preventing resistance; or

(6) the other person is less than [16] years old and the actor is at least [four] years older than the other person; or

(7) the other person is less than 21 years old and the actor is his guardian or otherwise responsible for general supervision of his welfare; or

(8) the other person is in custody of law or detained in a hospital or other institution and the actor has supervisory or disciplinary authority over him.

Sexual contact is any touching of the sexual or other intimate parts of the person for the purpose of arousing or gratifying sexual desire.

OFFENSES AGAINST PROPERTY

ARTICLE 220. ARSON, CRIMINAL MISCHIEF AND OTHER PROPERTY DESTRUCTION

Section 220.1. Arson and Related Offenses

(1) Arson. A person is guilty of arson, a felony of the second degree, if he starts a fire or causes an explosion with the purpose of:

Sum & Substance QUICK REVIEW of Criminal Law

(a) destroying a building or occupied structure of another; or

(b) destroying or damaging any property, whether his own or another's, to collect insurance for such loss. It shall be an affirmative defense to prosecution under this paragraph that the actor's conduct did not recklessly endanger any building or occupied structure of another or place any other person in danger of death or bodily injury.

(2) Reckless Burning or Exploding. A person commits a felony of the third degree if he purposely starts a fire or causes an explosion, whether on his own property or another's, and thereby recklessly:

(a) places another person in danger of death or bodily injury; or

(b) places a building or occupied structure of another in danger of damage or destruction.

(3) Failure to Control or Report Dangerous Fire. A person who knows that a fire is endangering life or a substantial amount of property of another and fails to take reasonable measures to put out or control the fire, when he can do so without substantial risk to himself, or to give a prompt fire alarm, commits a misdemeanor if:

(a) he knows that he is under an official, contractual, or other legal duty to prevent or combat the fire; or

(b) the fire was started, albeit lawfully, by him or with his assent, or on property in his custody or control.

(4) Definitions. "Occupied structure" means any structure, vehicle or place adapted for overnight accommodation of persons, or for carrying on business therein, whether or not a person is actually present. Property is that of another, for the purposes of this section, if anyone other than the actor has a possessory or proprietary interest therein. If a building or structure is divided into separately occupied units, any unit not occupied by the actor is an occupied structure of another.

ARTICLE 221. BURGLARY AND OTHER CRIMINAL INTRUSION

Section 221.0. Definitions

In this Article, unless a different meaning plainly is required:

(1) "occupied structure" means any structure, vehicle or place adapted for overnight accommodation of persons, or for carrying on business therein, whether or not a person is actually present.

(2) "night" means the period between thirty minutes past sunset and thirty minutes before sunrise.

Section 221.1. Burglary

(1) Burglary Defined. A person is guilty of burglary if he enters a building or occupied structure, or separately secured or occupied portion thereof, with purpose to commit a crime therein, unless the premises are at the time open to the public or the actor is licensed or privileged to enter. It is an affirmative defense to prosecution for burglary that the building or structure was abandoned.

(2) Grading. Burglary is a felony of the second degree if it is perpetrated in the dwelling of another at night, or if, in the course of committing the offense, the actor:

(a) purposely, knowingly or recklessly inflicts or attempts to inflict bodily injury on anyone; or

(b) is armed with explosives or a deadly weapon.

Otherwise, burglary is a felony of the third degree. An act shall be deemed "in the course of committing" an offense if it occurs in an attempt to commit the offense or in flight after the attempt or commission.

(3) Multiple Convictions. A person may not be convicted both for burglary and for the offense which it was his purpose to commit after the burglarious entry or for an attempt to commit that offense, unless the additional offense constitutes a felony of the first or second degree.

ARTICLE 222. ROBBERY

Section 222.1. Robbery

(1) Robbery Defined. A person is guilty of robbery if, in the course of committing a theft, he:

(a) inflicts serious bodily injury upon another; or

(b) threatens another with or purposely puts him in fear of immediate serious bodily injury; or

(c) commits or threatens immediately to commit any felony of the first or second degree.

An act shall be deemed "in the course of committing a theft" if it occurs in an attempt to commit theft or in flight after the attempt or commission.

(2) Grading. Robbery is a felony of the second degree, except that it is a felony of the first degree if in the course of committing the theft the actor attempts to kill anyone, or purposely inflicts or attempts to inflict serious injury.

ARTICLE 223. THEFT AND RELATED OFFENSES

Section 223.0. Definitions

In this Article, unless a different meaning plainly is required:

(1) "deprive" means: (a) to withhold property of another permanently or for so extended a period as to appropriate a major portion of its economic value, or with intent to restore only upon payment of reward or other compensation; or (b) to dispose of the property so as to make it unlikely that the owner will recover it.

(2) "financial institution" means a bank, insurance company, credit union, building and loan association, investment trust or other organization held out to the public as a place of deposit of funds or medium of savings or collective investment.

(3) "government" means the United States, any State, county, municipality, or other political unit, or any department, agency or subdivision of any of the foregoing, or any corporation or other association carrying out the functions of government.

(4) "movable property" means property, the location of which can be changed, including things growing on, affixed to, or found in land, and documents although the rights represented thereby have no physical location. "Immovable property" is all other property.

(5) "obtain" means: (a) in relation to property, to bring about a transfer or purported transfer of a legal interest in the property, whether to the obtainer or another; or (b) in relation to labor or service, to secure performance thereof.

(6) "property" means anything of value, including real estate, tangible and intangible personal property, contract rights, choses-in-action and other interests in or claims to wealth, admission or transportation tickets, captured or domestic animals, food and drink, electric or other power.

(7) "property of another" includes property in which any person other than the actor has an interest which the actor is not privileged to infringe, regardless of the fact that the actor also has an interest in the property and regardless of the fact that the other person might be precluded from civil recovery because the property was used in an unlawful transaction or was subject to forfeiture as contraband. Property in possession of the actor shall not be deemed property of another who has only a security interest therein, even if legal title is in the creditor pursuant to a conditional sales contract or other security agreement.

Section 223.1. Consolidation of Theft Offenses; Grading; Provisions Applicable to Theft Generally

(1) Consolidation of Theft Offenses. Conduct denominated theft in this Article constitutes a single offense. An accusation of theft may be supported by evidence that it was committed in any manner that would be theft under this Article, notwithstanding the specification of a different manner in the indictment or information, subject only to the power of the Court to ensure fair trial by granting a continuance or other appropriate relief where the conduct of the defense would be prejudiced by lack of fair notice or by surprise.

(2) Grading of Theft Offenses.

(a) Theft constitutes a felony of the third degree if the amount involved exceeds $500, or if the property stolen is a firearm, automobile, airplane, motorcycle, motorboat, or other motor-propelled vehicle, or in the case of theft by receiving stolen property, if the receiver is in the business of buying or selling stolen property.

(b) Theft not within the preceding paragraph constitutes a misdemeanor, except that if the property was not taken from the person or by threat, or in breach of a fiduciary obligation, and the actor proves by a preponderance of the evidence that the amount involved was less than $50, the offense constitutes a petty misdemeanor.

(c) The amount involved in a theft shall be deemed to be the highest value, by any reasonable standard, of the property or services which the actor stole or attempted to steal. Amounts involved in thefts committed pursuant to one scheme or course of conduct, whether from the same person or several persons, may be aggregated in determining the grade of the offense.

(3) Claim of Right. It is an affirmative defense to prosecution for theft that the actor:

(a) was unaware that the property or service was that of another; or

(b) acted under an honest claim of right to the property or service involved or that he had a right to acquire or dispose of it as he did; or

(c) took property exposed for sale, intending to purchase and pay for it promptly, or reasonably believing that the owner, if present, would have consented.

(4) Theft from Spouse. It is no defense that theft was from the actor's spouse, except that misappropriation of household and personal effects, or other property normally accessible to both spouses, is theft only if it occurs after the parties have ceased living together.

Section 223.2. Theft by Unlawful Taking or Disposition

(1) Movable Property. A person is guilty of theft if he unlawfully takes, or exercises unlawful control over, movable property of another with purpose to deprive him thereof.

(2) Immovable Property. A person is guilty of theft if he unlawfully transfers immovable property of another or any interest therein with purpose to benefit himself or another not entitled thereto.

Section 223.3. Theft by Deception

A person is guilty of theft if he purposely obtains property of another by deception. A person deceives if he purposely:

(1) creates or reinforces a false impression, including false impressions as to law, value, intention or other state of mind; but deception as to a person's intention to perform a promise shall not be inferred from the fact alone that he did not subsequently perform the promise; or

(2) prevents another from acquiring information which would affect his judgment of a transaction; or

(3) fails to correct a false impression which the deceiver previously created or reinforced, or which the deceiver knows to be influencing another to whom he stands in a fiduciary or confidential relationship; or

(4) fails to disclose a known lien, adverse claim or other legal impediment to the enjoyment of property which he transfers or encumbers in consideration for the property obtained, whether such impediment is or is not valid, or is or is not a matter of official record.

The term "deceive" does not, however, include falsity as to matters having no pecuniary significance, or puffing by statements unlikely to deceive ordinary persons in the group addressed.

Section 223.7. Theft of Services

(1) A person is guilty of theft if he purposely obtains services which he knows are available only for compensation, by deception or threat, or by false token or other means to avoid payment for the service. "Services" includes labor, professional service, transportation, telephone or other public service, accommodation in hotels, restaurants or elsewhere, admission to exhibitions, use of vehicles or other movable property. Where compensation for service is ordinarily paid immediately upon the rendering of such service, as in the case of hotels and restaurants, refusal to pay or absconding without payment or offer to pay gives rise to a presumption that the service was obtained by deception as to intention to pay.

(2) A person commits theft if, having control over the disposition of services of others, to which he is not entitled, he knowingly diverts such services to his own benefit or to the benefit of another not entitled thereto.

Section 250.2. Disorderly Conduct

(1) Offense Defined. A person is guilty of disorderly conduct if, with purpose to cause public inconvenience, annoyance or alarm, or recklessly creating a risk thereof, he:

(a) engages in fighting or threatening, or in violent or tumultuous behavior; or

(b) makes unreasonable noise or offensively coarse utterance, gesture or display, or addresses abusive language to any person present; or

(c) creates a hazardous or physically offensive condition by any act which serves no legitimate purpose of the actor.

"Public" means affecting or likely to affect persons in a place to which the public or a substantial group has access; among the places included are highways, transport facilities, schools, prisons, apartment houses, places of business or amusement, or any neighborhood.

(2) Grading. An offense under this Section is a petty misdemeanor if the actor's purpose is to cause substantial harm or serious inconvenience, or if he persists in disorderly conduct after reasonable warning or request to desist. Otherwise disorderly conduct is a violation.

Section 251.4. Obscenity

(1) Obscene Defined. Material is obscene if, considered as a whole, its predominant appeal is to prurient interest, that is, a shameful or morbid interest, in nudity, sex or excretion, and if in addition it goes substantially beyond customary limits of candor in describing or representing such matters. Predominant appeal shall be judged with reference to ordinary adults unless it appears from the ch*aracter of the material or the circumstances of its dissemination to be designed for children or other specially susceptible audience. Undeveloped photographs, molds, printing plates, and the like, shall be deemed that processing or other acts may be required to make to disseminate it.

XIII. TABLE OF CASES

TABLE OF CASES

References are to section numbers.